Living, Studying, and
Working in

Italy

Living, Studying, and Working in

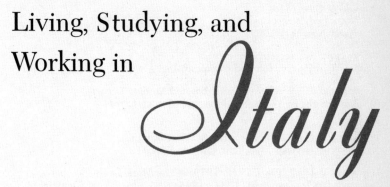

Italy

Everything You Need to Know to
Fulfill Your Dreams of Living Abroad

Travis Neighbor and Monica Larner

AN OWL BOOK
HENRY HOLT AND COMPANY   NEW YORK

For my family and friends,
companions on this epic journey
                                    T.N.

For Christine and Stevan Larner,
and their new life
                                    M.L.

Henry Holt and Company, Inc.
Publishers since 1866
115 West 18th Street
New York, New York 10011

Henry Holt® is a registered
trademark of Henry Holt and Company, Inc.

Published in Canada by Fitzhenry & Whiteside Ltd.,
195 Allstate Parkway, Markham, Ontario L3R 4T8.

Library of Congress Cataloging-in-Publication Data
Neighbor, Travis.
    Living, studying, and working in Italy : everything you need to
know to fulfill your dreams of living abroad / Travis Neighbor and
Monica Larner.—1st ed.
        p.   cm.
    "An Owl book."
    Includes index.
    ISBN 0-8050-5102-3 (alk. paper)
    1. Italy—Guidebooks.   2. Americans—Travel—Italy—Guidebooks.
I. Larner, Monica.   II. Title.
DG416.N44   1998   97-30702
914.504'92—dc21

Henry Holt books are available for special
promotions and premiums. For details contact:
Director, Special Markets.

First Edition 1998

Designed by Paula R. Szafranski

Printed in the United States of America
All first editions are printed on acid-free paper. ∞

10   9   8   7   6   5   4

Contents

Contents

Acknowledgments

We would like to thank our editors, Theresa Burns and Amy Rosenthal, for their enthusiasm and dedication, as well as the Italians we have encountered along the way who made us feel at home in their country.

I would like to thank Emiliano Neri for his love, creativity, and support, for which I will always be grateful; Jess Neighbor for being a great pioneer and friend; Teresa Neighbor and Ed Neighbor for believing in and supporting my dreams; Clelia Capelli and Luigi F. Solano for handing down the magic of Italy. Also special thanks to the Neri family; Marie Dolores Solano; Louisa Solano; Cathleen Fleck; Ivana Cangiano; Babettli Azzone; Vanessa Azzone; Brian Jay Ward; Rosanna Cirigliano; Andrea Biagini; Nina Roberts; Patrizia Deluise.
                    —Travis Neighbor, New York City, 1997

If it weren't for my parents' decision to move to Rome years ago, I might have never known that a person can fall in love with a place. For this, I thank them and the friends I found here: Joana Bentley, always near despite geography; Francesca Leondeff for showing me her country; Kate Carlisle, la Texana-Romana; Gabriella Quaroni for her generosity; Carolyn and Roland Muri; Silvia Sansoni; Andrea Scharff; Raphael Jesurum; Robert Glickman; Arturo Zampaglione of *La Repubblica*; John Rossant of *Business Week*; and my brother Michael, who doesn't know what he's missing.

                              —Monica Larner, Rome, 1997

Preface

When we first met for lunch in the summer of 1995 at Rockefeller Center in New York City, we were both working for American branches of Italian companies. We had spent more than ten years of combined experience living in Italy and had moved back to the United States just a short while before. With the magic of Italy strong in our minds, our friendship was born by comparing tales of life abroad. Over a sandwich and a cup of tea, we learned that our experiences had been very different and yet very much the same. One of the things we shared most was the feeling that the Italian sojourn had deeply influenced our personal development. We also shared a regret that in our early years there we hadn't known things we know now—things that only seasoned expatriates learn through direct experience. Our complaints, confusions, and questions had been the same, we discovered, and we'd encountered the same difficulty in finding solutions and answers. We agreed that we had yet to read a book that addressed the practical side of living, studying, and working in Italy.

This book offers experience and knowledge gathered during our years in the *bel paese*. It includes details of American expatriate life, down to the most minute things. Although much of the information is useful to other foreigners and even Italians, the perspective is American. You may be surprised to find no substantial reference to the artistic heritage of the country, no cataloging of monuments and sculptures.

In fact, you will not find any detailed information about Italian art, hotels, or restaurants. We leave those to the hundreds of tourist guidebooks, whose purpose is to do just that. Our focus is different: we are interested in providing you with information that will help you penetrate to the core of daily life in a country that is rapidly changing, things such as filling out paperwork, arranging an internship, looking for a job, and enrolling in school.

A few notes about the book. It includes many personal stories and insights we have gathered over the years. Because it was written by two people, to eliminate confusion we have used the pronoun "I" in personal stories and "we" in our advice to you. Some of our experiences may not apply to all of Italy since we have lived mainly in two cities, and each Italian city and region has its own customs. While we have tried, whenever possible, to fill you in on some of those differences, the adventure of discovering them is mainly left up to you. Regarding Italian vocabulary in the book, we have provided translations of words when we felt it necessary but have left out most of the basic words you can find in a dictionary. The Italian words we do give are written in italics.

Be sure to take into account that some of the information in the book may have changed since it was written. For example, if you are faxing a résumé to an Italian company, it is always best to call the company first to verify that the fax number we have listed is still valid. When it comes to prices, we have listed them only in certain instances to give you a general sense of the cost of things. These, too, are subject to change. For the sake of convenience, when we have listed prices in both lire and dollars we have based it on a 1,500-lire-to-the dollar exchange rate. Keep in mind that the rate does fluctuate. Italian tax laws also change frequently, and it is impossible to keep up to date without the help of an accountant. It is advisable to consult one before making any decisions concerning your finances, personal or professional. When it comes to work, working illegally is a reality of the Italian workforce, but be warned that while many people are doing it, illegal employment could ultimately lead to your being fined or even deported.

There are many Americans living, studying, and working in Italy—some who stay for months, others who stay for decades. We hope our book will help guide you through all stages of your experience, and most of all we wish you *buon viaggio*.

Before You Go

Children dressed in carnival costumes play with confetti in Rome's Piazza Navona.

CHAPTER ONE

A Place to Call Home

"If we want things to stay as they are, things will have to change," wrote Giuseppe Tomasi di Lampedusa in his 1958 novel, *The Leopard.* Although Lampedusa, the son of a nineteenth-century Sicilian landowner, was talking about the Risorgimento, which led to the birth of a unified Italy, his timeless remark characterizes a country that awkwardly straddles old and new, tradition and modernization. If one were to pinpoint the "magic" of Italy, it is precisely that: while its citizens cohabit with centuries of past history, Italy embraces new forces that catapult it into the new millennium. This is evident not only in the ancient ruins that rise up beside modern apartment buildings but in rich cultural traditions like the tightly knit family unit and the small-town socializing characteristic of even cities such as Milan and Rome. The Italians are a people of enormous fantasy and creativity who have successfully carried these traditions forward in a country that now stands among the world's richest and most powerful.

This comfortable space in which Italy exists between tradition and transition is what has attracted foreign visitors en masse for centuries. It is what made Americans in the past spend weeks traveling across the Atlantic Ocean in small trading ships to reach the Italian shores, and dismantle entire carriages at the Mount Cenis Pass in Switzerland to carry them across the Italian Alps. They went from Florence to Rome on foot, passing the bodies of executed highwaymen hanging from poles on the sides of the roads, and braved the Pontine marshes, famous for malaria-infested air and violent bandits. When they got to Sicily, they rode across the rocky, arid island territory on mules. They did whatever it took to go to Italy, and once they got there they inevitably fell in love with what they saw and wanted to stay for longer than they had planned.

Today, without these physical challenges of traveling, the number of Americans traveling to Italy each year has risen to more than 2.5 million, the number of other foreigners between 50 and 55 million. Most go for a modern version of the "Grand Tour," whisking about from town to town for a night and a day just to see the Roman Forum, the Uffizi Gallery, the canals of Venice, and the ancient city of Pompeii. But for some modern adventurers, this brief encounter is not enough. They want to dig deeper, not just to see the country but to live it. They come for a month, a summer, a year, sometimes a lifetime.

A Young Country

Despite a history rooted in antiquity, the Republic of Italy is not even 150 years old. Before 1861, Italy was a collection of regional principalities with independent governments, different dialects, and very separate traditions. The dialects, for example, were so different that a person from one town literally could not communicate with another even a few miles away. Despite these distinctions, Italy was proclaimed a united nation in 1861 following the Risorgimento, when Giuseppe Garibaldi marched down the peninsula with his army of "Redshirts" and united the territories in the name of King Vittorio Emanuele II and the Italian monarchy. In 1870, Rome was conquered and "Italy" as we know it was born.

Yet, even once "united," Italy largely remained a loosely assembled group of separate regions. Benito Mussolini, who led the nation into the Second World War by ruling with the iron grip of fascism, had visions of glorious conquests of an Italian empire complete with colonies in Africa. But an empire never was created, and even today many of the problems of old, such as distinct regional dialects, persist. The fact that the country has such a short history under one flag explains many of the contradictions inherent in it today, as well as why Italy is still going through an identity crisis of sorts. It has long been said that Italy is really unified only during the World Cup soccer matches, when Italians everywhere bring out the flag and join to support the national soccer team, as well as to chant to the glory of the country. Some modern-day Italians wonder if Italy is no more than a "geographic expression"—a land bounded by mountains and sea but not by a sense of nationality—while others would like to see the rich industrial north and the poor agricultural south split into two different countries.

The First Republic

Italy emerged from the darkness of fascism and the Second World War with a strengthened desire to rebuild as a unified nation. In 1946, the Italian Republic was formed following a popular referendum in which voters ousted the monarchy that had ruled them for seventy years. A year later, the Italian Constitution was approved and Italy became a democratic republic divided into twenty regions made up of *province* (provinces) and *comuni* (municipalities). A political structure was designed with the intention of never letting any one political party or individual politician gain too much power as Mussolini had, yet ultimately that structure has been largely responsible for many of Italy's problems in recent years. That structure consists of two houses of Parliament (a Chamber of Deputies and a Senate), the president (*presidente*) and the prime minister (*presidente del Consiglio*). The president is elected by the Parliament and functions as the official head of state, though he or she does not run the country. Instead, the prime minister, chosen by the president based on election results (not elected directly by the Italian people, who vote for parties and not candidates), runs the nation. The prime minister is also responsible for forming the actual government by choosing from members of his or her coalition party and appointing heads of the various ministries. Overlooking all of this is the Constitutional Court, consisting of fifteen appointed judges who define the power of the state and its regions and make sure new laws conform with the Constitution.

While this system has numerous built-in safety measures to make it theoretically stronger, in reality it amounts to a structure so weak that Italian governments fall on average every nine months (at the writing of this book there have been fifty-five Italian governments since the Second World War). With as many as thirty or forty competing political parties at one time, few can ever gain a significant enough percentage of votes to make a difference. In the end, the only way governments can be formed is by coupling various parties together in broad, poorly defined political alliances. In 1993, the electoral system was reformed to give a bit more direct voting power to the people, but the resulting "mixed system" based on two electoral principles (proportional and majority) is so confusing that it seems as though the lawmakers might have to go back to their drawing boards to change it once again.

Despite a weak government the postwar period brought enormous wealth to Italy. The decades of the 1950s and 1960s are known as the period of the "Italian Miracle" because industries in the north flourished and successful small businesses all over the country catapulted Italy into the same economic bracket as its prosperous northern European neighbors. The postwar period was also the era of the Cold War, with Italy serving as a crucial axis between East and West, and home itself to the largest Communist Party in the Western world. On the other side of the political spectrum, extreme right-wing parties with roots in fascism began to emerge. To keep the extreme right and left wings at bay, centrist political alliances held a virtual monopoly on power during those years. The common denominator was the Christian Democratic Party, which had strong ties to the Catholic Church and the United States. Italian governments were "revolving-door" governments back then: the same group of people went into and out of power with such frequency that no outsider could find a way to slip in. Like anything that stays in one place for too long, the revolving-door governments resulted in stagnation, a lack of political circulation, and ultimately a climate ripe for corruption.

The Second Republic

The corruption continued right up until the late 1980s. With the destruction of the Berlin Wall in November 1989, the division between East and West became blurred and Italy began a process of self-evaluation and renewal so dramatic that it has been called the "dawning of the Second Italian Republic." A group of dissident judges led by Antonio Di Pietro exposed the corruption that had permeated almost all political parties during the revolving-door frenzy, most especially the Christian Democrats and the Socialists. The judges, viewed by the people as modern-day Robin Hoods, forced Italians to acknowledge that Italy was rotten at its very core. Judge Di Pietro created computerized files on most major politicians, logging in their incomes and expenses and then cross-referencing the information to uncover discrepancies. The evidence he uncovered prompted him and his colleagues to commence the anticorruption investigation called "Operation Clean Hands." The investigations started roughly in 1992, but within three years more than five thousand businessmen and politicians had been implicated as well as three former prime ministers. At one point, Clean Hands had a third of the active Senate under criminal investigation! The city of Milan was dubbed "Tangentopoli," or "Bribesville," because so many of the local businessmen were found to have received or paid bribes. These bribes included everything from kickbacks paid to construction companies to bribes made to public officials.

The Tangentopoli madness spread, revealing that the nation was infected from top to toe; since then Italy has held a steadfast place on the Top Ten list of the most corrupt countries on the planet. Clean Hands brought Italy's entire postwar political order into question and inspired the nation to vote for change. Not only did it put an end to revolving-door governments, it obliterated long-standing parties such as the Socialist Party, whose leader, Bettino Craxi, is still hiding out in Tunisia avoiding charges of corruption. Seven-time Christian Democratic Prime Minister Giulio Andreotti, who was once nicknamed "Eternal Giulio" because he never left the political spotlight, was tried for association with the Mafia. Many parties desperately attempted to disassociate themselves from the proceedings by changing leaders, names, and political identity. In the political void following Clean Hands, Italians elected Silvio Berlusconi, a media tycoon–turned–politician, as prime minster. He was considered an outsider to the rotten group of politicians and was therefore elected by citizens as the only candidate with an "untainted" past, despite his making a political alliance with both federalist Umberto Bossi and right-wing Gianfranco Fini of the National Alliance Party. (Fini's previous political role was that of the leader of a party called Movimento Sociale Italiano, which had been founded by Fascists; Bossi, on the other hand, has gone on to dedicate himself to a secessionist movement to split the country in two.) Berlusconi's government lasted only eight months after it was revealed that investigators were probing for corruption in his media empire. This brought an end to the euphoria of the Second Republic once

Italian citizens flood the square in front of Milan's Duomo to protest the government in 1996.

it became apparent that the new guard was inflicted with the same problems as the old. Many were left to question if a second republic had indeed ever existed. One thing was certain: the aftermath of Clean Hands forced Italians to realize that changes must be made.

Today, Italy is faced with the pressures of the European Monetary Union (EMU): if the Italian economy is to remain competitive in the European Union, Italians must trim back on the carefree spending that came with the climate of corruption in its past. The Italian state has started to sell off and privatize many industries it owns, such as the telephone and electric companies, in order to raise revenue. Fiscal austerity has brought about the trimming of the generous pension plans the state offers to its citizens and subsidies it offers to businesses. Politically, the country is contemplating ways of changing the Italian Constitution to give more direct power to voters, to change the function of the Parliament, and to fix a maximum period of time for which a prime minister can remain in office. Italians, however, remain optimistic and enthusiastic about politics, and Italy still has one of the world's highest percentages of voter turnout even though Italians go to the polls more often than the citizens of any other European country.

North and South

A growing group of Italian citizens, however, do not view Italy as a
united country and would rather see most of the northern Italian territory, such as the regions of Veneto, Lombardy, and Piedmont, divided
from the rest of the nation and renamed "Padania." These separatists
point to the fact that the Italian north is eight times as rich as the south
and is therefore taxed more, yet much of the tax revenue goes to funding reconstruction and development of the impoverished Mezzogiorno,
or south. As the country functions now, all government ministries are
based in Rome and decisions concerning all regions are made in the
capital city. By separating themselves from their southern countrymen,
the northerners feel, they could keep their money and decision-making
powers to themselves.

These signs of separatism have crept up gradually. First there was
the Alitalia airplane pilot who, upon arrival at Milan's Malpensa Airport, announced, "The crew and I would like to welcome you to Padania." Then came a few maverick letters addressed to the fictional
country of Padania, which the post office actually delivered. Next, a
small "security force" called the "Green Shirts" appeared with the purpose of "securing the southern borders" of Padania. On September 15,
1996, Umberto Bossi, who was responsible for the idea of Padania, declared its "independence" from Italy and claimed it would soon have
its own Parliament and currency.

Padania's roots actually go back to 42 B.C., when the emperor Au-
gustus divided the Italian peninsula into eleven regions for administrative purposes. One region, called Gallia Cispadana, was bordered by
the Po River; the other, called Gallia Transpadana, lay south of the Italian Alps. Although Bossi is largely considered ludicrous for his the-
atrics and on a national level few take him seriously, he is nonetheless
a force to be reckoned with: in 1996, the city of Treviso in northern
Italy gave 42 percent of its votes to Bossi's political party in national
elections. But Bossi's influence does not come from his idea of creating
the independent nation of Padania; it comes rather from the fact that he
exposed a nerve in Italian society and pinched it hard, bringing the
problem of Italy's regional differences to the spotlight.

Before Bossi dedicated himself to creating Padania, he was one of
the first to insist that Italy should become a federalist nation, his idea

being to decentralize the Italian government by giving more autonomy to the individual regions, thereby letting them decide how to spend their tax revenue. His cries of *"Roma ladrona"* ("Rome the thief") made an impact on people around the country who were tired of seeing their income taxes thrown into the black hole of governmental bureaucracy and corruption.

Because of the lopsided north-south system of taxation, many Italians live with an enormous feeling of injustice, the northerners because their taxes are not recycled back into their region, the southerners because they have been forced into relying on government handouts. Bossi's idea of creating Italian federal states has caught on, and the current Italian government has been exploring this option as a possible solution for easing regional tensions. It is unlikely that Italy will be divided into two separate nations, but if the reforms under way are brought to term, Italy could become a nation of united states.

The Economy

Italy's economy has become the world's fifth strongest over the past few decades. It has done so despite a weak government and mainly on the merit of hardworking individuals. The setting for most of the nation's prosperity is not mile-wide and mile-high retail centers as in the United States, but little two-room *botteghe,* or small shops, concentrated in the north of the country. While other nations made their fortunes through big business and industry, Italians became rich by making things such as hand-produced eyeglasses and buckles for precision-crafted ski boots. Italy is exceptional in this regard: aside from a few large corporations such as Fiat and Benetton, the backbone of its economy is the mom-and-pop store. For while the state struggled in the past with the burden of maintaining the costs of its massive monopolies and subsidizing failing businesses (even the *panettone* cakes Italians love to eat during the holiday season are state-made), the individual Italian entrepreneur blossomed.

Following years of internal woes caused by the Clean Hands anticorruption investigations, Italy has now set its sights north of its border. The sobering effects of the post-Tangentopoli era have caused Italians to scrutinize their role as one of the founding members of the European Union, as well as their participation in the European Monetary Union, since it was revealed that regardless of a strong economy,

Italy was having trouble meeting the EMU requirements. As a result, the country, led by Prime Minister Roman Prodi, is on a crash diet to slash inflation and reduce the deficit through deregulation and privatization. State-run white elephants such as Telecom Italia, the phone company, are being auctioned off to private bidders. Other state monopolies such as the railroads, the electricity company, and many industrial holdings are soon expected to be split up into parts and sold off as well. Consumers, in the meantime, look forward to improved services.

When it comes to work, Italy's biggest problem is unemployment. Twelve percent of Italians do not have jobs, and in some areas of the south unemployment figures have hit an alarming 50 percent among recent college graduates. Steps have been taken to reduce unemployment, such as creating lower-paying training periods for young people trying to break into the workforce, offering employers incentives to hire, and decreasing work hours, thereby allowing more room for new employees. Italian labor is heavily unionized among the three main labor unions (all politically affiliated)—the Confederazione Generale Italiano del Lavoro (CGIL), the Confederazione Italiana Sindacati Lavoratori (CISL), and the Unione Italiana dei Lavoratori (UIL)—which make it extremely difficult for employers to fire unwanted employees. Because labor laws protect the worker and not the employer, many employers are reluctant to hire for fear of having to absorb high labor costs such as benefits and pensions, and some opt to hire illegally instead.

Immigration

At the beginning of this century, the volume of Italian emigrants to the Americas was so great that entire towns in Sicily and near Naples were practically emptied, left with only half or even a third of their natural population, with some smaller villages completely abandoned. Young men in search of work left their wives and children behind, promising to return with riches earned abroad. A few returned, but many more stayed away, settling in places such as the United States and Argentina. Not all emigrants went to the New World, however; many Italians ventured to the industrial north, to cities such as Milan and Turin, where they found positions in the new automobile and manufacturing companies there. Migration from the south to the north is what fueled a large part of the Italian economic miracle. Historians began to say that Italy "had the Third World within its borders" as the south provided a continuous supply of cheap labor for the successful factories of the north.

Since the beginning of the 1990s, immigration has taken over as foreigners from other countries flood Italy's gates, coming in from places such as North Africa, sub-Saharan Africa, Sri Lanka, the Philippines, Latin America, and eastern Europe, especially the former Yugoslavia and Albania. In 1995, Italy's population grew by more than 1 percent due to immigration, more than the natural growth of the country. Italy is now home to 58 million people and host to about 900,000 registered aliens (the number of illegal aliens is estimated to be just as high). For the first time, the nation is faced with the task of assimilating different races, cultures, and religions.

Unlike the Italian migration from the south to the north, which helped build a strong economy, today's immigrants are forced into the margins of society, holding jobs such as housecleaning, window washing, street vending, or crop picking. Many Italians feel that their presence is a burden on the economy, and, as in much of the rest of Europe, legislators are taking steps to curb immigration by instituting stiffer border patrols and by deporting immigrants lacking the proper stay permits. At the same time, steps have been taken to accept foreigners. Recently passed laws make it possible, for example, for some immigrants to vote in local elections and participate in the armed forces. Regardless, immigration is changing the way Italians perceive their own identity, and this new racial and ethnic mix is contributing to the overall cultural wealth of the country. In 1996, a young black woman won the "Miss Italy" beauty pageant, thus redefining the standards for Italian beauty.

The Mafia

On July 19, 1992, anti-Mafia prosecutor Paolo Borsellino was murdered with five members of his security escort on a highway in Palermo. A few months later another prosecutor, Giovanni Falcone, was murdered with his wife in a similarly gruesome manner. Then, one May night in 1993, Florentines awoke to a shattering blast that made the ancient walls of their houses tremble. Someone had planted a bomb near the Uffizi Gallery in Florence, leaving five people dead and forty injured, and destroying precious artworks in one of the world's most important collections. The explosion was the first of a rash of attacks. That same month, in Rome, another bomb was planted, believed to be intended to kill a television personality who had recently dedicated a program to condemning the Mafia. In July of that year, three car bombings—two in Rome and one in Milan—left another five dead and twenty-eight injured.

Although the circumstances of these attacks have not been made completely clear, the Italian Mafia is believed responsible for all of them, as it attempts to restore its diminishing power and influence. The car bombs in Rome damaged two of the city's most prized churches, and many believe it's more than a coincidence that the attacks against the church occurred just shortly after Pope John Paul II visited Sicily to urge the islanders to stand up against organized crime. It is also much more than a coincidence that the bombings all occurred around the start of the Clean Hands investigations, when organized crime lost its "influential friends" because many of them were put under criminal investigation. Unprecedented numbers of arrests of *mafiosi* themselves, including the arrest of the "boss of all bosses," Salvatore "Totò" Riina, suspected in the Borsellino murders, have served another equally effective blow to their power. Now it seems that almost every day the evening news reports new arrests and new trials convicting *mafiosi*. *Pentiti,* former gangsters turned police informers, are squealing on each other left and right, brushing aside their allegiance to *omertà,* or the code of silence, which was their protective shield for so long.

Yet whether the Mafia has been weakened is still to be determined. Without a doubt criminal organizations still hold a death grip on parts of the south. The "Super Mafia," as it was called in the 1970s, infested the country and lurked in every shadow, reaching the pinnacle of its power when isolation and underdevelopment of the south left people with little means to fight back. And while the "Super Mafia" is supposedly disappearing, the three main branches of the Mafia—known as "Cosa Nostra" in Sicily, "Camorra" in Naples, and "'Ndrangheta" in Calabria—still exist. They entice recruits with false promises of power and influence in a part of the country still suffering from high unemployment and economic difficulties. Businesspeople in the south are still forced to pay a *pizzo,* or bribe, to local criminals to have their businesses "protected." Many Italians worry that perhaps, in fact, the state's fight against the Mafia has not succeeded in diminishing the

Mafia's power, and some even suspect that the older generation of *mafiosi* sitting in jail cells is already being replaced by new, younger *mafiosi*—a breed more ruthless and violent than its predecessors. Southerners live in a state of fear, and the state's newly sponsored telephone crime hot line, designed to allow people to anonymously inform police of crime tips, has reportedly never rung. What exactly is the capability of this new generation of Mafia in the south remains, for now, unknown, but none can ignore its very palpable presence.

The Family and the Evolving Role of Women

Film and popular culture have depicted *la mamma italiana* as a black-scarved, kitchen-bound, overbearing matron. She is, in fact, one of the most cherished and essential figures in Italy, deeply respected as the pillar of the Italian home. But among younger women, the role of the *mamma* is changing. Forty percent of young mothers are also working women, and 10 percent of the Italian Parliament is female. Women have strong presences in professions such as politics, publishing, and journalism and have served as the head of the Chambers of Deputies and head of the state-run television networks—a big jump from when Italy was remembered as having a flashy porno queen named "la Cicciolina" ("The Cuddly One") as a parliamentary deputy.

As the role of the Italian woman has changed, *la famiglia,* the Italian family unit—considered by Italians the sturdiest building block of a healthy, stable society—has also undergone a metamorphosis. More Italian couples are opting to live together rather than get married, and it is not uncommon for Italy to have a zero birthrate some years. At the current negative birthrate, demographers predict that the Italian population will face extinction in two hundred years. In general, Italians have significantly fewer children than Americans and women from other European nations. When they do have children, they often have them at an older age (in some areas of the north, the average age for a mother giving birth to her first child is as high as twenty-seven). Italy also has one of the lowest abortion rates in the world. Although the options of both abortion and divorce were introduced to Italy relatively recently—both were made legal in the mid-1970s—their numbers are not high enough to be the sole cause of the changes in the Italian family. These changes stem rather from how Italians view themselves today:

Some things change, some things stay the same: a mamma italiana *in Palermo, Sicily.*

less as part of a family unit as in the past, and more as individuals with choices to make regarding careers and personal self-enrichment.

Nonetheless, Italian families continue to put enormous emphasis on eating together, taking care of grandparents, and making sure children can always count on their parents for support no matter what their age. Curiously, as the new Italian family evolves, a sentiment known as *mammismo* is on the rise. A *mammone* is the Italian equivalent of a "mama's boy," and *mammismo* is the trend of young people to live at home and be supported by their parents. Statistics show that fifteen years ago 47 percent of males between the ages of twenty-five and twenty-nine lived with their parents. In 1996, that figure rose to nearly 70 percent. *Mammismo* is due mostly to the country's high unemployment levels but also shows that the Italian family, despite the changes, still remains a coherent unit.

Old meets new: An electric bus zooms by the Colosseum.

Religion

Italy is primarily a Roman Catholic nation, Rome being home to the pope, Vatican City, Saint Peter's Basilica (the largest Catholic church on the planet), and more Catholic churches per square mile than any other place in the world. However, the religious identity of this country— once famous for miracle apparitions and crying Madonna statues—is changing quickly. Immigration from foreign continents has brought many faiths to Italian shores. Only a few miles away from the Vatican sits one of the biggest Islamic mosques in the Western world. A thriving Italian Jewish community flourishes throughout the country, and in fact some of the traditional Roman cuisine is based directly on Jewish recipes. Sects of Buddhism have popped up in recent years, regularly holding conferences that attract members from all over the world. It often surprises foreigners to learn that Italians themselves in general are not practicing Catholics (in fact, according to a poll published in *Newsweek* magazine in 1993, the United States actually has a higher percentage of believers in its population than Italy does, and more Americans believe in life after death than do Italians). Italians, however, still follow many of the Catholic traditions such as celebrating weddings in church and closing businesses on local saint's days.

Italy and the New Millennium

Italy will be the site from which the year 2000 is inaugurated. Not only the Vatican but all cities from Venice to Palermo are preparing themselves for the massive numbers of pilgrims and tourists expected to visit. They are launching Internet sites, making improvements to transportation systems, and mapping out new artistic-historical itineraries. Paintings and monuments are being restored, bridges and underpasses are being built, parking lots are being constructed, and airports are being enlarged. The Year 2000 Jubilee, celebrating two thousand years of Christianity, will be more than a religious event: it will be the moment in which the world looks to Italy to celebrate two thousand years of civilization. In the spirit of the event, Italians are embracing everything the new millennium will bring. The countdown has already started, making this one of the most exciting times to be in Italy.

CHAPTER TWO

Getting Ready for Take Off

So you're ready to take off and move to Italy? Chances are, you haven't thought of many things that will make your transition smoother and your life there more convenient and comfortable. In the long run, the key to successful planning for the move overseas is anticipating the things from home that you will miss and doing the paperwork that must be completed in the United States. Planning before you go will minimize your culture shock and help you feel "at home" in your adopted country from the start.

Visas

Due to Italy-America agreements, if you're going to Italy as a tourist for less than three months, you don't need to apply for a visa. However, you will need one if you are planning on staying longer or if you are going there to study or work. Some visas are harder to get than others, some nearly impossible. One obstacle you'll inevitably encounter is that the application process can take an excruciatingly long time to complete: in some cases you must wait nine months between submitting your application and receiving a response. The delay is explained by the fact that your paperwork must be sent to Italy, be evaluated by the appropriate ministries, and then be sent back to the Italian Embassy or Consulate in the United States. From the colorful, frame-worthy stamp in your passport to the sense of accomplishment you'll have, getting a visa will make you feel as though you've received a diploma in a course called "Italian Bureaucracy 101."

While the exact requirements for each visa differ, there are some basic requirements common to all. First of all, you will have to go in person to the consular office of the embassy in Washington or to one of the ten consulates located in major cities across the United States. You will be asked to complete multiple copies of an application form stating where you plan to go and for how long, as well as your reasons for going. You will also be required to present a series of documents, which vary according to visa. The important thing is to bring at least seven copies of each document as well as the original. In order to apply for any visa, you must bring the following general documents:

- a valid passport
- passport-sized photos (sometimes six to eight are required)
- proof that you are a resident of the area where the consulate is located
- a letter stating why you're going, for how long, exactly where you'll stay, and the names of any people who will accompany you
- a valid round-trip ticket or proof that you intend to travel from Italy to another country before returning to the United States
- proof of financial means while in Italy (this must be a letter from your bank on its letterhead stating your account number(s) and balance(s); if you are retired, bring recent pension checks)
- the visa of any country you intend to visit after Italy, if this is the case

The Italian Embassy is located in Washington, D.C., while consulates are located in Boston, Chicago, Detroit, Houston, Los Angeles, Miami, New Orleans, New York, Philadelphia, and San Francisco. There are also vice consulates scattered about smaller cities, but their function is limited. Most offices are open in the mornings for visits and during the afternoon for telephone calls. They are usually swamped with work—the Italian Consulate General of New York receives more than 1,200 calls per day—which means you should go knowing what you want and armed with the correct documents. The offices are closed on weekends and holidays except for emergencies, and the busiest times of the year are summer, Christmas, and Easter. Because the embassy in Washington and the consulates in New York and San Francisco have sites on the Internet, you can find some information on line, perhaps saving yourself a trip in person.

While a visa allows you to enter Italy with a certain legal status, once in the country you are under the jurisdiction of the Italian police and no longer the consulate that issued the visa. More specifically, the visa determines how you are viewed by the *questura* (the local police headquarters) in Italy when you go to apply for a *permesso di soggiorno* (stay permit). It also determines which kind of *permesso* you can apply for. Visas with solid backing (e.g., letters from Italian employers) tend to get higher priority and a faster response, and visas for study abroad students enrolled in major American universities are often granted within a few days. The important thing to keep in mind is that there is no real relation between the visa and the permit. For example, even if you enter Italy with a work visa, the *questura* officials can decide not to give you a work permit. Or you might get a work visa from the consulate for two years, only to receive a work permit from the *questura* for one. If you do enter Italy without a visa, once you arrive you are supposed to apply for a general stay permit lasting three months, though many shorter-term visitors don't do this. That permit can then be renewed for another three months before you must leave the country. (All this is discussed in detail in Chapter 4.)

RESIDENCY VISA

If you are going to Italy for a longer period of time and can afford to live there without working, you may want to consider getting a *visto per dimora*, or residency visa. This visa is often used by foreigners who have retired and collect income from a pension plan or Social Security. You can apply for a residency visa by taking only the general visa documents described above.

FAMILY VISA

There are two kinds of family visas. The purpose of both is to allow family members of Italian citizens, or family members of American citizens who already have Italian visas, to go to Italy. Neither allows the visa holder to work or study there. Which visa you get depends on the relative location of the various family members at the time of applying at the Italian Embassy or Consulate. For the first visa, the *visto per coesione familiare,* all family members must be in the United States when the visa application is filed. If some family members are in the United States and some are already in Italy, the second visa, the *visto per ricongiungimento familiare,* should be requested. In this second case, in addition to filing the application with the Italian Embassy or Consulate in the United States, those who are in Italy must go to the local *questura* to file an application for their relatives to join them. For both visas, in addition to the general visa documents described previously, you will have to bring documents proving your familial relations.

STUDENT VISA

The *visto per motivi di studio,* or study visa, is for students who are already enrolled in a school in Italy and is one of the easiest and fastest visas to obtain. Keep in mind that the Italian Embassy and Consulates have an Ufficio Studenti (Students' Office), which offers a variety of services such as assistance with enrolling in an Italian university. To apply for this visa, take the general visa documents described earlier, as well as the following to the consulate:

- an acceptance letter from a school or university in Italy, showing when your studies will begin and end
- proof of health insurance that will cover you while overseas
- a letter from your parents', guardians', or own bank stating their account number(s) and balance(s)
- a notarized letter signed by your parents or guardians (if you are financially dependent on them) or yourself (if you are financially self-supporting) taking financial responsibility for you during your stay in Italy

WORK VISA

There are four basic kinds of work visas you should know about, each one with different requirements. There are also other specific work-related visas, such as visas for professors on sabbatical. If you don't fall into one of the following four categories, call the Italian Embassy or Consulate for more information.

EMPLOYMENT VISA   You must first have an employer who is willing to vouch for you in order to obtain the *visto di lavoro subordinato,* or employment visa. A year could easily pass from the time your employer files the necessary paperwork to the time you receive the visa. Unless you are already employed by an Italian company in the United States or are living in Italy, it's virtually impossible to find a company willing to go through the long bureaucratic hassle involved. If you do have an employer willing to help you, in addition to the general visa documents you must take authorization from the Ispettorato Provinciale del Lavoro (Provincial Labor Office) from the Italian district where you are going to work; this must be requested by your employer in Italy and signed by the local *questura*.

VISA FOR WORKING IN ITALY AND GETTING PAID FROM THE UNITED STATES There is a special visa just for employees of an Italian company who will be paid by a foreign company while in Italy, called the *visto di lavoro subordinato per un 'azienda italiana retribuito da una compagnia estera*. This is needed, for example, if you work for a company in the United States and are transferred to Italy but will continue to be paid by the home headquarters. In addition to the general visa documents required, take the following to the Embassy or Consulate:

- a letter from you stating that: (a) you are an employee of the company; (b) you are being transferred to the Italian branch of your company (make sure to specify the location of the Italian office); and (c) the U.S. office will continue to pay your salary directly
- a letter from your American employer stating the same information that your letter does; your employer's signature must be notarized by a public notary, authenticated by a county clerk, and stamped by the State Department with a seal
- a letter from the director of the Italian company confirming that the information in the home company's letter is correct (in this case, restating the information is necessary); the director's signature must be authenticated by an Italian *notaio*, or notary public

FREELANCING VISA The *visto per lavoro autonomo o indipendente*, or visa for self-employment/freelance work, is a real Catch-22. The visa permits you to freelance in Italy, but you cannot get it without an Italian company willing to state that it will hire you as a "consultant." Ultimately, this can create a hassle for the company, and therefore most companies are not willing to make the effort. In order to obtain a self-employment visa, you must take the general visa documents required to the embassy or consulate, as well as the letter from the Italian company saying why it wants to hire you as a consultant; this must be notarized by an official Italian notary public.

Although the Italian Embassy and Consulate do not require it, it may be useful to take copies of any documentation proving you are a freelance professional in your field. For example, if you're an actress, bring your portfolio and copies of any playbills that show your acting experience. Also, take copies of your résumé and a list of professional references, just in case. If you're a tax consultant, for example, take any diplomas and official certificates you have earned, as well as proof of professional associations you might belong to. All of these things could help persuade the authorities in Italy.

GENERAL BUSINESS VISA   If you're planning to engage in any general commerce in Italy, the *visto per affari* is for you. In addition to the materials required for the self-employment/freelance visa listed above, you must also take a letter that describes the kind of business activity you plan to engage in, the name of your company, the city and street address of your company, and proof of registration with the local Italian chamber of commerce (*camera di commercio*).

Preparing to Go

LAST-MINUTE PAPERWORK
    Aside from applying for a visa, there are other bureaucratic preparations to make, the most obvious being that you have to obtain a passport. Passport applications can be filed with a U.S. Passport Agency, at a post office, or in many state and federal courts. If you already have one, don't forget to check the expiration date. Also, make photocopies of it for safekeeping, since there are few things as worrisome as losing your passport overseas. In addition, in many cases where you think an actual passport might be needed—such as cashing traveler's checks—often a photocopy will suffice.

    If you're planning to take a lot of personal goods with you, or if you want to take expensive professional equipment, contact the Italian Embassy or Consulate for the latest customs regulations. Generally, you can take limited numbers of items to Italy without paying custom duties, such as cameras, jewelry, a bicycle, skis, and small amounts of tobacco, alcohol, and coffee. However, *all* items must be for noncommercial use, which means that you aren't planning to sell them. If you plan to take a pet with you, you will have to obtain an official certificate from a state-registered veterinarian declaring that the animal is in good health and has had a rabies vaccination at least one month, but no longer than one year, before departure.

MAKING FINANCIAL PREPARATIONS

The most important financial preparation to make before you move overseas is planning your budget. When you do so, count on things in Italy costing as much as they do in the United States. This is true for rental apartments, restaurants, and groceries. Usually, cities tend to be more expensive than suburbs, especially if you live in the downtown area.

Saving Money   One way to save money is by applying for a calling card with a U.S. telephone company such as MCI, AT&T, or Sprint. Italian long-distance rates are infamously high and can make a big dent in your funds. Also, consider investing in a portable computer and fax modem before you go so that you can have access to electronic mail. E-mail will let you communicate with all of your professional contacts, friends, and family back home almost free of charge. If you won't be going to Italy for long, signing up with CompuServe before leaving the United States may be a good choice (see Chapter 10).

Getting Money   If you have an international ATM bank card with your bank in the United States, you can almost always make withdrawals from Italian bank machines. However, you should make sure before you go that your secret personal identification number, or PIN, is composed of numbers and not letters, since many Italian ATM machines have only numerical keypads. For example, if your code is I-T-A-L-Y, change it to 4-8-2-5-9. Also, keep in mind that many Italian ATM machines cannot accept a code that has more than five digits. Since the international PIN issue varies from bank to bank, call your local U.S. branch for specific directions. If you are planning to take a lot of money with you to Italy, you may want to consider opening a *conto estero,* or foreign currency account, with an Italian bank before leaving the United States. If, instead, you plan to use traveler's checks abroad, remember to purchase them before leaving (American Express and Thomas Cook are the most widely accepted). It is also extremely useful—in fact, "essential" according to most seasoned travelers—to have a major American credit card as well (in general, Visa, American Express, and MasterCard are the most common in Italy). If you already have a credit card, don't forget to notify the card company of your change of address.

Anticipating U.S. Banking and Tax Needs   If you have regularly occurring debts to pay in the United States (such as mortgage installments, student loans, or building maintenance payments), you should prepay them before leaving or devise a system whereby a bank or a trusted person will pay them for you. If you plan to continue paying U.S. bills from Italy, you will most likely need to pack your checkbook. Once in Italy, you will have the option of making U.S. tax payments through the American Embassy or Consulates, but if you prefer not to do this you will have to do it with the assistance of someone back home. Finding a reliable accountant or friend who will have access to your W-2 forms should not be left for the last minute. Also, keep in mind that if you file estimated taxes quarterly, you can prepay all annual taxes due to the IRS in one lump sum. If you want someone else to have access to your bank account to assist with your payments, you must give that person a "power of attorney" before you go by filling out paperwork at your bank. Lastly, if you receive Social Security or other monthly payments (e.g., dividends or interest) in the United States, arrange to have them deposited directly in your U.S. bank account before leaving.

Last-Minute Reminders   It is always a good idea to keep a few hundred dollars with you as dollars, not changing them into lire, for they will come in handy when you fly back to the States. In addition, you should arrive in Italy with some dollars already converted into lire to cover small initial expenses such as a taxi from the airport. However, don't change too much—it's always better to avoid changing lire back into dollars, since you normally lose money during the exchange. (For more information about money, banking, and taxes, see Chapter 5.)

CLOSING YOUR HOME IN THE UNITED STATES

If you own a home in the United States, it is generally preferable to terminate all utility contracts if you'll be gone for a long time. If you plan to rent out your home, make sure the new tenants put their name onto the utility bills so that you are not responsible for their charges. But, whether you own or rent a home in the States, it's advisable to prepay any housing bills before you leave. You can overpay basic bills (e.g., electricity, gas, phone, and any other bills that generate a minimum monthly charge) so that the utility companies can then subtract the payments due from the existing credit. As an alternative, you can arrange for automatic payment through your U.S. bank or credit card, which is actually the norm when you subscribe to an American Internet access or e-mail provider.

You should also instruct the U.S. Postal Service to forward your mail to your Italian address—which it will do for a fee up to one year after you move—or hold it in storage for up to three months. Otherwise, you should arrange to have someone in the United States collect your mail for you. If you expect to do a lot of mailing from Italy once you've arrived, look into setting up an account with American shipping companies and overnight express mail services (e.g., Federal Express or DHL) before you go. These services are more expensive in Italy, and setting up an account with an American one may save you money in the long run. Also, pack a roll of U.S. postage stamps in case you need to send self-addressed stamped envelopes to the States. If you need to ship furniture or a car overseas, shop around for freight-shipping companies in your area. When you call, make sure to ask if customs taxes are included in the price.

KEEPING TRACK OF CONTACTS BACK HOME

Create a directory of the phone numbers of your bank, credit card company, and health insurance company before you go (toll-free and non-toll-free, since you sometimes can't call 1-800 numbers from Italy—though if you dial 1-880 instead of 1-800, or 1-881 instead of 1-888, you can access them but will pay regular long-distance rates). If the "1-800" number you want is created with words (e.g., 1-800-ITALIAN), write down the corresponding numbers, since your Italian phone won't have letters on the dialing pad (see Appendix for a conversion table). Also, collect the phone numbers and addresses of companies you regularly use in the United States, especially ones that ship overseas, such as bookstores and mail-order companies. You may want to make a photocopy of your address book and leave it with someone in the States, although you can dial 176 for U.S. directory assistance from Italy.

PREPARING FOR GOOD HEALTH ABROAD

Insurance and Physicians   In order to avoid being caught unprepared with a health problem, check if your insurance company will cover you overseas. If it doesn't, look into buying an international policy with another company. If you are on Medicare, look into getting a supplement reimbursement plan, since Medicare itself won't cover you abroad. You may also want to call the International Association for Medical Assistance to Travelers (IAMAT) and request their list of English-speaking doctors in Italy before you leave. Arrange for a last round of medical, gynecological, and dental checkups before you go, and write down a clear summary of your medical history, including allergies to medicines.

Medicine and Toiletries   If you take prescription medicine, including birth control pills, take an extra supply with you or arrange for someone to send you refills. Also, get the generic names of the prescription medicines from your pharmacist or doctor at home; this may make it easier to find equivalents in Italy. If you have favorite over-the-counter medicines, such as Advil, Bufferin, or Tylenol, pack a supply, since these are often hard or impossible to find in Italy. You should take all medicine in its original containers so that Customs officials don't mistake them with narcotics, and pack your prescriptions with them just to be on the safe side. Take all the brand-name toiletries you are accustomed to using, too. Italy has its own variety of toiletries and carries many American ones as well, but if you're particularly attached to things like ChapStick lip balm or Secret deodorant, you might not like using a substitute. If you wear contact lenses and prefer a specific brand of solution, take it with you, as American brands can be hard to find in Italy.

Last-Minute Purchases   There are a few things you can buy before leaving that may come in handy later. These include an American health guide or dictionary and a portable scale from the States, since Italian scales are in kilos and not pounds (though some Italian stores sell scales that display readings in both). (For more information, see Chapter 7.)

PLANNING FOR YOUR HOME AWAY FROM HOME

Cooking and Baking   Americans abroad inevitably begin to miss American food, so take a good supply of culinary supplies with you. Unlike U.S. Customs, the Italian authorities will allow you to bring food from abroad, and I have one friend who once brought over a frozen turkey one Thanksgiving. One way around the problem of missing American dishes is to make the food yourself, and this becomes especially important around the holidays. An American cookbook and an American calendar with the dates marked will be helpful for planning these events. Because Italy uses the metric system, you will need to take American measuring spoons and cups, and a meat thermometer calibrated in both Celsius and Fahrenheit, with you. Other hard-to-find baking items include muffin tins and American-size pie pans. No matter what, don't forget to pack the most essential ingredient: a can of baking powder. You can't buy American baking powder in Italy, and it's too confusing to try to figure out the equivalent amounts using Italian brands of yeast.

Electronics   Some Americans make the mistake of packing lots of American movies on videotape, only to find the tapes cannot be used in Italian videocassette recorders. Unless you have a video player in Italy that will play both PAL (the Italian system) and NTSC (the U.S. system), don't take VHS movies on cassette. The same goes for American hair dryers. Using them in Italy tends to cause electrical surges, so hair dryers are best left at home and bought new once there. For all electrical appliances and electronics, purchase 110-to-220-volt, 50-hertz AC transformers and plug adapters. You can buy them in Italy, but they are sometimes hard to find. Also, bring American three-to-two-prong plug adapters, which are impossible to buy in Italian stores, in case you need one in order to plug your appliance into the transformer.

Computer Supplies   If you have a computer, stock up on American software before leaving, since it's difficult to buy the English-language version of most programs once there, though Italian versions of system software and the most popular word processing programs are available. If you plan to make frequent purchases, find out if your American computer supplier will ship overseas. Some companies, such as PC & Mac Connection in New Hampshire, do all of their business through mail order, and information about these can be found in the back of computer magazines. If your printer model is older or has been discontinued, take a supply of printer cartridges, too. (See Chapter 10 for details.)

Student Planning

If you are a college student, you will have to meet with an academic adviser at your school to discuss the issues of graduation requirements, transfer credit, and taking a leave of absence. Make sure to get all the necessary forms as far in advance as possible or arrange to have someone in the States send them to you in Italy. If your enrollment in the American college is based on a scholarship, find out from a financial adviser if you can take a leave of absence without losing that funding. If you are planning to apply to an American graduate school or a summer internship program while in Italy, you will need to get official copies of your school transcripts from the bursar's office before leaving the States. This is also true of any recommendation forms and letters from professors, as well as application forms and school catalogs you might need. National exams, such as the GRE or GMAT, can be taken in Italy, but you should look into registration before you go. Also, because it is much more difficult to find the test study books in Italy, buy the ones you might need before leaving the United States.

If you want to get the International Student Identity Card (ISIC) for discounts to some museums and travel, contact the Council on International Educational Exchange (CIEE) before leaving. This card costs less than $20 and is especially useful when it comes to buying discount plane tickets. Unfortunately, in Italy it accomplishes little else, since most museums do not give discounts when you present it. Also, if you want to buy a Eurailpass, the discount train ticket for Europe, you must purchase it from CIEE or other travel agencies before leaving the States since it cannot be bought in Europe (see Chapter 9 for details).

Preparing to Work in Italy

When it comes to working in Italy, there are some basic details which, when anticipated in advance of leaving the United States, can make your stay easier and more enjoyable. For example, if you will need to prepare reports to send back home, take reams of American paper with you. Italian paper is narrower and longer and won't fit correctly into American folders or files (this can be a huge problem and should not be underestimated). If you're planning to send letters on your American letterhead from Italy, pack a supply of stationery and envelopes. If you have any subscriptions to special trade magazines, arrange to have them mailed to you in Italy. Find out first if those same magazines are available on the Internet, since you can save yourself money by reading them on line. Most of the major business guides published in English, such as *Hoover's* or *The Red Book,* cannot be bought in Italy except through mail order. If you know you'll need any in particular, take them with you.

Useful Addresses

EMBASSY OF ITALY

1601 Fuller Street, N.W.
Washington, DC 20009
tel (202) 328-5500
fax (202) 328-3605
www.italyemb.nw.dc.us:80/italy

ITALIAN CONSULATE GENERALS

BOSTON:
100 Boylston Street, Suite 900
Boston, MA 02116
tel (617) 542-0483
fax (617) 542-3998

CHICAGO:
500 North Michigan Avenue, Suite 1850
Chicago, IL 60611
tel (312) 467-1550
fax (312) 467-1335

DETROIT:
535 Griswold
1840 Buhl Building
Detroit, MI 48226
tel (313) 963-8560
fax (313) 963-8180

HOUSTON:
1300 Post Oak Boulevard, Suite 660
Houston, TX 77056
tel (713) 850-7520
fax (713) 850-9113

LOS ANGELES:
12400 Wilshire Blvd, Suite 300
Los Angeles, CA 90025
tel (310) 820-0622
fax (310) 820-0727

MIAMI:
1200 Brickell Avenue, 8th Floor
Miami, FL 33131
tel (305) 374-6322
fax (305) 374-7945

NEW ORLEANS:
630 Camp Street
New Orleans, LA 70130
tel (504) 524-2271
fax (504) 581-4590

NEW YORK:
690 Park Avenue
New York, NY 10021-5044
tel (212) 737-9100
fax (212) 249-4945
www.planetitaly.com/New/Consulate/

PHILADELPHIA:
1026 Public Ledger Building
100 South 6th Street
Philadelphia, PA 19106-3470
tel (215) 592-7329
fax (215) 592-9808

SAN FRANCISCO:
2590 Webster Street
San Francisco, CA 94115
tel (415) 931-4924
fax (415) 931-7205

STUDENT INFORMATION

Educational Testing Service (ETS) of the College Board
Princeton, NJ 08541-6000
tel (609) 921-9000
Publications about the GRE, MCAT, etc:
tel (800) 537-3160
Council on International Educational Exchange (CIEE)
205 East 42nd Street
New York, NY 10017
tel (212) 822-2600
www.ciee.org
(Or call (888) COUNCIL toll-free for the office nearest you)

Living

Soldiers from the Garibaldi Brigade play tribute to the country and its traditions.

CHAPTER THREE

Making the Adjustment

Sept. 26, '92.—Arrived in Florence. Got my head shaved. This was a mistake. Moved to the villa in the afternoon. Some of the trunks were brought up in the evening by the contadino—if that is his title. He is the man who lives on the farm and takes care of it for the owner, the marquis. The contadino is middle-aged and like the rest of the peasants—that is to say, brown, handsome, good-natured, courteous and entirely independent without making any offensive show of it. He charged too much for the trunks, I was told. My informant explained that this was customary.

Sept. 27.—The rest of the trunks brought up this morning. He charged too much again but I was told that this also was customary. It is all right, then. I do not wish to violate the customs.

—Mark Twain, *Autobiography,* 1892

Moving to Italy means culture shock. It means replacing the familiar comfort of your routine back home with a new one and listening to a language you don't understand. In Italy, you have to explain how you feel about America yet often feel out of tune with the things going on there, especially where popular culture is concerned. It also means missing what you cannot replace—the minute, physical details of daily life at home—and discovering aspects you may like just as much or even more. There's no doubt that it is an exciting and daring experience, but it can also be scary. The best way to deal with your fear is to accept that culture shock is a normal part of living abroad and try to do things to take the "shock" out of your transition. Many Americans tend to avoid other Americans in the early stages because they feel that speaking English will hamper their learning of Italian. At first that may be true, but ultimately your contact with fellow expatriates will be important as you learn to rely on them for your local connection to home. However, whether your friends be American or Italian, it cannot be overstated that a good command of the Italian language will be crucial to your success.

Culture Shock

THE THREE STAGES OF CULTURE SHOCK

Foreigners go through similar stages of culture shock no matter how well they are integrated into Italian society. From our experience, there are three main stages common to all:

EXCITEMENT AND CURIOSITY You are thrilled to be in Italy and anxious to learn as much as possible about your new home. You are outgoing and happy, ready to make new friendships and to try activities you've never done before. You find the lack of technology in Italy "quaint" and are happy to be free from your world of shopping malls and voice mail. You embrace these differences because you see them as romantic. You enjoy what you see as the "quirky" things about daily life (e.g., stores closing for a few hours at midday) and start to believe that such things make Italy a more "human" place than the States. You admire the Italians' attention to fashion, and you become more conscious of what you wear. Most of all, you don't want to stick out as a foreigner, especially an American.

DISBELIEF AND FRUSTRATION At a certain point you start to notice things about Italy that you don't like. This often happens following a frustrating encounter with the local bureaucracy, an argument with a bank teller who doesn't offer the same customer service you're used to, or a bus strike. You can't believe that people could live with such problems on a regular basis. You begin to resent the lack of technology and miss things from home. You wonder why you're making your life more difficult by living in a foreign country—and of all places, in Italy. Furthermore, you are sick of having Italians ask you about American culture. Their curious questions (e.g., "Which do you like better, America or Italy?") once seemed charming but are now irritating. This is the hardest period to get through. It can last a week, a month, or more than a year. If there are enough things about the country that you truly like, patience will help you make it to the next phase. If there aren't enough, you may end up moving back home.

SATISFACTION AND BELONGING Eventually you begin to see that things aren't as bad as you thought, and you learn the shortcuts that Italians themselves use to get around frustrating obstacles. You feel that fitting into Italian society does not require giving up your true self, and you find ways to use your American experience to create solutions

A country road in Tuscany.

for yourself. You become fluent in the language. You appreciate Italian culture as different from your own yet also part of who you are. You have finally understood how to get things done. That sense of magic you felt at the beginning returns, and you feel lucky to be living overseas. You accept the distinctions of being an expatriate and learn to value your unique experience as that of an American abroad.

FACTORS THAT MAY CONTRIBUTE TO YOUR SENSE OF SHOCK

There are many things that contribute to your sense of culture shock, from little things such as vegetables you've never seen before to bigger ones such as codes of conduct required if you don't want to offend someone. Since the number of differences you will encounter is so great, here are a few descriptions of what you're in for and of some of the blunders Americans inevitably make.

MANNERS AND SOCIAL BEHAVIOR We Americans may joke that the British pay too much attention to manners, but keep in mind that the British based many of their social codes on Baldassare Castiglione's *Il libro del cortegiano*, which was translated as *The Book of Courtesy* in 1528 and became a best-seller in the United Kingdom. In modern

Italy, social status and manners still abound. In fact, Italians unconsciously assess other people's age and relative social standing seconds before the first words of greeting are exchanged, altering their grammar and vocabulary appropriately. Theoretically, noble titles were abolished in Italy when Victor Emmanuel III abdicated in 1946, yet many people who otherwise would have had titles still flaunt them whenever possible.

Staying in an Italian home overnight can be a cultural adventure in itself, since your normal manners may not only clash with but directly contradict those of your Italian hosts. For example, the first time you come into an Italian kitchen in your bare feet, you'll realize that it's not the norm in Italy—Italians always wear slippers or shoes around the house. Or when you show up at the breakfast table in pajamas, that's not acceptable either, since Italians put on a bathrobe or come dressed to the table. Even when it comes to gift giving, you may run into problems, thinking it's better to buy a gallon bottle of less expensive wine for dinner because "the more the merrier." On the contrary, Italians will have a pretty good idea what the wine cost and would bring a regular-sized bottle of more expensive wine themselves. In general, Italians don't like "bargains" the way Americans do; they believe in quality over quantity, they pay attention to the way clothing is stitched, and the brand name on goods is vital. To be safe, always bring a smaller, more expensive, yet appropriate gift.

CIGARETTE SMOKING   When I arrived at the Rome airport on my first visit to Italy, I was amazed to find so many people puffing away inside the terminal at six in the morning. In the train station people smoke as they wait in line; in shoe stores there are ashtrays strategically placed around the showrooms for the convenience of the smokers. I have seen more than one butcher cut meat with a butt dangling from his lips. Even in the government offices where VIETATO FUMARE (no smoking) signs are posted on the walls, the employees often sit smoking as they stamp people's documents. When you go out to eat, there aren't any "no smoking" sections, and you may find yourself enjoying your pasta to the smell of tobacco. In addition, Italian smokers don't normally ask if you mind when they want to smoke, and anti-smoking laws exist but are rarely enforced.

NUDITY   Nudity in the media can be disconcerting to unaccustomed Americans. Half-naked and naked women often appear on the covers of the leading Italian newsmagazines, and prime-time TV shows regularly feature scantily clad dancing girls. With all of the nudity around, American men may think it's okay to walk the streets without a shirt on. Yet while women may go topless on the beaches, Americans should be warned that it is generally illegal for men to go topless in cities.

PHYSICAL CONTACT AND INTIMACY   Starting with the kiss on each cheek Italians routinely give when greeting, Italian physical contact makes many Americans seem rigid and detached. Italian girls are often seen holding hands, adult friends walk arm in arm during Sunday strolls, and male friends (as well as fathers and sons) often hug and kiss each other when they meet. You'll notice the lack of personal space if you ride a public bus. Even if the bus is virtually empty, another passenger will not hesitate to sit in the seat next to yours. When people speak together, they often touch each other's arms or hands to emphasize a phrase. You will often see people stroking each other's cheek affectionately as they converse. In fact, hands are of utmost importance— so much so that Italians can have entire conversations from a distance using a complex system of hand gestures with no risk of miscommunication. Learning the common gestures is as fundamental as learning the language, for the same gesture used in different ways can mean entirely different things. For example, there is one gesture in which the index and pinkie fingers are extended in the shape of horns: pointed at the ground, it wards off bad luck; pointed at someone else, it accuses him or her of being a cuckold. When it comes to intimacy, Italians draw a sharp distinction between the words *ti amo, ti voglio bene,* and *mi piaci. Ti amo* (I love you) is used only in romantic relationships, while *ti voglio bene* (I care about you) is also used for close friends and family. Normally, saying *"ti voglio bene"* in a romantic situation is interpreted as a lack of total commitment or sense of uncertainty about the relationship. *Mi piaci* (I like you) is the most casual expression of all.

MYTHS AND STEREOTYPES

The Italian interest in all that is American can work for or against your culture shock. On the one hand, it's a pleasant surprise to hear American songs constantly on the radio and watch American films or TV shows dubbed in Italian. Italian media often seem to dedicate as much space to American news as to local news. You'll meet many Italians who are obsessed with all things American (songs, movie titles, actors' names, brand names), and Italians covet their Levi's and Timberlands as we might covet an Armani suit. One thing that is amusing to Americans in Italy is that Italians often misunderstand names of American things and mispronounce them without realizing what they're doing. When you try to explain to them that they're wrong, they are often disappointed. For example, try to tell Italians that Darth Vader from *Star Wars* is not called "Dark Venner," as they were introduced to him; chances are that they will not be swayed.

Yet it can also be irritating to find yourself up against all the Italian myths and stereotypes of America, especially the unflattering ones. Some Italians will claim that Americans have no history, tradition, or culture. They even have a phrase—*È un'americanata!*—to describe not only multimillion-dollar American action films but anything that is tacky or an exaggerated waste of money. Some of the most pervasive stereotypes include: American women are promiscuous; all Americans are obese; all Americans are rich like the characters on *Dallas;* and many American schoolchildren go to classes carrying guns. Unfortunately, try as you may, there's little you will be able to do to debunk these myths.

Networking

One of the best things you can do to make your Italian life more satisfying and productive is network. Networking—be it for social or professional purposes—is a full-time activity in Italy. For work it is more essential than in the United States, especially since potential employers most likely haven't heard of your college, don't care about your GPA, and aren't impressed by letters of reference from unknown faces overseas. In other words, you are what they see and nothing more, so you have to make personal connections in order to get ahead. One good thing to keep in mind is that most Italians love to meet foreigners, which means that for you networking will often be nearly effortless. You will meet people at the bus stop, at bars, and in *piazze.* You may find that the barber cutting your hair has a son who just failed an English exam at school and needs tutoring or that the person on the exercise bike beside you in the gym happens to work for an import-export company. For example, I met a lot of Italians through a kayaking club I joined. Italy is an endless chain of *contatti* that you can become an active part of if you get out there and network.

The question is, how do you make the first step? First of all, be adventurous. Do something you've never considered doing back home.

For me it meant joining the boat club; for you it could mean becoming part of a theater group, taking up mountain biking, or learning how to make pottery—anything that puts you into touch with Italians and Italian culture. (We have included a list of some Italian sports federations at the end of this chapter that can help you find local athletic clubs and associations.) Also, continue doing activities you've always pursued (whether it's dance, political activism, or Bible study), and search for clubs and organizations you can do them with. Remember that networking often means offering and receiving help in one form or another as well as showing you're planning to stick around—if people don't think you're intent on staying, they won't go to the effort of giving you a helping hand.

THE ENGLISH-SPEAKING EXPATRIATE NETWORK

In some Italian towns, foreigners often seem to outnumber the Italians, and Americans in particular have created a vast network. By becoming involved, you'll find yourself surrounded by others who can help you with anything from finding a plumber or lawyer who speaks English to identifying the best shops in your neighborhood. There is an expatriate club for just about every interest, from women's clubs to drama groups. For example, the American International League is for people interested in participating in charity work and social events. The multiple chapters of both Democrats Abroad and Republicans Abroad (the overseas branches of the Democratic and Republican National Committees) organize events related to politics. There are expatriate associations geared toward pooling professional information and experience, such as the Professional Women's Association. Another, called Network, is a group of native-English-speaking female residents of Florence and Tuscany, which meets once a month for buffet dinners and guest lectures, exchanging information, ideas, and friendship. (The Network newsletter is also a great source for job and apartment hunting.)

Often the expatriate circles are organized around a central element such as the embassies and consulates. In particular, the American Embassy organizes lectures, concerts, and social activities such as parties for the Fourth of July and Halloween (I once went to a chili cook-off stocked with American beer, chips, chocolate chip cookies, and brownies, and instantly felt back in the United States). It also has a Culture Desk that can help Americans orient themselves and has lists of some expatriate clubs and events. Every one or two weeks the various

English-speaking embassies organize social nights, including "TGIF" (USA), the "Churchill Club" (England), "Beaver Bar" (Canada), and "Roo Bar" (Australia). American overseas schools (see Chapter 19 for addresses) organize baseball and basketball leagues, fairs, and potluck dinners. They also sponsor Cub Scouts, Girl Scouts, and Boy Scouts. The American universities and the American Academy in Rome have lectures, concerts, and exhibitions that are often open to the public. In addition, there are more than thirty-five English-language churches and synagogues in Italy that sponsor bake sales, cultural activities, and outings. By taking advantage of these resources, you can create a new "home away from home" more similar to the one you left behind than you'd ever imagined possible.

LOCAL ENGLISH-LANGUAGE RESOURCES

Thanks to industrious expatriates and business-minded Italians, Italy has excellent English-language resources that make life abroad much easier. Because expatriates tend to come and go, smaller clubs also tend to open and close. If you can't find a group that shares your interests, you'll have to create it yourself. The most prominent resources include the following.

THE *ENGLISH YELLOW PAGES* The *English Yellow Pages* (*EYP*) is a phone book published by and for the English-speaking expatriate community in the cities of Rome, Florence, Bologna, and Milan. It has addresses and phone numbers of associations, professionals, and companies that address expatriate needs. It also provides useful regional information, such as addresses of local hospitals, outdoor markets, and post offices. You can buy the *EYP* at English-language bookstores or order it by mail or phone (see address at end of this chapter).

ENGLISH-LANGUAGE PUBLICATIONS Aside from the international editions of *Newsweek, Time,* and *Business Week,* as well as the *International Herald Tribune* and *The European,* which can all be bought at newsstands (in Rome and Milan, *The New York Times*—two to three days late—has also been spotted), there are English-language publications produced locally in Italy. Each one varies in tone and focus. *Vista* has articles and information related to Florence and Tuscany that travelers, students, and residents will find useful. These include reviews of local art exhibitions, news pertaining to expatriates, information about places to go on weekends, and calendars of cultural events. The *Time Out* guide to Rome is published once a month and provides mainly listings of cultural events and services in the Eternal City. *Metropolitan* has both feature articles and classified listings as well as calendars of events in Rome. *Yes, Please* is a fashion magazine in English that comes out every three months. *Wanted in Rome* has an abundance of classified ads, plus some travel information for trips around the city. *The Informer* provides more general technical information and practical advice for expatriates all over the country.

ENGLISH-LANGUAGE BOOKSTORES   There are more than fifteen English-language bookstores in Italy. For networking, their bulletin boards, full of "SOS" messages from Americans looking for good conversation and roommates, come in handy. Many expatriates consult these boards religiously. (See Chapter 15 for addresses.)

ENGLISH-LANGUAGE MOVIE THEATERS AND VIDEO STORES   There are Italian cinemas throughout the country that offer movies in English, though most only show them on certain nights of the week. The main ones include: Astro and Goldoni (Florence); Angelicum, Anteo, Arcobaleno, Mexico, and Odeon (Milan); Alcazar and Pasquino (Rome); and Adriano (Bologna). The Pasquino in Rome and Astro in Florence are two good exceptions that show exclusively movies in English on all days. These are great places to meet other Americans. There are also video stores that rent movies in English, including Blockbuster Video, which has branches everywhere and offers a wide selection of original-language titles. (If you can afford to get a satellite dish for your home, you can even watch the NBC Super Channel, CNN, and MTV in English.)

GAY RESOURCES

Compared to the United States and some northern European countries, Italy has less to offer the homosexual community in terms of support networks and events. Only the largest cities have gay clubs and bars, and there is only a handful of associations catering to the needs of gays and lesbians. Gay activism is less vocal than in the States, and gay issues rarely reach the media spotlight, though the Italian media often seem obsessed with homosexuality in the United States. The Catholic Church condemns homosexuality, and the words *frocio* and *finocchio* (literally, "fennel") are hostile words used for gays by the general population. As a result, gay rights have not emerged into the mainstream and gay couples still don't feel comfortable publicly expressing their affection for each other. In general, homosexuality is tolerated by Italians, but many prefer not to discuss it, leaving it instead a matter of privacy, many taking a "don't ask, don't tell" attitude. On the other hand, homosexuals have made some of the most important artistic contributions to the country's cultural heritage. From poet and movie director Pier Paolo Pasolini to director Luchino Visconti, Italian cinema, literature, and fashion are famous also thanks to the artistic genius of some of the country's most prominent homosexuals.

The gay and lesbian networks that do exist in cities such as Rome, Milan, Florence, and Turin are small but include things like gay beaches, bookstores, restaurants, cinema festivals, dance clubs, and bars. Some cities have a gay map called "Pianta Gay," available at newspaper kiosks, with English-language listings of activities and night life. Or you can buy *Babilonia,* a gay culture magazine with a lesbian section, at the kiosks as well. The biggest association for gays with some resources for lesbians is Arci Gay and Arci Lesbica. Its national headquarters is in Bologna, but local chapters can be found in every large Italian city from Turin to Palermo. They offer such services as free psychological and legal counseling, an AIDS information hot line for clinics and testing, and a hotline for information on gay and lesbian festivals and nightlife. The Circolo Mario Mieli in Rome and Informa Gay (with chapters in Turin, Genoa, Rome, Ravenna, and Perugia) offer similar services, and the Circolo also has a lesbian hotline. Ompo's Gay House in Rome, founded by Massimo Consoli (an important gay rights activist and founder of the Italian gay rights movement), claims to have the largest European gay library and more than fifteen thousand works available on the Internet at www.publibyte.it/promo/consoli. The Collegamento tra Lesbiche Italiane (CLI), based in Rome, is the nation's main lesbian group along with Arci Lesbica. CLI publishes a monthly magazine with a calendar of lesbian events and workshops, and a list of clubs and restaurants. All of the associations mentioned above can give you information about social and health resources available in other Italian cities.

RESOURCES FOR PEOPLE WITH DISABILITIES

There are approximately 4 million people in Italy who live with disabilities, 40 percent of whom are part of the Italian workforce. Yet this is not to say that Italy is equipped to accommodate disabilities as the United States is, generally due to a lack of technology and adequate architectonic restructuring. For example, I have never seen a regular Italian public bus equipped to take a wheelchair, and while many buildings are not even equipped with elevators, those that are often have elevators too small to accept wheelchairs. Universities usually lack adequate transportation, computers, and financial assistance for people with disabilities. However, some improvements are being made. Young men who opt for civil service over the military draft sometimes serve as readers for blind students. Traffic lights in some larger cities emit signals for the blind. Universities have created telephone hot lines for people with handicaps. In particular, the University of Rome "La Sapienza" has a library of more than three hundred university textbooks in Braille and on cassette, and a few classes are taught in sign language.

There are numerous smaller associations in Italy that people with disabilities can join, and some of the main ones are listed at the end of this chapter. When it comes to sports and free time, you may want to contact the Associazione Tempo Libero per gli Handicappati (ATLHA, or Free-Time Association for People with Handicaps). ATLHA organizes trips within Italy and abroad for both Italian and foreign people with disabilities, as well as other recreational activities such as museum trips, concerts, and sporting events. The Federazione Italiana Sport Disabili (FISD) is the Italian sports federation for people with disabilities. It can point you in the direction of regional clubs and sporting events for anything from swimming to archery. For legal issues, the Lega per la Difesa dei Diritti degli Handicappati (LEDHA), based in Milan, can advise you as to getting jobs, enrolling in school, and other legal issues. The Associazione per lo Sviluppo di Progetti Informatici per gli Handicappati

---

Getting Beyond Culture Shock: The Basics

✦ Learn Italian well, spoken and written; make a concerted effort to learn about Italian culture, history, and art; watch Italian films and TV. A list of books and films is included in the appendix at the back of this book.

✦ Be clear about why you're in Italy in the first place; set some personal goals (professional and social) for yourself while there, and try to maintain them.

✦ Make an effort not to berate Americans or the United States in an effort to fit in; ultimately, this can make you feel isolated from both yourself and your background.

✦ Try not to get caught up in the habit of complaining constantly about problems in Italy.

✦ Brush up on your American history and geography so you can give some concrete answers to Italians' questions about the United States.

(ASPHI) is a nonprofit association with branches in Milan, Rome, and Bologna. It provides computer-related courses for people with all sorts of disabilities, to keep you up to date on the latest technology. After you pass a qualifying exam, all courses are free. If you have Internet access, check out its great Web site with descriptions and definitions of useful Italian terms, as well as information about other local associations in Italy.

Useful Addresses

You will note that for some associations and clubs, only phone numbers have been listed. This is in cases where the organization has no official address and the president has requested that his or her home address not be given.

English-Language
Publications

English Yellow Pages
Via Belisario, 4/B
00187 Roma
tel (06) 4740861
fax (06) 4744516
eyp@isinet.it

The Informer
Via dei Tigli, 2
20020 Arese (Milano)
tel (02) 93581477
fax (02) 93580280
informer@mondoweb.it

Metropolitan
Via IV Novembre, 152
00187 Roma
tel/fax (06) 6798595

Vista Florence and Tuscany
Borgo degli Albizi, 15
50122 Firenze
tel (055) 2342898
fax (055) 244130
www.dada.it/vista

Wanted in Rome
Via dei Delfini, 17
00186 Roma
tel (06) 6790190
fax (06) 6783798
wantedinrome@compuserve.com

Time Out
Via Tomacelli, 146
00186 Roma
tel (06) 68809123
fax (06) 68809149
timeout@itaca.com

Yes, Please
Via Aristo, 2
20145 Milano
tel (02) 462185
fax (02) 4813660

Movie Theaters Showing
English-Language Films

BOLOGNA:
Adriano
Via San Felice, 52
40122 Bologna
tel (051) 555127

FLORENCE:
Astro
Piazza San Simone
50122 Firenze

Goldoni
Via Serragli, 109
50129 Firenze
tel (055) 222437

MILAN:
Angelicum
Piazza Sant'Angelo, 2
20121 Milano
tel (02) 6551712
Anteo
Via Milazzo, 9
20121 Milano
tel (02) 6597732
Arcobaleno
Viale Tunisia, 11
20124 Milano
tel (02) 29406054
Mexico
Via Savona, 57
20144 Milano
tel (02) 48951802
Odeon
Via S. Radegonda, 8
20100 Milano
tel (02) 874547
ROME:
Alcazar
Via Merry del Val, 14
00184 Roma
tel (06) 5880099
Pasquino
Vicolo del Piede, 19
00153 Roma
tel (06) 5803622

EXPATRIATE ASSOCIATIONS AND CLUBS

American Business Group Milan
tel (02) 809816
fax (02) 89501233
American Club of Rome
c/o Marymount
Via di Villa Lauchli, 180
00191 Roma
tel (06) 3295843
American International League
Uff. Postale, 33
Via G. Silvani
50124 Galluzzo (FI)
tel (055) 4250126
**American Women's Association of Rome
(AWAR)**
Savoy Hotel

Via Ludovisi, 15
00187 Roma
tel/fax (06) 4825268
Americans in Milan
tel (02) 466746
**Democrats Abroad Italy
Milano**
tel (0332) 820788
fax (0332) 227795
**Democrats Abroad Italy
Rome**
tel (06) 8080133
fax (06) 8080134
Fie Theater
Via delle Gore, 8
50141 Firenze
tel (055) 4361959
**FLAGG—Federated League of Americans Around the Globe
Rome**
tel (06) 4820147
fax (06) 4871149
Music Box Theater Company
Piazza Antonio Meucci, 23
00146 Roma
tel (05) 5592405
Network
c/o Syracuse University
Piazza Savonarola, 15
50132 Firenze
tel (055) 481449
tel (055) 571376
**Professional Women's Association
Milan**
tel (02) 48001427
fax (02) 29512793
**Professional Women's Association
(PWA)**
Savoy Hotel
Via Ludovisi, 15
00187 Roma
tel (06) 8551632
fax (06) 4744141
**Republicans Abroad Italy
Rome**
tel/fax (06) 635316

Welcome Neighbor
Via Barbarano Romano, 15
00189 Roma
tel (06) 30366936
fax (06) 30361706

RELIGIOUS ORGANIZATIONS
(ENGLISH-LANGUAGE)

FLORENCE:
Baptist Church
Borgo Ognissanti, 4
50123 Firenze
tel (055) 210537
Comunità Israelitica (Jewish)
Via L. Farini, 4
50121 Firenze
tel (055) 245252
fax (055) 241800
Lutheran Evangelist Church
Via dei Bardi, 20
50125 Firenze
tel (055) 2342775
**St. James American Church
(Episcopalian)**
Via B. Rucellai, 9
50123 Firenze
tel (055) 294417
St. Mark's English Church (Anglican)
Via Maggio, 16/18
50125 Firenze
tel/fax (055) 294764
MILAN:
All Saints Anglican Church
Via Solferino, 17
20121 Milano
tel/fax (02) 6552258
**Church of Jesus Christ of Latter-Day
Saints**
Viale Don Orione, 10
20132 Milano
tel (02) 2828846
fax (02) 2896292
English Roman Catholic Church
Santa Maria del Carmine
Piazza del Carmine, 2
20121 Milano
tel (02) 86463365
fax (02) 86462828

Methodist Church of Milan
Via Porro Lambertenghi, 28
20159 Milano
tel/fax (02) 6072631
NAPLES:
Christ Church
Via S. Pasquala a Chaiai, 15b
80100 Napoli
tel (081) 411842
PALERMO:
Church of the Holy Cross
Via Mariano Stabile
90100 Palermo
tel (091) 581787
ROME:
Anglican Church of All Saints
Via del Babuino, 153
00187 Roma
tel (06) 36002171
Jewish Synagogue
Lungotevere dei Cenci
00186 Roma
tel (06) 6564648
Methodist Church Ponte Sant'Angelo
Via Banco di S. Spirito, 3
00186 Roma
tel (06) 6868314
fax (06) 6896981
Rome Baptist Church
Piazza San Lorenzo in Lucina, 35
00186 Roma
tel (06) 6876652
Saint Andrew's of Scotland
Via XX Settembre, 7
00187 Roma
tel/fax (06) 4827627
St. Patrick's Church
Via Boncompagni, 31
00187 Roma
tel (06) 4885716
fax (06) 48903742
St. Paul's Within the Walls
Via Napoli, 58
00184 Roma
tel (06) 4883339
fax (06) 4814549
stpaul@mclink.it

San Silvestro in Capite
("Meeting Point")
Piazza San Silvestro, 1
00187 Roma
tel (06) 5121925
Santa Susanna
Via XX Settembre, 14
00187 Roma
tel (06) 4882748
fax (06) 4740236
VENICE:
Jewish Synagogue
Ghetto Vecchio
30135 Venezia
tel (041) 715012
Lutheran Evangelical
Campo SS. Apostoli
30135 Venezia
tel (041) 5220704
Methodist
Campo Santa Maria Formosa
30135 Venezia
tel (041) 5227549

GAY RESOURCES
Arci Gay and Arci Lesbica Nazionale
Piazza di Porta Saragozza, 2
40123 Bologna
tel (051) 580563
fax (051) 6446722
Circolo Mario Mieli
Via Corinto, 5
00146 Roma
tel (06) 5413985
fax (06) 5413971
CLI (Collegamento tra Lesbiche Italiane)
Centro Femminista Separatista
Via San Francesco di Sales, 1/a
00153 Roma
tel/fax (06) 6864201
Informa Gay
Via Santa Chiara, 1
10122 Torino
tel (011) 4365000
fax (011) 4368638
Ompo's Gay House
Via Ghiberti, 8/b

00153 Roma
tel (06) 93547567
fax (06) 93547483
www.publibyte.it/promo/consoli

ASSOCIATIONS FOR PEOPLE
WITH DISABILITIES (ITALIAN)

GENERAL HANDICAPS:
ASPHI
(Associazione per lo Sviluppo di Progetti Informatici per gli Handicappati)
Via Arienti, 6–8
40124 Bologna
tel (051) 277811
fax (051) 224116
ASPHI
Via Gozzadini, 7
20148 Milano
tel/fax (02) 40091878
www.asphi.it
ATLHA
(Associazione Tempo Libero per gli Handicappati)
Via Cascina Bellaria, 90
20150 Milano
tel (02) 6070564
fax (02) 6070578
FISD
(Federazione Italiana Sport Disabili)
Via Gregorio VII, 120
00165 Roma
tel (06) 39376846
fax (06) 39376843
LEDHA
(Lega per la Difesa dei Diritti degli Handicappati)
Viale Monte Santo, 7
20124 Milano
tel (02) 6570425
fax (02) 6570426
DOWN SYNDROME:
AIPD
(Associazione Italiana Persone Down)
Viale delle Milizie, 106
00192 Roma
tel (06) 3722510
fax (06) 37351749

Unione Italiana Down
Via A. Volta, 19
16128 Genova
tel (010) 592883
fax (010) 541527

EPILEPSY:

AICE
(Associazione Italiana contro
L'Epilessia)
Via Tommaso Marino, 7
21121 Milano
tel/fax (02) 809799

HEARING PROBLEMS:

AUDIES
(Associazione Nazionale per la Lotta
alla Sordità e la Tutela degli Audiolesi)
Via Pestrino, 6
30035 Mirano (Ve)
tel (041) 430079
fax (041) 431989

ENS
(Ente Nazionale Sordo Muti)
Via Gregorio VII, 120
00165 Roma
tel (06) 39366697
fax (06) 6380931

Istituto dei Sordomuti di Torino
Viale S. Pancrazio, 65
10044 Pianezza (TO)
tel/fax (011) 9677048

VISION PROBLEMS:

ANS
(Associazione Nazionale dei Subvedenti)
Via Clericetti, 22
20133 Milano
tel/fax (02) 70632850

Associazione Promozione Sociale
Disabili Visivi
Via Lima, 22
00198 Roma
tel (06) 8550260
fax (06) 8844800

UIC
(Unione Italiana dei Ciechi)
Via Borgognona, 38
00187 Roma
tel (06) 699881
fax (06) 6786815

SPORTS CLUBS (ITALIAN)

(*Note:* Ones marked with an asterisk are
all located in Viale Tiziano, 70, 00196
Roma)

FOR INFORMATION ABOUT ALL SPORTS:

Comitato Olimpico Nazionale Italiano
(CONI)
Palazzo delle Federazioni Sportive
Foro Italico
00195 Roma
tel (06) 36851
fax (06) 36857697

ARCHERY:

Federazione Italiana Tiro con l'Arco
Via Cassia, 490
00189 Roma
tel (06) 3312404
fax (06) 3663860

AVIATION:

Aero Club d'Italia
Viale Maresciallo Pilsudski, 122124
00196 Roma
tel (06) 879641

BASEBALL & SOFTBALL:

*Federazione Italiana di Baseball e
Softball
tel (06) 36851

BASKETBALL:

Federazione Italiana Pallacanestro
Via Fogliano, 15
00199 Roma
tel (06) 8863071
fax (06) 8444091

BOATING/SAILING:

Lega Navale
Sezione Roma
Via XXIV Maggio, 11
00187 Roma
tel (06) 6784706

BOXING:

*Federazione Pugilistica Italiana
tel (06) 36858276

CANOEING AND KAYAKING:

Federazione Italiana Canoa Kayak
Via Flaminia, 357
00196 Roma
tel (06) 3242050

CYCLING:
Federazione Ciclistica Italiana
Via Marsala, 8
00185 Roma
tel (06) 36857255

EQUESTRIAN SPORTS:
*Federazione Italiana Sport Equestri
tel (06) 36858344

FENCING:
*Federazione Italiana Scherma
tel (06) 36858520

FISHING:
*Federazione Italiana Pesca Sportiva
tel (06) 394754

GOLF:
Federazione Italiana Golf
Via Flaminia, 388
00196 Roma
tel (06) 394641
fax (06) 3220250

MOTORCYCLING:
*Federazione Motociclistica Italiana
tel (06) 36858371

ROWING:
Federazione Canottaggio
Via Crescenzio, 14
Roma
tel (06) 366596

RUGBY:
Federazione Italiana Rugby
Via Leopoldo Franchetti, 1
00194 Roma
tel (06) 3610821

SAILING:
Federazione Italiana Vela
Viale Brigata Bisagno, 2/17

16129 Genova
tel (010) 565723

SOCCER:
Federazione Italiana Giuoco Calcio
Via Gregoria Allegri, 14
00198 Roma
tel (06) 84911

SWIMMING:
Federazione Italiana Nuoto
Piazza Lauro De Bosis, 2
00196 Roma
tel (06) 3219001

TENNIS:
*Federazione Italiana Tennis
tel (06) 36858210

TRACK AND FIELD:
Federazione Italiana Atletica Leggera
Via della Cammilluccia, 703
00148 Roma
tel (06) 326831

VOLLEYBALL:
*Federazione Italiana di Pallavolo
tel (06) 3964651

WINTER SPORTS:
Federazione Italiana Sport Invernali
Via Piranesi, 44/b
20137 Milano
tel (02) 75431
fax (02) 7380624

WRESTLING, JUDO, HAMMER:
*Federazione Italiana Atletica Pesante
tel (06) 36858230

CHAPTER   FOUR

Understanding Paperwork

"Verba volant, scripta manent" means "spoken words fly away and writ-ten ones remain" in Latin and summarizes the justification Italians give to their obsession with paperwork. Many words have been used to de-scribe Italian bureaucracy, few of them positive. It has been called chaotic, Byzantine, labyrinthine, and Medieval. One of the only posi-tive aspects is that if you ever find yourself in a bind for conversation material at a dinner party, the topic of Italian bureaucracy is a foolproof way of initiating lively and heated debate. A few years back a major Italian newspaper published an article entitled "Good-bye *questura* Line, in Bologna Passports Can Be Issued in Half an Hour!" Thirty Italians lined up at the office to apply for a passport, and they received it that same day. The article described the feat as *"roba da Guinness,"* or "stuff worthy of world records." Don't get your hopes up, though, for like world records, improvements to the Italian bureaucracy don't come often.

Documents You'll Need
and Where to Get Them

In this chapter are discussed many bureaucratic procedures you must go through, each of which requires that you bring a series of documents and often passport-sized photos. Because the exact requirements for each procedure can change, double-check with the appropriate authorities in Italy about what is needed. There are, however, two basic elements of Italian paperwork you should immediately become familiar with: the *marca da bollo* and *carta bollata*. The *marca da bollo* is a tax stamp. It varies in value and can be purchased at the tobacco store, and it is always used for official documents. *Carta bollata* is paper that already has the tax stamp printed on it; this, too, can also be bought at the tobacco store. Whether you use the *marca* or the *carta* depends on the individual document. In addition, you should keep in mind that all important documents you bring with you from the United States—including your birth certificate and marriage certificate—will eventually have to be translated into Italian and authenticated by the U.S. Consulate or Embassy.

THE QUESTURA

The *questura* is the main police headquarters in any Italian city, and it will become an essential part of your life in Italy. It is the office where, among other things, *permessi di soggiorno* (stay permits) are issued to foreigners and passports are issued to Italians. It is also where you file a police report in the event of an accident, burglary, or any other crime. Most foreigners in Italy—as well as most Italians—will agree that the *questura* is not a friendly place. From the first guard who greets you roughly at the front door to the person behind the desk who takes your documents, you have the sense that this is a group of impatient and indifferent people. The *questura* is also difficult to navigate. There is no voice mail menu of options if you try solicit-

Important Vocabulary	
Questura	Italian police headquarters
Comune	Municipality where you live
Circoscrizione	Subdivision of a *comune*
Anagrafe/ Ufficio di Stato Civile	Bureau of Vital Statistics/ Census Office
Ispettorato Provinciale del Lavoro	Provincial Labor Office
Permesso di soggiorno	Stay permit
Libretto di lavoro	Work card
Permesso di lavoro	Work permit
Codice fiscale	Individual taxpayer number
Partita IVA	VAT tax number
Carta d'identità	ID card
Nulla osta	"No obstacle" permit
Marca da bollo	Tax stamp
Carta bollata	Paper with tax stamp on it

ing information by phone. If you are able to get a free line (which is nearly impossible), the receptionist will curtly tell you that information is given out only in person. Once you get to the *questura,* you will find no written guide and the information desk, when it exists, is located inside the station and therefore inaccessible until you get in. There is always a long line of foreigners out front, all there for different purposes. Because the *questura* is open for only half the day and refuses to make appointments, you may find the door closed in your face just before your turn comes up. Don't expect to be given the privilege of a guaranteed first place in the next day's line—you will just have to start again from the beginning. Yet some *questure* have offices or counters specifically for Americans where the wait is often shorter, so ask the guard at the door if there is one before you get in line. Some *questure* also list information on the Web sites of local town halls (see Chapter 10 for additional information on Internet access).

The *Comune*

The *comune* is the municipality where you live. Each *comune* has its own government administration, including a *sindaco* (mayor), and the office of the *comune* resembles the American town hall in terms of function. Its history goes back to feudalism, when residents of smaller geographic areas rose up against landowners in a desire for self-government. A *comune* may be divided into smaller entities called *circoscrizioni.* For example, the city of Rome is one *comune* but has twenty *circoscrizioni.* If you buy property or move from one *comune* to another, you will have to pay a visit to the *comune* office. You can locate it by looking in the phone book (we have provided a few numbers at the end of this chapter).

The *Anagrafe*

Each Italian *comune* has an *anagrafe* (bureau of vital statistics or census office). It is sometimes called the Ufficio di Stato Civile. The *anagrafe* is responsible for keeping track of demographic data such as deaths, births, and marriages and for issuing related documents. There's even an *anagrafe canina* for your dog's paperwork. Some Italian *comuni* offer a service called *anagrafe a casa,* whereby you can request the *anagrafe* documents over the phone and the documents are delivered to your home within forty-eight hours for a small additional fee. The individual *circoscrizioni* also have smaller census offices

The Palazzo Vecchio, home to the comune *of Florence.*

called *uffici anagrafici nelle circoscrizioni,* but they often forward you to the main *anagrafe* of your *comune.* Millions of documents are generated by the *anagrafe* each year, including:

- ID cards, or *carta d'identità*
- birth certificates, or *certificato di nascita*
- death certificates, or *certificato di morte*
- marriage certificates, or *certificato di matrimonio*

- residency certificates, or *certificato di residenza*
- criminal record documents, or *certificato di carichi pendenti* or *casellario giudiziario*
- certificates of citizenship, or *certificato di cittadinanza*
- family status documents, or *stato di famiglia*

FROM VISAS TO STAY PERMITS

Once you arrive in Italy, you must apply for a *permesso di soggiorno* (stay permit) within eight days. However, you cannot apply for a specific permit unless you have entered Italy with the appropriate visa, as discussed in Chapter 2. There are many types of stay permits, the most common being the *permesso di soggiorno per turismo,* the *permesso di soggiorno per ricongiungimento familiare,* the *permesso di soggiorno per coesione familiare,* the *permesso di soggiorno per studio,* the *permesso di soggiorno per dimora,* and the *permesso di soggiorno per lavoro.* The *turismo* permit is for anyone who comes to Italy as a tourist. Technically, even tourists planning to stay for one week should apply, but this rarely happens. This permit cannot extend for more than three months and can be renewed only once. The *ricongiungimento familiare* permit is for spouses, children, and dependent parents of Americans who are married to Italian citizens. This is given when family members come from the States to join others already in Italy. The *coesione familiare* is for the American spouse or children of an Italian citizen who have moved to Italy together. The *dimora* is for Americans establishing residency in Italy who do not intend to work or study. The *studio* permit is for students and requires the student visa.

The *lavoro,* or work permit, requires that you have a specific work visa. Providing the Italian Labor Ministry has approved your or your employer's work petition for you, the *questura* will issue you a work permit that lasts ninety days. During this time you must enroll in the Italian social security system, sign a labor contract with your employer, and obtain final authorization to work from the Provincial Labor Office. When this is done, the *questura* will give you a work permit, which is good for two years or as long as the job lasts.

To apply for any of the *permessi,* you must bring the following documents: a passport, the *permesso* application (obtained at the *questura*), a *marca da bollo* (the amount varies from year to year), at least three passport-sized photographs, and a previous *permesso* if you are renewing one. Make four photocopies of each to bring with you. Some *permessi* require other documents as well, such as your marriage certificate or your birth certificate and proof of financial means. Students must bring a certificate of enrollment and proof of health insurance.

THE *CARTA D'IDENTITÀ* (ID CARD)

Any citizen or resident of Italy can request a state-issued *carta d'identità* (ID card) at the *Anagrafe*. It is the standard form of Italian photo identification. The *carta d'identità* will enable you to travel to other EU countries without a passport. Italian law requires that you carry some form of photo ID with you at all times; if you do not have the *carta d'identità*, carry your passport or a photocopy of it.

THE *LIBRETTO DI LAVORO* (WORK CARD)

Do not confuse the *libretto di lavoro* with the *permesso di lavoro*. The *libretto* is a work card that all citizens and residents of Italy need to be legally employed, for it serves as a register of all employment positions you have had. It is obtained from the Ispettorato Provinciale del Lavoro (see local phone book for address) and is valid for ten years before it must be renewed. The *permesso di lavoro* (the work permit), on the other hand, is good for only as long as you are employed and is available to nonresidents as well.

THE *NULLA OSTA*

The *nulla osta*, or "no obstacle," document is a permit issued by the state confirming your eligibility to be a full-time employee, or *dipendente*, and serving as proof that you are an upstanding citizen. It is usually issued only after you have been offered legal employment and before you actually start working. It can be obtained at the Ufficio di Collocamento (Employment Office) of your *comune* or from the Ispettorato Provinciale del Lavoro. The *nulla osta* is good only for as long as you are employed with the given company or employer. *Nulla osta* permits are required for getting a job and for getting married.

THE *CODICE FISCALE*

The *codice fiscale* is an individual taxpayer number, the closest Italian equivalent to the U.S. Social Security number in that it is required of any individual—Italian or foreign—engaged in financial transactions. While it does not permit a foreigner to work, it is necessary for getting paid legally. It is also necessary if you invest in real estate, buy a car, open a bank account, pay bills or taxes, buy shares in an Italian company, apply for a professional license or authorization, register with the *Camera di Commercio* (Chamber of Commerce), or register as a member of an *albo* (professional order). It is an indispensable tool when dealing with bureaucracy and is becoming increasingly necessary in everyday living as many forms and applications require it. Recently, legislation was passed that made obtaining the *codice fiscale* mandatory for all Italian citizens.

Anyone moving to Italy should get a *codice fiscale* as it is easy to get and free of charge (having it does not mean you automatically have to pay Italian taxes). In order to get a *codice fiscale*, you must go to the Ufficio delle Imposte Dirette or Anagrafe Tributaria of your district with a valid ID or passport. If you are a foreigner, it's best to bring your passport and your *permesso di soggiorno*, although you might not be asked for it. You will be required to fill out a form providing information such as your name, gender, and place and date of birth. Within a few hours you should receive your *codice fiscale* number. The final plastic *codice fiscale* card, complete with magnetic strip, will be mailed to your home address. If your civil status changes (e.g., you get married or divorced), you must apply for a new *codice fiscale*. If you discover a mistake in the information on your card, you have up to six months to report the changes to the Ufficio delle Imposte Dirette; otherwise, you can incur a fine.

THE *PARTITA IVA*

The *partita IVA* is the Italian value-added tax (VAT) number, IVA standing for *imposta sul valore aggiunto*, which is the same as VAT. The *partita IVA* is required of all self-employed professionals, including freelancers and small-business owners. All individuals selling a service or product are required to charge the 19 percent standard IVA tax or the 38 percent luxury IVA tax and must have a special *partita IVA* number so that the government can keep track of their finances. In addition, they must register income and expenses on special stationery and file an income tax return. Many professionals using the *partita IVA* choose to let an accountant handle this complicated procedure, especially when it comes to keeping invoices and *registri* (books) in order. If you want to apply on your own, you should request a *partita IVA* from the Ufficio Provinciale IVA in your *comune* within thirty days of starting your professional activity. In order to get it, you need to bring your *codice fiscale,* your photo ID and copies of it, and proof that you have paid an annual fee to the Ufficio Provinciale IVA's account at the post office. This fee can be expensive and will include annual renewals. You will also have to buy special *registri* and leave them with the Ufficio Provinciale IVA for registration. After a few days you will get them back and can start writing invoices for your services. If your activity ends, you have thirty days in which to cancel your *partita IVA.*

Becoming a Resident

There are many good reasons for obtaining residency. With residency you can get health care through the Unità Sanitaria Locale; buy a house, apartment, or land; buy and register a new or used car, open a bank account, get a *libretto di lavoro* (work card; note: you are not guaranteed the work permit with residency); apply for an Italian driver's license; get an Italian identity card; and send your children to Italian public schools. In short, you have almost everything you could possibly want except the power to vote in Italian elections. There is, however, one good reason why you might not want to obtain it: Italian property owners avoid renting to residents because Italian tenancy laws make residents hard to evict.

To apply for residency, you must start the paperwork trail from the beginning in the United States, at least nine months before you want to leave. Get a residency visa from the Italian Consulate or Embassy, then get a *permesso di soggiorno per dimora* from the *questura.* Next, go to the Ufficio Stranieri of the *comune* where you live and apply for *residenza.* If you are requesting residency because you are married to an Italian citizen, you will obtain a family visa and family stay permit instead. Make sure to bring a copy of your marriage certificate (if it's in English, it must be translated into Italian and authenticated by the U.S. Embassy or Consulate).

Once you have been granted residency, you will be required to register yourself as a resident with the *anagrafe;* then you will have to wait at least three months until your residency confirmation is final. Sometimes the local police will pay you a visit to make sure you actually live where you say you do. You can lose residency by letting the permits expire or by not notifying the *anagrafe* of a change in address.

Carabinieri, *the Italian military police, sport fashionable Armani uniforms.*

Marrying an Italian Citizen

If you want to marry an Italian citizen in the United States, contact the city hall in the city where you plan to marry and ask which documents are required. Generally, your future spouse just needs to bring a passport, although sometimes blood tests are required. Also contact the local Immigration and Naturalization Service (INS) office and ask which documents are required so that your spouse can stay in the United States without problems after the wedding. There is an INS office in Rome and at the U.S. Consulate in Naples that can provide information.

If you plan to marry in Italy, the process is more complicated. Whether you decide to have the actual ceremony in a church or in the town hall, you must partake in a civil ceremony. When you are married in church, the civil part is incorporated into the ceremony. In both cases you must notify the *anagrafe* of your union so that it can change your civil status on the necessary documentation. You will have to obtain a long series of documents at various offices all over the city, and all foreigners must get a *nulla osta* document as well. An announcement of upcoming weddings is posted at the *comune* for two weeks prior to the ceremony, to give others the chance to object to it to prevent bigamy from occurring. (In 1996, Italy's most eligible bachelor, Giovanni Alberto Agnelli, hoped to wed his American sweetheart in secret, but his plans to keep the news from the media were botched when he was required to make his wedding public in advance by posting a notice.) At the civil ceremony you also have the option to sign a sort of prenuptial agreement called *la separazione dei beni,* which determines how your finances and property will be shared. Women who marry in Italy keep their maiden names, although many adopt their husband's surname for social purposes. Doorbells and bank accounts list two surnames, one for the wife and one for the husband. Children take their father's name unless the parents are not married or the father does not officially recognize the child as his own at birth.

Obtaining Italian Citizenship
or Dual Citizenship

Some Americans choose to obtain dual citizenship or even to renounce their American citizenship in favor of the Italian one (in 1992, Italians were permitted to hold dual citizenship for the first time). There are many reasons for becoming a dual citizen, the most outstanding being the right to certain state jobs, the right to vote in Italian elections, and the elimination of the need to apply for stay permits. If you are young and male, you might be wary of becoming an Italian citizen if you don't want to serve in the obligatory military draft, seen as a total waste of time by many young men who have completed it. Before you apply for Italian citizenship, contact the Immigration and Naturalization Service in the United States to see whether having Italian citizenship can compromise or cancel your American one, as the laws change. As of the writing of this book, the dual status will not affect your U.S. citizenship negatively at all. You may be able to obtain Italian citizenship if:

- You were born in Italy and are over twenty-one years of age.
- One of your parents is Italian.

- You've been living legally in Italy for at least ten years.
- You're married to an Italian citizen.
- You have Italian ancestors.
- You've worked for at least three years in an overseas office of the Italian government.
- You've been living in Italy for at least two years and you've given particular services to the nation, such as serving in the Italian military.

Most Americans obtain citizenship via marriage or Italian ancestors. In the case of marriage, you can request citizenship after six months of marriage if you and your spouse live in Italy or after three years if you live abroad. In the case of ancestors, you will have to prove that you are eligible by demonstrating a certain knowledge of their history, such as the fact that your Italian relative did not renounce his or her Italian citizenship. In order to do this, you will have to obtain documents such as the ship records from when your relative arrived in the United States and his or her naturalization forms. These documents will have to be obtained from various American authorities. Other documents required include your relatives' birth certificates. For example, if your maternal grandfather was born in Italy, you will have to get both his birth certificate and your mother's. Because the laws and requirements change, consult the Italian Embassy or Consulate in the United States before doing anything.

Ultimately, whatever your reason for requesting citizenship, you will have to go to the courthouse, or *prefettura*, of the *comune* you live in and bring three copies of many documents *in bollo* (with the tax stamp on them). If you are obtaining citizenship through marriage you must go to the local Ufficio Cittadinanza. All documents in English must be translated into Italian by an official translator, such as one at the U.S. Embassy, and must be made on *carta bollata*. Once your request has been accepted, you will receive a letter from the president of the Republic or Interior Ministry welcoming you to Italian citizenship. You should expect to wait approximately six months to two years before receiving this response. Once you have received your citizenship letter, you are cleared to apply for an Italian passport, which normally doesn't take long to procure.

The U.S. Embassy and Consulates

The U.S. Embassy is located in the heart of Rome on the fashionable Via Veneto in the former palace of Princess Margherita. There are three consulates, located in Florence, Naples, and Milan, as well as consular agents in Genoa, Turin, and Palermo who can handle some of the consular duties. There are many things that these offices will do for Americans, but be aware that they will not help you find housing or a job, obtain stay permits or dual citizenship, or deal with the Italian government in any way. You can count on the embassy for the following things:

EMERGENCIES

If you find yourself in the hospital, consular agents will visit you, or if a loved one has died while abroad, they will make arrangements for sending the body home. If you are jailed, they will send a representative to visit you in prison and notify your family. They will relay messages for you and make sure you receive proper medical treatment, but their only function is to ensure that you are treated equally. They cannot help you legally because they have no influence over Italian laws. You can contact the "officer on duty" at the embassy or consulate nearest you at any time including nights, weekends, and holidays. Call the number of the consulate or embassy and make a note of the emergency cellular phone number provided on their answering machine.

PAPERWORK

The embassy keeps a record of all Americans living in Italy that register with it as residents abroad. It is a good idea to register so that the U.S. Embassy knows where to find you in case of emergency. However, registering will not influence your standing with the Italian government as far as stay permits and residency are concerned (many Americans never register). You can also register births and deaths at the embassy. If you need notary public services, official translations, or authentication of documents (these services are necessary for much of the Italian paperwork), you can get them done here. If you have lost or damaged your passport, the Citizens' Services Office will give you a replacement passport for a fee. You can also renew your passport there. If you marry an Italian, you and your spouse will be sent to the U.S. Immigration and

Naturalization Service office in the American Consulate of Naples to complete the paperwork and interview for your spouse's U.S. visa.

FINANCIAL INFORMATION

There are tax specialists at the embassy and consulates who will help you with various aspects of tax filing and provide basic information (see Chapter 5 for more information). You can also file taxes at these offices. If you're expecting Social Security benefits, or if you have questions about payments, the Federal Benefits Unit at the embassy can provide information and assistance.

SOCIAL ASSISTANCE

The Community Liaison Office organizes meetings with the American Abroad Association and the American Chamber of Commerce. These meetings will give you a basic overview of the American community in your area. There is also an American Citizens Service Center to help expatriates deal with culture shock. The embassy and consulates will provide you with a basic reference list of English-speaking lawyers, doctors, accountants, tax preparers, translators, or schools for your child but will not make recommendations. For general questions about U.S.-Italy relations, contact the Press Office in the embassy.

Absentee Voting
in American Elections

If you are interested in voting in federal American elections while abroad, you can arrange to do so either before you leave the United States or once you have arrived in Italy. In the States, go to the Election Commission Office of the district you are registered to vote in and ask to apply for an "absentee" ballot. Requirements and deadlines vary from state to state, and in some states you can even vote absentee in local and state elections as well. If you want to vote in the presidential elections in November from Italy, contact the American Embassy or Consulate at least three months prior to the elections and request overseas voter information. Given that you meet the voting requirements, these offices will also provide you with a ballot and will mail it to the United States in its special Foreign Service mail system. Another option is to contact the Italian offices of the Republicans Abroad or Democrats Abroad (see Chapter 3 for addresses) for information.

Useful Addresses

In addition to the addresses and phone numbers of the *questure* and *comuni* that we have listed below, you can find information about the one nearest you in front of the local phone book under *numeri di pubblica utilità.* Go to these offices early in the morning, as they are usually closed in the afternoon. If you ever have questions concerning the latest laws, check the *Gazzetta Ufficiale,* a paper available at any newsstand, which publishes an updated list of the most recent legislative changes.

THE AMERICAN EMBASSY

American Embassy
Via Vittorio Veneto, 119/a
00187 Roma
tel (06) 46741
fax (06) 4882672

THE AMERICAN CONSULATES

American Consulate General—Milan
Via Principe Amedeo, 2/10
20121 Milano
tel (02) 290351
fax (02) 29001165
American Consulate General—Florence
Lungarno Amerigo Vespucci, 38
50123 Firenze
tel (055) 2398276
fax (055) 284088
American Consulate General—Naples
Piazza della Repubblica
80122 Napoli
tel (081) 5838111
fax (081) 7611869

AMERICAN CONSULAR AGENTS

Via Dante, 2
16100 Genova
tel (010) 584492
Via Re Federico, 18/bis
90100 Palermo
tel (091) 6110020
Via Roma, 15
34100 Trieste
tel (040) 660177
fax (040) 631240

COMUNI

BOLOGNA:
tel (051) 203111
FLORENCE:
tel (055) 27681
MILANO:
tel (02) 6236
NAPLES:
tel (081) 7951111
PALERMO:
tel (091) 7401111
ROME:
tel (06) 67101

QUESTURE

(*UFFICIO STRANIERI,* OR OFFICES FOR FOREIGNERS)

FLORENCE:
Via Zara, 2
50123 Firenze
tel (055) 4977665
MILAN:
Via Montebello, 26/28
20100 Milano
tel (02) 62263400
NAPLES:
Via Medina, Questura
80133 Napoli
(081) 7941111
ROME:
Via Genova, 3
00184 Roma
tel (06) 46862987

CHAPTER   FIVE

Money, Banking, and Taxes

Italy is the most highly taxed nation in the EU, and the level of tax dodging is known to be higher in Italy than in other European nations. It seems that every time you want to do anything—from registering a used moped to filling out a form at the police station—there's yet another *bollo* tax stamp to buy for yet another tax. Most of the time you don't even know exactly what the *bollo* is for, but you know that without it you can't complete your task. There are annual taxes you would never even dream of, on things like owning a car radio or pets, using credit cards, and having a driver's license. Some American expatriates end up evading taxes either because they don't understand the tax laws or because they feel they are too difficult to follow. More often than not, they don't understand even whether they're supposed to file with the U.S. Internal Revenue Service or with the Italian tax authorities. One of the most important things to remember is that you should file a U.S. tax form every year, regardless of whether you are earning money or not.

If you're technologically savvy, some of your banking and taxes can be cleared up via the Internet, and many major American banks permit you to access your account information on line. Some Italian banks already have Web sites, too, and local on-line banking should soon appear. The IRS itself has created a vast database of on-line information and allows you to file forms electronically. You can even purchase

American tax software programs that take you right through the IRS's tax-filing procedure. Even the Fisco, or Italian tax authority, has tax guides and databases on the Web. However, there is one thing that cannot be stressed enough: even though the technology has improved, tax laws change frequently. You should always consult a *commercialista,* or accountant, for updates on the latest tax requirements before making decisions concerning your money.

But whether you have a lot of money or a little, Italy makes you feel richer. There's a difference between spending 2 million lire and $2,000. In fact, the additional zeros may confuse you so much that at first you have to be careful not to give people 50,000-lire bills instead of 5,000-lire ones. Although Italy has often claimed it would subtract a few of the zeros from its currency to make things simpler, so far it has not done so. In fact, the changes that have been made have only heightened the confusion. For example, sometimes there are as many as three different coins minted for the same denomination. Counterfeiting in Italy is such a problem that the Ministry of Finance redesigns the currency every few years. The bills are full of little security devices, such as a thin metal ribbon that runs down the bill, watermarks, and special color coding. One thing, however, always stays the same: how to calculate the exchange rate. If you start with dollars, multiply the dollars by the exchange rate (e.g., 1,500 lire to the dollar); if you start with lire, divide the lire by the exchange rate.

The Benefits of Sticking with American Banks Abroad

On a short-term basis, it is easier and cheaper to continue banking with your bank in the United States than to open an account with an Italian bank. Even on a long-term basis, many Americans prefer not to deal with Italian banks because of the often poor customer service and high bank fees. Generally, each major American bank has a special "worldwide" department that handles Americans residing overseas. Some charge a modest annual fee ($25 average) for its services, which often include having your monthly statements and bank correspondence sent to your Italian address.

You have many options for accessing money, each with different advantages and disadvantages. Aside from cash and traveler's checks, the most common are described on the following pages.

THE INTERNATIONAL ATM CARD

Practical experience has shown that the easiest option is to leave your money in an American account and access it using an ATM card for withdrawals in lire. The greatest risk of the ATM card is, of course, that it may be stolen, lost, or eaten by a hungry "Bancomat" (Italian ATM). Many of the Italian banks are part of an international network such as CIRRUS or NYCE, and many machines even offer instructions in English. If your PIN number includes letters, make sure you ask your bank about changing it to digits before leaving for Italy. You may also have to get a specially formatted "international PIN number" depending on your bank. The advantage of using your American ATM card is that you have money immediately, while the disadvantage is that there is a (usually 3,000 lire or $2) fee per *prelievo*, or withdrawal, plus whatever fee your home bank may charge.

CREDIT CARDS

Italians are not big believers in plastic. In fact, they are openly suspicious of it. You can't buy many things with credit cards that you can in the States, and credit card payments by phone are uncommon. When eating out or shopping around town, expect to see heads shake "no" when you pull out your card. In fact, you should always inquire at smaller hotels and restaurants before making reservations if you plan to pay with a credit card. As a result, many Italians walk around with huge wads of cash crammed into their pockets. In addition to the amount of the purchase and any regular card fees, there is generally a 1 percent currency conversion fee applied to purchases made abroad. Using your cards to draw cash advances is unwise because they normally involve sky-high interest rates and an extra 3 percent overseas fee (2 percent for the transaction fee plus 1 percent for the conversion fee).

WIRING MONEY FROM YOUR U.S. BANK

Wiring money from your U.S. bank to a bank in Italy is a good option if you won't go hungry if the money doesn't arrive on time. They say it should take five to seven days, but from our experience it can take ten to fourteen. Sometimes a transfer doesn't arrive at the right branch and you have to track it down on your own. If you send transfers often, you will also spend loads of money on fees at both ends. The fastest way to transfer funds is to have an account in Italy and an account in the United States. If both branches are part of the "Swift" system of international transfers, your American bank can send the money directly to your Italian branch. If your American branch isn't part of it, you can always wire the money from an Italian bank in the United States; if your Italian branch isn't part of the Swift system, money can be wired to your Italian bank's headquarters, which will then transfer it domestically to your local Italian branch.

THE AMERICAN EXPRESS MONEYGRAM AND WESTERN UNION MONEY TRANSFER

The American Express Moneygram and the Western Union Money Transfer are fast but expensive ways to send money to Italy. They take only ten to fifteen minutes to arrive overseas, cost approximately $50 to $60 to send $1,000, and can be sent from hundreds of places in the United States. In Italy, you can pick up the money in lire at one of the five local Amex offices (two in Florence, one in Milan, one in Rome, one in Venice) or from one of the many Western Union representatives.

PERSONAL AND CERTIFIED U.S. BANK CHECKS

Don't even think about writing a personal check on your U.S. account and cashing it in Italy. Neither people nor banks will accept them. The only thing they are useful for is paying bills back home. The one exception we have found is American Express, which will accept U.S. checks for your Amex credit card payments if you make the payment in person at one of their offices. You can also use your U.S. checks there to buy traveler's checks. Getting a certified check, or *assegno circolare,* from your American bank is not advisable either. Italian banks will not cash certified checks unless you have an account with them, and if you do have one it may take a while for the tellers to be convinced that your check is valid. If you're studying with an American college in Italy, however, the school may have a special check-cashing deal with a local bank.

The Italian Banking System

If you have more complex banking needs, or if you plan to live in Italy for a long time, you will want to open an account with an Italian bank. Frequently situated in antique stone palaces adorned with frescoed ceilings and smooth marble counters, Italian banks offer all of the regular teller services as well as twenty-four-hour ATM machines (Banco-

A branch office of the Banca Nazionale di Lavoro, located in the Piazza della Repubblica in Florence.

mat). Bancomat cards can now be used for making payments in some stores and for paying bills at the post office, too. You can also check your balance and make withdrawals using a Bancomat machine; you cannot, however, use it to make deposits. If you have an Italian account, your bank can automatically pay housing bills for you, and you can pay other bills with a bank-to-bank transfer called a *bonifico* (the *bonifico* can also be used to send money abroad). Bank branches are generally open to the public from 8:30 A.M. to 1:00 or 1:30 P.M. and 2:30 to 4:00 P.M. or 3:00 to 4:30 P.M., Monday through Friday. Some banks in city centers are also open on Saturdays from about 9:00 A.M. to 12:00 P.M. The downside to Italian banks is that they charge notoriously high fees for everything from cashing checks to closing an account. The upside is that they often offer higher interest rates than American ones do.

DIFFERENT ACCOUNT OPTIONS

As an American, you must have Italian residency and a *codice fiscale* (Italian individual taxpayer number) to open a *conto corrente* or *conto interno* (account). The *estratto conto* or *resoconto* (bank statement) is sent to you at the end of every month or every three months, depending on the bank. There are different kinds of accounts that you can open, including a *libretto di conto* (passbook savings) and a checking account with a *libretto di assegni* (checkbook). You can also apply for a Bancomat card with your accounts, but remember that generally daily withdrawals on it cannot exceed 500,000 lire. Any dollars you deposit (*versare*) must be first converted into lire. If you plan to open a joint account, keep in mind that there are two types: a *conto corrente cointestato* (where either person can make transactions without the other's signature) and a *conto corrente a firme congiunte* (where both signatures are needed for even the smallest transaction). Italian citizens can also open an account in a foreign currency called a *conto in valuta*. You can even open a savings account at the post office called a *conto postale*, which works like a bank account but has no credit card or Bancomat card attached. This type of account does come with *assegni postali*, special checks that can be used to pay bills at the post office.

Note that any transfer of money or deposit from an American bank of $10,000 or more will be automatically reported to the IRS by that bank. When the money arrives in Italy and goes into an Italian account, start a paper trail in case the IRS wants to know what happened to it or if you repatriate it later.

IL CONTO ESTERO

A nonresident American planning to stay awhile can open a *conto estero*, or foreign currency account. This account must be opened in a specific currency, such as dollars, and any money withdrawn from it will be withdrawn in that currency and then can be converted into lire. The source of funds must originate from outside Italy, meaning that if you have a check drawn on an Italian bank in Italy you cannot deposit it into your *conto estero*. You can, however, deposit cash you have brought with you from the States. This type of account can be opened through the American branch of an Italian bank, but the procedure is generally much more complicated as some banks will require a minimum deposit of about $10,000 as well as various letters of reference. The easier alternative is to open a *conto estero* once you get to Italy.

DIFFERENT TYPES OF BANKS

Some Italian banks function on a national level, making banking a lot simpler because you can find their branches everywhere. Two of the larger ones include the Banca Nazionale del Lavoro and the Banca Commerciale Italiana. Even the city banks such as Banca di Roma and Banco di Napoli have branches all over the country. On the other hand, some banks function only locally, making travel less convenient. More than one hundred Italian banks already have Internet sites that provide information about their services. For example, the Banca Commerciale Italiana is at www.bci.it. The Banca di Roma is at www.bancaroma.it. For a partial list, try *Topnet* site (www.topnet.it). Go to the *indice per argomenti* (index by subject) and choose *Istituti di Credito On-line*. For information about the Banca d'Italia, or Italian Central Bank, go to the *Codework* section of Inrete (www.inrete.it/cdwk/cdwk.html).

Taxes: American and Italian

Whether you should pay taxes to the American or Italian government largely depends on how much money you earn, where you are a legal resident, and whether you have dual or single citizenship. Italy and the United States have income tax treaties to protect their citizens from double taxation, and there are advantages to paying in one country over the other. If you're earning lire in Italy, it can be costly to pay American taxes in dollars because of the exchange rate.

U.S. citizens are subject to U.S. tax no matter where they live. However, if you pay foreign taxes on your income, you are eligible for a foreign tax credit, provided that the income is not what the IRS calls "excluded income." This credit normally applies only to income earned from a foreign source, such as an Italian company. There are two ways to deal with foreign taxes you have paid or accrued. The first is to take them in the form of a credit; this makes your U.S. income tax smaller on a dollar-for-dollar basis. The second is to take them in the form of an itemized deduction; this reduces the amount of your income that is subject to U.S. tax. An important factor to keep in mind is that not all levies that foreign countries call "taxes" are considered taxes by the IRS.

The general rule is that you don't pay U.S. tax on foreign source income if the foreign tax rate is higher than the U.S. rate. If the foreign rate is lower, you will have to pay U.S. taxes on the difference between the rates. If you earn less than $70,000 per year in Italy and pay Italian taxes on it, you are not required to pay taxes in the United States as well. This is called the "$70,000 exclusion." However, you must file

IRS Forms 1040 and 2555 or 2555-EZ to claim your exclusion. The latter form is also used to report taxes paid on real estate owned in Italy. No matter what your situation is, a "failure-to-notify" penalty can be charged to anyone who doesn't report a foreign tax status to the IRS. In other words, even if you don't earn money in Italy, you must report to the IRS at the end of the year. Because the tax guidelines change every year, you should check out the newest ones before you file.

CONTACTING THE IRS FROM ITALY

The Internal Revenue Service has an office located at the American Embassy. You can obtain the current and previous year's tax forms, make an appointment for assistance, and even file taxes at this office. You can also obtain an estimated tax payment schedule. This office will help you with any technical questions or problems, and you can even work out payment plans. All of the American Consulates have a legal office and arrange for a special traveling tax consultant, who provides free advice around the time taxes are due. The U.S. and Foreign Commercial Service of the embassy in Rome also offers accounting and legal guidelines for U.S. companies operating in Italy. There is also an International Taxpayer Service division of the IRS in Washington, D.C., which you can contact for information and forms. All addresses are listed at the end of this chapter.

FILING FOR AN EXTENSION AND GETTING A REFUND

If you're going to submit a Form 1040 based on the calendar year, the normal date for filing is April 15 each year. If you live in Italy and your tax home is there, you are automatically granted a two-month extension, but you will have to pay interest on any unpaid money during those two months. When you file, you will have to attach documents proving you qualify as an overseas resident (see Publication 54). If you will qualify as a resident after the two-month period has expired, you can apply for a special extension by filing Form 2350 before the due date. If you expect a refund, you can have it deposited directly into your U.S. bank account. You will have to complete Form 8888 and attach it to your return (e.g., Form 1040).

IRS TAX FORMS AND PUBLICATIONS FOR EXPATRIATES
- Publication 776, "General Overseas Tax Package"
- Publication 901, "U.S. Tax Treaties"

- Publication 593, "Tax Highlights for U.S. Citizens and Residents Going Abroad"
- Publication 54, "Tax Guide for U.S. Citizens and Residents Abroad"
- Publication 554, "Tax Information for Older Americans"
- Publication 516, "Tax Information for U.S. Government Civilian Employees Stationed Abroad"
- Publication 4, "Student's Guide to Federal Income Tax"
- Publication 953, "International Tax Information for Businesses"
- Publication 514, "Foreign Tax Credit for Individuals"
- Publication 520, "Scholarships and Fellowships"
- Forms "Package X," Two volumes of income tax forms and information
- Form TD F 90-22.1, "Report of Foreign Bank and Financial Accounts"
- Form 8822, "Change of Address"
- Form 888, "Direct Deposit of Refund"
- Form 2350, "Filing Extension"
- Form 2555 or 2555-EZ, "$70,000 Exclusion"
- Form 2555 or Form 2555-EZ, "Foreign Earned Income Exclusion"
- Form 5471 Schedule M, "Foreign Corporation Controlled by a U.S. Person"
- Form 5471 Schedule N, "Foreign Personal Holding Company"
- Form 3903F, "Foreign Moving Expenses"
- Form 1116, "Computation of Foreign Tax Credit: Individuals, Fiduciary, or Nonresident Alien Individual"
- Form 1118, "Computation of Foreign Tax Credit-Corporations"

THE MAIN ITALIAN TAXES TO WATCH OUT FOR

The Ufficio delle Imposte Dirette, the office in charge of collecting taxes in Italy, is also known as the *Fisco*. Because of the *Fisco*'s inflexibility toward the taxpayer, many people have adopted a common philosophy: when in doubt about your taxes, overpay and apply the money due back to the following year's taxes, since you'll probably never see a refund. To avoid being left in the dark, there are a few Italian taxes you should become familiar with. The first is IRPEF, which stands for *im-*

posta sul reddito delle persone fisiche. This is personal income tax and ranges from approximately 12 percent to more than 60 percent of gross earnings. Generally speaking, if you live in Italy for more than half the year or if you do most of your business there, you are subject to this tax. Corporate income tax is IRPEG (*imposta sul reddito delle persone giuridiche*); it applies to limited partnerships and limited liability companies, Italian stock companies, and cooperatives. In some cases it also applies to foreign companies as well as noncommercial entities and foundations. IRPEG is taxed at a fixed rate (in recent years it was 36 percent). Companies have to pay an annual registration tax called the *tassa di concessione governativa.* Individuals, associations, and companies also pay a local income tax called ILOR (*imposta locale sui redditi*). Other local taxes may also be applied, depending on your business. IVA (*imposta sul valore aggiunto*) is value-added tax. The rate of IVA varies, but the standard rate is 19 percent for regular items and 38 percent for luxury goods. Other taxes you might encounter include: *imposta di registro* (registration tax), *imposta comunale sull'incremento di valore dei beni immobili,* or INVIM (a form of capital gains tax), *imposta successioni e donazioni* (estate and gifts tax), *imposta di bollo* (stamp tax), *imposte ipotecarie e catastali* (land registry and cadastral tax), and *imposta di fabbricazione* (manufacturing tax).

ITALIAN TAX FORMS

The tax forms that you file in Italy are similar to American forms but more difficult to understand. The *modello 740* tax form is the Italian equivalent of the American Form 1040. It is the standard form people use to complete their *dichiarazione dei redditi* or declaration of income. This form can be bought in specialized stationery stores for less than $5. The *modello 740 semplice* and the *modello 730* are simplified versions of it. Corporations file the *modello 760* with attachments, including reports by the board of directors and auditors. One form you might receive from employers is the *modello 101,* the equivalent of the American W-2 form. In Italy, this form is kept by the employee and is not filed unless the employee also has other forms of income; in that case it is attached to the *modello 740.* The *modello 201* is the version of the 101 for retired people. It is obtained from the Istituto Nazionale Previdenza Sociale (INPS, or Italian social security administration) or from a private social security fund, when applicable.

Social Security

As long as you live in Italy, you can continue to receive your U.S. Social Security benefits thanks to the U.S.–Italy social security agreement created in 1978. Items covered under this agreement include Social Security taxes (including the U.S. Medicare portion), retirement, disability, and survivors' insurance benefits. In Italy it includes family allowances, too. Items not covered include benefits under the U.S. Medicare program and Supplemental Security Income (SSI). The two governments differ in how often they provide benefit checks and how much those benefits are.

When you pay Social Security taxes, you are actually accumulating what are called Social Security credits. Ultimately, these credits will be converted into Social Security benefits, the money you receive once you retire. Americans who work in both Italy and the United States can acquire these credits in both countries. The key factor in determining whether you will acquire American or Italian credits is the residency status of your employer. If you are self-employed, you are covered in the United States. If you have dual citizenship, you can choose which country to be exempt from. Whether you receive U.S. or Italian benefits also varies depending on your situation. In some cases Americans who have both Italian and American credits can earn only partial U.S. benefits.

It is your responsibility to declare which country you will pay social security taxes to and therefore in which you will earn credits. You do this through the Social Security Administration in the United States or through the provincial office of the INPS. Both the U.S. Embassy in Rome and the U.S. Consulate in Naples have offices that handle Social Security benefits, called Federal Benefits Units (see Chapter 4 for addresses). For more details, order U.S. Social Security Administration Publication No. 05-10137 ("Your Social Security Checks While You Are Outside the United States"), using the address at the end of this chapter.

Sources of Financial Assistance

If you are earning money or own property in Italy, you should consult a *commercialista* (accountant) who specializes in the tax laws of both countries. The American Embassy in Rome can provide a list of local

English-speaking accountants and financial advisers. The *English Yellow Pages* also has listings, and *The Informer* regularly prints American and Italian tax deadlines. A handful of major American accounting firms and tax assistance companies have offices in Italy, mainly in Rome. If you have Internet access, *Taxline* on the Telecom Italia Net site (www.tin.it) under *Economia e finanza* (see *Canali di Video On Line* on the home page) and *Fisconet* (www.finanze.interbusiness.it) include guides to tax forms, indices to the top Italian tax books and magazines, tax software, and an archive of related legal information. For the IRS on line you have a few good options: via the World Wide Web (www.irs.ustreas.gov), FTP (ftp.irs.ustreas.gov), or Telnet (iris.irs.ustreas.gov).

Useful Addresses

MONEY TRANSFERS

American Express Moneygram
(in the U.S.) tel (800) 926-9400
Italian headquarters:
Piazza di Spagna, 38
00187 Roma
tel (06) 67641
fax (06) 6782456
Western Union Money Transfer
(in the U.S.) tel (800) 325-6000
Italian headquarters:
Via del Babuino, 51
00187 Roma
tel (06) 36001815
toll-free tel (1670) 16840
fax (06) 3208152

AMERICAN TAX ASSISTANCE IN ITALY

Arthur Andersen
Piazza Malpighi, 4/2
40123 Bologna
tel (051) 230515
fax (051) 230874
Arthur Andersen
Via della Moscova, 3
20121 Milano
tel (02) 636131
fax (02) 6571844

Arthur Andersen
Via Campania, 47
00187 Roma
tel (06) 478051
fax (06) 4746680
Arthur Andersen
Galleria San Federico, 54
10121 Torino
tel (011) 55971
fax (011) 544756
Coopers & Lybrand
Via Vittor Pisani, 20
20124 Milano
tel (02) 67831
fax (02) 66981433
Coopers & Lybrand
Via delle Quattro Fontane, 15
00184 Roma
tel (06) 4620071
fax (06) 4814636
Deloitte & Touche
Palazzo Carducci
Via Olona, 2
20123 Milano
tel (02) 88011
fax (02) 433440

Deloitte & Touche
Via Flaminia, 495
00191 Roma
tel (06) 3338300
fax (06) 3333347
Merrill Lynch
Via Manzoni, 31
20121 Milano
tel (02) 29002663
fax (02) 29000384
Merrill Lynch
Largo della Fontanella di Borghese, 19
00186 Roma
tel (06) 683931
fax (06) 68393231
Price Waterhouse
Corso Europa, 2
20122 Milano
tel (02) 77851
fax (02) 7785240
Price Waterhouse
Via G. B. De Rossi, 32/b
00161 Roma
tel (06) 441921
fax (06) 44244890

THE INTERNAL REVENUE SERVICE

For technical questions about international tax laws and treaties:
Office of the Associate Chief Counsel, International
Internal Revenue Service (IRS)
1111 Constitution Avenue, N.W.
Washington, DC 20224
tel (202) 622-3800
fax (202) 622-4484
For questions about international filing and forms:
Customer Service Division
International Taxpayer Service
Internal Revenue Service
950 L'Enfant Plaza, S.W.
Washington, DC 20224
tel (202) 874-1460

To request forms by phone:
tel (800) 829-3676
To request forms by fax:
(703) 487-4160
IRS
American Embassy
Via Veneto, 121, 2nd Floor
00187 Roma
tel (06) 46742560
fax (06) 46742223

SOCIAL SECURITY

For general information from the United States:
Office of Public Inquiries
Social Security Administration
6401 Security Boulevard
Baltimore, MD 21235
tel (410) 965-7700
To file a claim in the United States:
Social Security Administration
Office of International Operations—Totalization
P.O. Box 17049
Baltimore, MD 21235
tel (410) 965-8018
For information about the Italy-U.S. agreement:
Social Security Administration
Office of International Policy
P.O. Box 17741
Baltimore, MD 21235
tel (410) 965-3545
To file a claim with Italian authorities:
INPS—Direzione Generale
Servizio Rapporti e Convenzioni Internazionali
Via della Frezza, 17
00186 Roma
tel (06) 59056493
fax (06) 59056405

CHAPTER SIX

Setting Up House

Housing in Italy is not just about agents, contracts, and property value. It's about architecture and archaeology, about feeling intimately connected to the ghosts of tenants who have come before you. When I lived in a former schoolhouse in Rome's Trastevere neighborhood that dates back to the thirteenth century, I made repairs to the walls and discovered they had been covered with thick layers of hard paint. Intrigued by what the paint might be concealing, I chipped away at them until I came to a faded pastel fresco that might have covered all the walls in the house but had been destroyed by centuries of humidity. As I continued to make repairs, I discovered the original handmade terracotta floor below the machine-made tiles I so despised. I have heard of other homeowners finding wooden beams hidden in ceilings and marble columns behind stuccoed walls.

But discoveries aren't limited to the inside of your home. Who wouldn't stop to admire the frescoed buildings along the Ligurian coast, the secret courtyards tucked away within the buildings of Naples, or the ancient farmhouses of the Tuscan countryside? Often, when I stop to look up at a particularly ornate window frame, a recently polished copper gutter, or a heavy wooden *portone*, a little crowd of Italians gathers to join me. They're not sure what they're looking at, but they're curious. "*Ma che c'è lassù?*" ("What's up there?") they ask. I answer by asking them if they've ever noticed these precious details embedded in the cityscape. *"Certo,"* they reply and continue on their way. It's not nonchalance, for they cherish their surroundings as much as I do; they've just had more time to get used to them.

Finding a house, however, is a challenge, as is understanding housing bills. Keeping up to date on how to pay the bills, how they're calculated, and whom to pay is harder than keeping up on payments. Not only are they more expensive than what you're used to in the United States, but there are many more of them, making for an extra financial burden. In addition to the basic utilities, you'll have to pay for things such as water, trash collection, and even owning a television. Make sure you account for these additional expenses when planning your monthly budget.

Cercasi Casa: Renting and Buying a Home

SHORT-TERM RENTALS

If you expect to live in Italy a few weeks or a few months, or if you want to test a neighborhood before settling in for good, you have two options: to stay at a "residence" or to lease an apartment for a short period of time. A room in a residence can be rented for any length of time, just like a hotel room. There is a concierge desk, room service, and laundry service. The difference is that these rooms usually include a small kitchen and are cheaper than hotels in the long run. To find the residence nearest you, look in the phone book or call Rescasa, an official residence finder service in Milan, for suggestions. You may find their listings are limited to major cities (see the end of this chapter for address). In general, expect to pay 600,000 lire ($400) to 1,350,000 lire ($900) per week. If that's too expensive, you might find a better deal renting a furnished apartment or room. Renting a room costs about 500,000 lire ($330) per month in the city, and renting a one-bedroom apartment will cost that much per week. The further you go outside of the city centers into the *periferie,* the cheaper the housing.

LONG-TERM LEASES

Americans have better access to Italian rental properties than Italians themselves. Tenancy laws make renting to foreigners the safest bet for *padroni* (property owners), who are scared of renting to Italian *inquilini* (tenants) because they are difficult to evict. If Italian tenants can prove they have no other home in the district other than the one they are rent-

Colorful signs advertising apartments clutter street corners.

ing, they have the right to stay for as long as they want. Americans who are not legal residents of Italy are not protected by these laws and are therefore considered ideal tenants because they are easier to get rid of.

When looking to lease rental property, you will want to be familiar with some terms, including *affittasi* (for rent), *vendesi* (for sale), *attico* (top-floor apartment), *monolocale* (studio apartment), *ammobiliato* (furnished), *centro storico* (historic center), *casale* (farmhouse), *piano terra* (ground floor, or what Americans call the first floor), *servizi* (kitchen, bathroom), *portiere* (doorperson), *angolo cottura* (small corner kitchen), *riscaldamento autonomo* (independent heating), and *condominio* (condominium fee). To find rental listings you can look through published ads, place an ad yourself, or simply walk through your favorite neighborhood looking for AFFITTASI ("For rent") signs. Otherwise, you can turn to the help of a real estate agent. Owners will ask you to pay the first month's rent plus two months as deposit up front. Some even ask for three months. In addition, if you find your home with the help of an agency, you'll generally have to pay one month's rent for its services.

Equo canone, or "fair rent," is the Italian equivalent of rent control. Rent prices are stabilized by the government depending on the quality of the property and the services included. Usually, *equo canone* rent contracts are made out for a period of four years and can be renewed almost indefinitely with very small increments in rent. Again, nonresident Americans don't qualify for *equo canone*. Foreigners sometimes ask for a *contratto di foresteria*, which is a shorter lease (usually less than the standard four years) and is more expensive. It lasts for as long as agreed upon by the tenant and the landlord. This arrangement offers flexibility if the foreigner moves often or plans to leave the country altogether. Often rental agreements are made without any written contract whatsoever, which can be risky on a long-term basis but tempting for shorter stays.

DEALING WITH REAL ESTATE AGENTS

Using the services of an *agente immobiliare* (real estate agent) in Italy can be a trying experience. When I was looking for an apartment, my main problem was trying to avoid agents. Almost all of the classified ads I called had been placed by agencies hungry to unload property on me that wasn't what I wanted. When I deliberately sought their help, they never had more than two apartments at a time, which meant that I had to contact about fifteen different agents just to get a good selection to choose from. In addition, even when I agreed to the price they asked for without protest (rent prices in Italy are usually negotiable), inevitably they would call back to say they had forgotten to include a certain tax or mysterious building fee so I would have to pay more. Ultimately, if you plan to rent for less than a year, using an agent is not cost-effective. If you rent for only a few months, make sure to negotiate a 10 percent commission instead of the usual one month's rent.

If you need the help of an agent it is recommended that you check their credentials with the nearest *camera di commercio,* or chamber of commerce. If you are renting from the United States, always make arrangements and agreements via fax to avoid misunderstandings. You can find agents in the *English Yellow Pages* and the Italian phone book, and a few specializing in American clients are listed at the end of this chapter. Some Internet sites have also been set up as on-line agencies and real estate bulletin boards, most of which include lengthy descriptions and photographs of the properties. Be sure to research the validity of the properties before you sign any agreements. Though most of the names include the word "villa" in them, the agencies normally also have apartments as well. A few such sites include: *Italian Villas* (www .italian-villas.com), a Washington-based agency; *Overseas Villas* (www .overseasvillas.com), the site of the Overseas Connection, featured in *Forbes* and *InStyle* magazine; *Cyberrentals* (http://cyberrentals.com), awarded four stars by *NetGuide* Magazine; and Cuendet's *Rentals in Italy (and Elsewhere!)* (www.rentvillas.com), run by a California agency called Rentals in Italy. As for my own saga, like so much else in Italy I finally found the perfect place through a friend of a friend despite two months of searching through just about every agency in Rome.

FINAL SUGGESTIONS WHEN RENTING

If you are renting, ask if the condominium fee is included in the rent. Also, make sure the owner doesn't expect you to pay 19 percent IVA tax on top of rent. (When apartments are owned by companies and not individuals, this is sometimes the case.) In addition, ask if there's a *buon uscita* or *buon entrata*. This is "key money" you sometimes must pay to buy off the previous tenant's rent. Avoid property that requires it because it is illegal. If you have children or pets, ask your condominium board if there are rules against them.

In terms of utilities, specifically ask if the home has gas for heating and cooking. I was moments away from signing a rent contract when I realized there were no heaters. When I asked about it, I discovered that not only was there no heat but that the kitchen and bathroom had only cold water. If there is gas, check if it's autonomous or central. Most renters prefer *riscaldamento autonomo* because they can keep their gas bills low. If you are renting for less than two months, check that heat and electricity are included in your rent. If you are renting for longer, you'll have to pay all utility and housing bills separately. Check the water pressure; otherwise you may find yourself doing a rain dance in the shower as many older buildings with antique pipes have little pressure. If you want air conditioning, plan to install your own since in Italy few homes have it. Check for screens on windows and doors—there are few in Italy, which makes for a nocturnal feeding fest in summer months. If it's true that mosquitoes are attracted to sweet blood, then Italian mosquitoes have found Paradise in the land of *la dolce vita*.

Buying Property

The real estate market went into crisis in 1992, and for the first time since World War II property prices were reduced by as much as 40 percent. As of the writing of this book things haven't gotten better, and the signs of hard times are everywhere. Street corners are plastered with neon-colored VENDESI ("For sale") signs advertising property for sale that no one is buying. Because property taxes weren't collected until recently, some wealthy families could afford to keep multiple homes uninhabited, never to invest in their maintenance. The decaying buildings in Venice are a prime example of this neglect. If there's a good to come from the property tax, it's that it has caused an ownership turnover. New owners armed with the money and enthusiasm to restore these forgotten properties are finally entering the market.

If you want to buy real estate in Italy, you should protect yourself by enlisting the help of as many professional sources as possible. Most important is the *notaio* (notary public), who will check for encumbrances on the property and will register the sale with the proper authorities. Also, get advice from an *avvocato* (lawyer) and a *commercialista* (accountant). You can hire a *geometra* (surveyor) to check for structural problems and to make an estimate of repairs needed.

If you and the owner agree on a price you make a *proposta d'acquisto* (offer) and sign a document called the *compromesso,* or preliminary sales agreement. It is accompanied by a *caparra* (down payment) of about 10 to 30 percent of the negotiated price. The *compromesso* determines the final date by which the transfer of ownership will take place. A *notaio* will prepare this document as well as the next one, called the *rogito.* The *rogito* is the final deed and marks the official change in ownership. Most important, the *rogito* records the sales price of the property as agreed upon by the buyer and seller. The *rogito* is usually signed several months after the *compromesso* to give the seller time to move out and the buyer time to collect the necessary funds. When the *rogito* is signed, the buyer must pay the remaining balance due. If the buyer walks out on the agreement after the *compromesso*, he or she loses the down payment. If the seller pulls out, he or she must return the *caparra* or sometimes pay back twice the amount as a penalty.

If you sell your property in Italy at a profit and have capital gains, you will have to pay a capital gains tax even if you repatriate the gains. Remember that you can subtract expenses such as the real estate broker's fee, improvements made to the property, legal fees, and depreciation (if your property was a business). If you break even after subtracting these expenses, you don't pay tax on the gain. But you must be able to prove all of them.

One of the most common practices in the Italian real estate business is *sottodichiarazione* (literally, "underdeclaration"). This is when the buyer and seller agree to declare officially on the *rogito* that the sales price is lower than what was really paid. It is usually about 50 to 60 percent less and saves both the buyer and seller money in taxes since all of the expenses, taxes, and commissions paid in relation to the sale are based on the *rogito* price, including the real estate agent's 3 percent commission and the *notaio*'s 2 or 2.5 percent. The practice of *sottodichiarazione* is very common, but be aware that it is illegal. A common problem some expatriates face is that when they want to repatriate the profits on the property they sold in Italy, they have to pay a U.S. tax on the capital gain—an amount that is larger than the sum declared in Italy if they underdeclared. The solution some turn to is keeping their fingers crossed that the IRS and Italian tax authorities don't compare notes.

FINANCING AND MORTGAGES

Italians prefer cash even when it comes to real estate and they shy away from mortgages and loans. A *mutuo* (mortgage) involves months of paperwork and a long approval process and covers only about 50 percent of the bank's appraised value of the property. Mortgage payments are made every six months and you'll have to register the mortgage with the Ufficio del Registro. Interest runs at about 17 percent for a ten-year loan—so high that it really doesn't make sense to get a loan from an Italian bank except if you are an EU member since EU policy mandates a lower interest rate. You could have your American money transferred to a *conto estero* in Italy, or you could take out a second mortgage on your U.S. home to avoid the high Italian interest rates.

PROPERTY TAX

ICI (*imposta communale sugli immobili*) is the property tax for home owners that was introduced in 1993. If you own property, you must pay ICI at the post office in two installments—one in June and one in December. It is calculated on the size of your house, the area you live in, and other factors such as the age of your building. There is an "easy" formula for calculating ICI, but most Italians leave the math in the hands of expert accountants because they have few chances for a refund if they overpay. For the past several years the state has miscalculated the number of ICI forms to print and there have been drastic shortages, leading property owners to fight over the few forms available at the post office as if they were in a clothing bargain basement.

HOME PROTECTION

Taking defensive procedures against burglary is a wise move for all property owners and in particular foreigners who leave their Italian homes unoccupied in the winter, since house robberies are the most common crimes committed in Italy. In one recent case, a country house was robbed of everything, including the copper pipes and sink faucets. Buying insurance can be expensive, and you'll have difficulty receiving claim payments. It's best to install as many locks on your door as you can. A *porta blindata* (armored door with a steel rod locking system), bars on windows, and *serrande* (metal curtains) to block access from balconies and windows are all effective crime deterrents, though they are also terrible eyesores. A good Italian *fabbro*, who does the work of the whole "smith" clan in the United States from blacksmith to locksmith, will install these security devices and give you tips on how to blend them with the appearance of your home.

RESTORATION AND REMODELING

Remodeling your home is not as simple as mixing concrete and knocking down walls; it's a complicated bureaucratic procedure that starts with obtaining a special permit. Most of Italy is covered by laws that protect the historic-aesthetic integrity of the landscape and the buildings, making it nearly impossible to alter the appearance of an old home. Even modernizing a kitchen or bathroom can be an enormous hassle. Because obtaining this permit is so difficult, many property owners decide to do *abusivo* construction, meaning they alter the property illegally. However, it is your responsibility to buy an apartment or house exactly as it appears in the blueprint, so if you notice, for example, a window that has been enlarged since it was recorded on the blueprint, ask to see the building permit for that alteration. If the seller doesn't have a permit, you are probably buying a house with an illegal change, and if it is discovered you will have to pay the fine.

The *vigili urbani,* police officers who roam the streets, have orders to keep an eye on what you throw out. If they notice plaster, broken tiles, or construction material in your trash, they will assume you are building illegally and will come to inspect your home. As a result, people dispose of construction evidence handful by handful with the normal trash over months, like prisoners digging an escape tunnel. Whenever the government is strapped for cash, a *condono* is issued. This is a sum of money property owners can pay to get pardoned for the illegal work done to their home. If you think illegal alterations have been made to yours, paying the *condono* is cheaper than facing eventual fines. It might seem like bribery, but it's in your best interest to pay it. In extreme cases police will destroy illegal construction. In the past this happened when houses were built on prime Sardinian coast locations and between the ancient columns of the temples in Agrigento, Sicily.

FINAL SUGGESTIONS WHEN BUYING

Ask your *notaio* to check that the property doesn't have any encumbrances such as unpaid taxes or prior mortgages. If your property was previously owned by a company that went bankrupt, the liquidator can reverse the sale of the property and claim it. You will be reimbursed—if you are lucky—the amount declared on the *rogito,* which was probably underdeclared. Also, check that the property is not part of a contested will. If you buy property from someone who has recently inherited it, the other heirs have five years after the death of the deceased owner to contest the will and claim back all or a part of it. Also, confirm that all utility and housing bills have been paid up until the time the property changes hands. The only way to be sure is to ask to see receipts.

Don't even contemplate buying real estate with a tenant inside. To get a successful *sfratto* (eviction) is nearly impossible—in fact, only 15 percent of all requests are actually executed each year. I know of an American couple who mistakenly believed the tenant would leave when they bought an apartment. Years passed, the couple exhausted all legal alternatives, and they still weren't able to evict her. They even cut off the water, but the resilient tenant could not be persuaded to move.

The couple was doomed to admiring their real estate from a street corner as the tenant made trips to the nearest fountain to get water.

Find out if nearby construction is planned. A campaign has started to restore Italy's ancient buildings and monuments. Although it's fascinating to watch as smog-stained buildings are brought back to their original colors, you wouldn't want to live through the process. Restoration can take years and involves covering the entire building with dark scaffolding. The process produces so much dust that opening your windows is unpleasant, if not unhealthy. If you are buying in the country, make sure no major construction, such as a new highway, is in the works on or near the property. Also, keep in mind that the stone and sandy cement used in Italian construction make humidity a huge problem because water is pulled up from the ground into the walls of your home. The only effective solution is to build an inner wall, leaving a little air space between it and the old wall. This will take up a considerable chunk of your living area.

If you are buying a home in the country, make sure it's connected to a telephone line, water pipes, gas, and electricity. If it's not, find out why the previous owners failed to make the necessary improvements. When buying in the country, also keep in mind the *diritto del coltivatore* (farmer's right). If your farmer neighbors earn more than 70 percent of their income from agriculture, they have the option to buy parts of your property within two years of your purchasing it if you don't intend to use it for agricultural purposes.

Useful Real Estate Publications

Case e Casali, which can be bought at newsstands, is a colorful real estate magazine in English and Italian, full of photos. If you love Italian country farmhouses, this magazine will make your mouth water. Classified ad publications on sale at newsstands, such as *Porta Portese* (Rome), *Seconda Mano* (Milan, Bologna, Florence), and *La Pulce* (Florence), all have real estate listings for both renters and buyers. Virtually all Italian newspapers include a real estate supplement at least once a week for no additional cost. English-language publications such as *Metropolitan* and *The Informer* have a few classified ads that are mostly placed by agents. If you live in Rome, the biweekly *Wanted in Rome* is almost entirely dedicated to classifieds. The Italian Government Tourist Board will help you look for homes to rent from the United States, or you can consult the Azienda Autonoma di Soggiorno or the Ente Provinciale per il

Turismo offices in the Italian region you live in for suggestions. In the United States, overseas listings can be found in the back of many magazines, including university alumni magazines and *The New Yorker*. Travel magazines, such as *Condé Nast Traveler* and *Travel & Leisure*, also have ads for American agencies specializing in overseas property.

Utilities and Housing Bills

Utility bills (*bollette*) look the same, and most come every two months. They are divided into two main sections. Half of the bill contains information on how to pay it and your account information; the other half contains both the remittance slip and the receipt for your records. The *numero utente* is your account number, the *importo lire* is the amount you owe, and the *scadenza* is the bill's due date. The *conto corrente* is the utility company's account number, which you will need for making payments. The most important thing to keep in mind is that many bills, including the phone bill, are not automatically itemized. This can be quite a shock to Americans. Some bills also require you pay a base fee regardless of whether you used the utilities or not.

SETTING UP SERVICE

For new service, you must call each utility company and ask for their *servizio nuovo contratto* department to receive instructions on how to proceed. You can find the relevant phone numbers by consulting the *"Numeri di Pubblica Utilità"* section of the Italian phone book. In general, utility companies are state-owned monopolies and are therefore the same no matter what part of the country you live in:

Electricity	ENEL
Water	ACEA
Gas	Italgas
Phones	Telecom Italia
Mobile phones	TIM or Omnitel

Many homes in rural areas aren't connected to electricity and phone lines or water and gas pipes, and connecting them will cost you a lot. Depending on which utility you are missing, you should consider getting a water storage tank, buying pressurized gas containers called *bombolone,* hooking up an electric generator, or getting a cellular phone. This might sound extreme, but if you spend only a few months a year in your Italian home, it's probably not worth hooking up to the main lines. If you do need to set up service from scratch, make sure you get a *contatore,* or meter, installed for electricity, water, and gas. ENEL, ACEA, and Italgas, respectively, will install them for you.

METHODS OF PAYMENT

Forget the send-the-check-in-the-mail attitude you learned in the United States, for Italian housing bills are rarely paid by check and are never paid by mail. Instead, you have three options for making payments:

Paying at the Utility Company   You can pay each bill by going to the office that issued it. This method is highly inconvenient because it means waking up early, traveling across town to the different utility companies, and waiting in line at each one.

Paying at the Post Office   It makes more sense to wait until you receive a couple of different bills and pay them all at once at the post office. Go to any branch, preferably in the morning, and step up to one of the *sportelli* (windows) for paying bills. A few post offices have installed a new service that allows you to use your Bancomat, or ATM bank card, to make payments if you don't have the cash on hand. Even if you don't have the actual bill, you can still pay it if you know the utility company's *conto corrente* number. This is a routing number that ensures your payment goes to the appropriate place.

Having Your Bank Pay for You   The easiest way to handle housing bills is to have your bank pay them for you. Banks will debit the amount due from your account for an extra 3,000 to 5,000 lire per bill. You should call your utility companies and replace your current billing address with the bank's address. The bank will pay bills mailed to it and keep track of payments on your monthly bank statement. In addition, the utility company will mail you a receipt of payment. Some companies, including most local Internet providers, will ask that you pay with a *bonifico,* a onetime wire transfer from your bank to theirs.

TELEPHONE SERVICE

The old telephone company, called the "SIP," had an awful reputation for static-disturbed lines, crossed wiring that superimposed a stranger's voice onto your own, and international connections that frequently failed. But the SIP no longer exists. It has been replaced by Telecom Italia, which has dramatically improved both the quality and services offered, and many expect it will only get better as the phone monopoly is broken up. Examples of improved service include call forwarding, call waiting, and ISDN lines.

Nevertheless, Telecom Italia has inherited some of SIP's bad habits. First, phone service is very expensive—so much so that it makes more sense to use a U.S. calling card for long-distance calls. Italian phone bills are calculated by *scatti,* or clicks, which cost 150 lire each. If you make a local call, it's only a couple of *scatti,* but if you call the United States from Italy, there's one *scatto* every few seconds. Depending on when you call, a minute on the phone to the United States can cost up to 5,000 lire ($3.50). Sometimes you can actually hear the *scatti* clicking away, making for a very uncomfortable conversation as you concentrate on counting *scatti* and not on the person talking to you.

If you want to set up new phone service, dial 187 (this number is good for the whole country). Setting up a new line costs about 300,000 lire ($200) and takes five days. Call 189 for questions about installing a second line or ISDN line for your fax or modem. Telecom Italia bills arrive every second month and are not itemized. If you request it, the phone company can itemize them for you, but the service is costly and does not offer as much detail as you get on American bills. If you spend a lot of time on the Internet, or have children or housemates who spend hours on the phone, you should ask the phone company about ways of keeping track of your *scatti*. Other things you can do include asking Telecom Italia to enable your phone to handle incoming calls only or restrict it from making long-distance ones. If you buy a fax machine in Italy, keep in mind that the slower Italian baud rates mean hundreds of extra *scatti*.

If you run up a high bill, Telecom Italia has a strange way of dealing with you. It will send a telegram demanding that you come to its offices in person within forty-eight hours to claim responsibility for the calls, otherwise it will cut off service. This can happen despite a perfect history of timely payments. The phone company calculates your average monthly usage, and if you go above that average, reds lights flash and telegrams are mailed out. I know a woman who spends only half the year in Italy and has a low average phone usage. Every time she comes back and starts using the phone regularly again, she gets one of those nasty telegrams and has to make the annual pilgrimage to the Telecom Italia office.

The Appeal of Cellular Phones

The cellular phone is a symbol of mobility, power, and technology that Italians find irresistible. What's more, it is the perfect instrument for maintaining the *bella figura*, that elusive and all-important "look" that earns you admiration and respect. A common joke in Italy is that Italians use their cellular phones to convey just four words at the end of the day: *"Cara, butta la pasta"* ("Honey, throw the pasta into the water"). *Piazze* all over the peninsula are dotted with people aimlessly wandering through the pedestrian and street traffic, too absorbed in their cellular conversations to avoid collisions. Enjoying a meal out on the town can sometimes feel more like a midday recess in a telephone switchboard center. When a phone rings at one table, all patrons enthusiastically check their breast pockets and purses to see if the incoming call is theirs. These actions, coupled with the characteristic hand gestures and high-volume voices, makes watching Italians on their cellular phones a spectator sport while sitting at an outdoor café. Almost no public place in the major Italian cities is free of the incessant rings of *"telefonini,"* or "little phones," as cellular phones are affectionately called.

You can get cellular phone service through Telecom Italia Mobile (TIM) or a private company called Omnitel Pronto Italia (OPI). Cellular service is expensive, but because of the competition between the two providers you can often get discounted rates and free sign-up. A third cellular phone service provider is expected in the near future. When signing up for service, make sure to ask for a GSM phone which has greater roaming capacity than others.

ELECTRIC BILLS

ENEL (Ente Nazionale per l'Energia Elettrica), the electricity company, provides service contracts that range from 1.5 to 6 kilowatts for private homes and higher wattage for businesses that need it. Most Italian households run on 3 kilowatts, which is very little. Forget toasting *bruschetta* while watching television and drying your hair at the same time, because you could blow a fuse. Your washing machine alone can use 3 kilowatts, which means you must turn off every single other appliance before washing clothing. The limited number of kilowatts is why so few Italian households have clothes dryers. When you move into your new home, make sure you know where the fuse box is and how to reset the system if you overload it. Also, use a power surge protector with important equipment such as a computer, because the current can fluctuate and you could lose documents. The amount ENEL bills you every second month reflects how much electricity it estimates you use based on how many kilowatts you get, meaning that even if you turn off the current for a summer, the electricity bill will not reflect zero consumption. You will receive a statement reflecting exact usage at the end of the billing cycle each year, with credit if you used less or a supplementary charge if you used more.

WATER BILLS

Italians have a love affair with water, whether it be going to the beach or relaxing by the soothing gurgles of a city fountain. Foreigners come to the country to see its water: from the canals of Venice to the Tivoli Gardens to the Bay of Naples. Italians themselves make cross-country pilgrimages to the best natural-water springs just to drink a few glasses and return home. Others bathe in outdoor thermal pools because they believe they will be cured of arthritis and respiratory problems. Buying water is more than pulling just any bottle off a shelf. Italian housewives stand in supermarket aisles trading secrets of their favorite brands: "This one is too heavy" or "This one has body" or "This one helps me digest." At dinner parties guests eye the brand of bottled water on the table as others would look under china settings for a seal.

Historians believe ancient Romans lived an average of thirty-five years because of the high lead content in their water. Today Italian women have a low incidence of osteoporosis, perhaps because of their water's high calcium content. A chef will tell you that pasta always tastes better in Italy because the calcium-rich water it boils in adds a savory quality. That same cook will also tell you it's a real nuisance to wash calcium-encrusted pots and pans.

Like anything else that is cherished, Italian water comes at a high price. Running water can cost you 100,000 lire ($65) every month for a medium-sized house. Each local district determines pricing for water with ACEA (Azienda Comunale Energia e Ambiente), the water company, and that price can vary depending on where you live. For example, if you live in an area with large gardens, expect a higher water bill. Most apartment buildings have a single water meter (*contatore*) that measures the amount of water in cubic meters used by the entire building. The total water bill is divided up by the number of apartments in the building. I once lived in a studio apartment with a restaurant on the ground floor and paid as much for water as the owners despite their twice-daily dishwashing extravaganza. Always turn off your water before going on a trip, because old pipes tend to burst, especially during the hot summer months, and cause destructive flooding.

GAS BILLS

Methane gas is used for heating water and cooking and is billed by Italgas, the gas company, every second month. You'd be surprised how many Italian homes, even in the cities, are not hooked up to gas lines and rely on expensive electricity for heating and cooking or on *bomboloni,* gas tanks that are attached to the stoves. If you do have gas, there are two systems for regulating it: *riscaldamento autonomo* (autonomous heating) or *riscaldamento centrale* (central heating). Autonomous heating lets you regulate the temperature of your home and water through the *caldaia,* or boiler, and you can keep costs down by shutting it off when you don't need it. However, you are required to pay for the maintenance of the boiler and the cost of a mandatory annual *caldaia* checkup. With central heating you pay as much as your neighbors do. The frustrating thing about central heating is that buildings are required by law to turn it on or off on preestablished dates in the fall and spring, and the actual day varies by region; if it's unseasonably warm or cold before that date, you will either sweat or shiver.

CONDOMINIUM FEES

As in the United States, some apartment buildings have *spese del condominio* (condominium fees) to cover expenses such as cleaning the hallways, paying the *portiere* (doorperson), and keeping the elevator running. Sometimes ACEA water is included in the condominium fee. Even renters are expected to pay a condominium fee if it hasn't been included in their monthly rent.

THE GARBAGE TAX

Don't take the *tassa comunale dei rifiuti* (garbage tax) lightly, since it's one of the most revered taxes in the land. No matter how often you move, that tenacious trash tax will catch up with you. A foreigner who lived in Italy returned to the country after a ten-year absence and was prohibited from registering with the local *comune* because it was discovered she had a decade-long outstanding garbage bill. Many cities require that you place your garbage outside at absurd hours, such as not after 6:00 A.M. and not before midnight. The city of Rome recently decided that garbage cans on the street were too ugly, so they were removed. At the same time, the mayor announced that fines would be given to those who did not properly dispose of their garbage. Afraid of the fines, citizens carefully divided their daily rubbish into little morsels that they secretly left in dark corners.

The money you pay is for the removal of your garbage, but many regard it as a form of property tax because it's calculated on the number of square meters you own. Many districts are currently considering changing the way the tax is calculated, and some have even suggested basing the tax on the number of garbage bags each private citizen produces. The question, of course, is who will count them. Citizens may eventually have to purchase special garbage bags from the *comune* that they will be required to use. For now, the trash tax can be paid once a year or in four *rate*, or installments, and because it's a tax you can pay it only at the post office. Trash is collected by different companies, which vary according to the region you live in. For example, in Rome garbage is collected by AMA (Azienda Municipale Ambiente), in Florence by a company called Fiorentina Ambiente, and in Milan by AMSA (Azienda Municipale Servizi Ambientali). You should call the trash-collecting company listed in the phone book of your neighborhood if you need to have large or recyclable items taken away.

TELEVISION TAX

Italians pay a television tax, which costs about 170,000 lire ($115) per year. When you buy a new television, your name will automatically be registered with the TV tax authorities, but many Italians get out of the tax by buying a used set or by making an "arrangement" with their vendor. If variety shows, American reruns, and government programming don't get you hooked, you can get pay-TV called Telepiù with a satellite dish. The dish will let you watch CNN, MTV, and even the NBC Superchannel, a European version of NBC, including *The Jay Leno Show* and *Dateline*.

DISPUTING A BILL

To dispute a housing bill, go to the utility office in person with the bill in question, but don't count on it being easy. Even if you convince the utility company that you were overcharged, it will be hard to convince it to issue a refund. In 1996, it was discovered that ENEL had overcharged many of its customers an extra 33 lire per kilowatt and reportedly pocketed $1 billion thanks to the mistake, but apparently no customer has seen a refund yet. If you do want to dispute a bill, make sure you back your claim with hard evidence. For example, if you get a 500,000-lire water bill and were out of the country for the period cited on the bill, take your airline ticket with you as proof of your absence, though you will probably be told you left your faucet running while you were away. In that case, get a neighbor to testify that you turned your water main off before leaving. The best thing you can do is to take precautionary measures to avoid having to dispute a bill. For example, regularly check your water, gas, and electricity meters to make sure the dials don't move after these utilities are turned off.

Useful Addresses

Italian Government Tourist Board
630 Fifth Avenue, Suite 1565
New York, NY 10111
tel (212) 245-4822
fax (212) 586-9249
Italian Government Tourist Board
401 North Michigan Avenue
Chicago, IL 60611

tel (312) 644-0990
fax (312) 644-3019
Italian Government Tourist Board
12400 Wilshire Boulevard,
Suite 550
Los Angeles, CA 90025
tel (310) 820-0098
fax (310) 820-6357

Rescasa
Federazione Italiana Residence
Via Serbelloni, 7
20122 Milano
tel (02) 76008770
fax (02) 794372

REAL ESTATE AGENTS IN ITALY

FLORENCE:
American Agency
Via Ponte Rosso, 33/r
50129 Firenze
tel (055) 495070
fax (055) 475053
Agriturist Toscana Vacation Houses
Piazza S. Firenze, 3
50122 Firenze
tel (055) 287838
fax (055) 2302285
The Best in Italy
Via Ugo Foscolo, 72
50124 Firenze
tel (055) 223064
fax (055) 2298912
Milligan & Milligan
Via dei Servi, 34
50122 Firenze
tel (055) 268256
fax (055) 268260
milligan@iol.it
MILAN:
Core Cocchini Relocation
Via Sirtori, 13
20129 Milano
tel (02) 29512793
fax (02) 29513075
Foster Agency Italy
Via Melzi d'Eril, 29
20154 Milano
tel (02) 312626
fax (02) 33104244
Property International
Via Correggio, 55
20149 Milano
tel (02) 4980092
fax (02) 48194170

NAPLES:
Gabetti
Via Afiteatro Marmoreo, 7
80035 Nola (NA)
tel (081) 5125383
fax (081) 5125719
Grimaldi
Via Pergolesi, 102
80078 Pozzuoli (NA)
tel (081) 5265233
fax (081) 5265240
ROME:
Homes International
Via Bissolati, 20
00187 Roma
tel (06) 4881800
fax (06) 4881808
Property International
Viale Aventino, 79
00153 Roma
tel (06) 5743170
fax (06) 5743182
Rainbow International Services
Via Venanzio Fortunato, 50
00136 Roma
tel (06) 35346122
fax (06) 35453687
VENICE:
Gestioni Finanziarie Immobiliari
Piazza San Marco, 144
30124 Venezia
tel (041) 5287750
fax (041) 5287475
House Deal Consulting
Castello San Lio, 5274A
30122 Venezia
tel (041) 5223920
fax (041) 5289671

CHAPTER SEVEN

Salute! *Staying Healthy Abroad*

Italians are not preoccupied with vitamins, "health food," or weight loss products the same way Americans are. They tend to eat what they want, and their diet has been hailed by experts worldwide as the healthiest around, thanks to their regular use of olive oil and fresh produce. When they have a health problem, their attitude is often *lascia stare*, or "let be," because they'd rather treat a problem at home than seek outside help for minor problems. Doctors in turn seem to take a more relaxed approach as well, often attributing physical problems to cold drafts, a bad night's sleep, or problems with the *fegato* (liver). The holistic attitude often borders on the tradition of old wives' tales, and many Italians firmly believe in the curative properties of herbs and fresh air (hence the existence of so many *erboristerie* or herbal stores). Once when I had a chest cold, the doctor didn't prescribe any medicine but told me to inhale steam perfumed with Eucalyptol, an over-the-counter version of liquid eucalyptus oil mixed with other natural herbs and flowers. I was skeptical, but after a few steam sittings I actually did feel better. Other natural remedies used religiously include lemon juice gargles for sore throats, nightly aspirin-induced sweats for colds, and chamomile tea with honey for bronchial infections. Of course, Mamma's homemade chicken broth is still the ultimate preventive therapy.

As a foreigner residing in Italy, you must understand your health care options in order to avoid feeling vulnerable when you need to seek care.

Not being able to speak Italian is a problem in itself, although many Italian doctors understand English or are at least able to read it. Sometimes it helps to write down your symptoms, and having a short written summary of your medical history on hand always comes in handy. One of the most intimidating aspects of the system can be the cultural differences, starting with the Italian thermometer, which is in Centigrade and must be placed under your armpit, not in your mouth. Another difference is that doctors don't send bills but expect you to pay in cash on the day of your visit.

If you are new to Italy, finding a doctor may seem difficult, but the American Embassy and Consulates can provide a list of English-speaking doctors in the area, as can International Association for Medical Assistance to Travelers, or IAMAT (see "Finding Additional Help"). At the end of this chapter is a list of private facilities and medical associations geared toward foreigners. As always, the best way to find specialized health care is by asking people you know and trust.

Overseas Health Options

In Italy, your health insurance options include becoming part of the public Italian health care system or purchasing a private plan from an Italian insurance company. However, getting an American traveler's insurance policy that covers you during your first year overseas is the easiest route to take. Later on, you can decide whether to delve into the Italian alternatives. If you work for an Italian company or the overseas branch of an American company, you will probably be enrolled in its in-house medical plan. If you're not covered by a company, you will quickly discover that it's harder than you would imagine to find an American insurance company that offers extended overseas coverage lasting more than one month. Four commonly used ones are Wallach & Company (MedHelp Worldwide), Travel Guard, Travel Insured International, and the Travel Safe Insurance of the Chester Perfetto Agency (see end of this chapter for addresses). The problem with most American plans is that you have to pay for services up front and then wait to get reimbursed, which can often take three months. Remember that the Social Security Medicare program will not cover you abroad, though some Medicare supplement plans will offer reimbursements for medical coverage of things that would be covered by Medicare at home. Also, most of the American or international hospitals in Italy that will accept American insurance take only Blue Cross/Blue Shield.

The Pros and Cons of the Italian
Public Health Care System

The greatest thing about the Italian national health care system, or Servizio Sanitario Nazionale, is that all citizens have the same right to health care regardless of how much they contribute in taxes, whether they have preexisting conditions, or if they are employed. Much coverage is free or nearly free, and you have to pay only a small percentage of the cost of medicine. Whether you get a minor operation or open-heart surgery, you spend practically nothing. Even if you decide to use a private clinic, you can get a partial reimbursement from the state as long as you first get permission from the public health offices. You can even get free house calls if you arrange them early enough in the morning.

Notwithstanding the advantages, complaints among the locals are endless. They say that they can't get the public services they need when they need them. The waiting lines are long and the facilities often decrepit. Patients usually have to get to the hospital at dawn to avoid sleeping in the corridor. I once accompanied a friend to the first aid station of one of Florence's most prestigious state-run facilities. It had been moved from its usual location to the basement due to construction work. Paint was peeling off of the walls and debris was everywhere—hardly a sanitary atmosphere. You often hear bureaucratic horror stories, such as that of a man who had a knee operation and ended up staying two extra weeks in the hospital simply because the person who had to authorize his discharge had gone on vacation. Furthermore, the state requires that when you stay home from work, your doctor must write an official letter stating your condition and send a copy both to your employer and to the government health office. It also has inspectors call or visit your home between certain hours each day (usually in the early morning and late afternoon) to make sure you are really there. Because of the inconvenience, many Italians decide to use vacation days if they are sick for one or two days instead of the official company "sick days."

Nonetheless, Americans without health insurance feel more protected in Italy than they do at home, partly because Italian doctors often treat foreigners in hospital emergency rooms at no cost. It is also because Italy has a long tradition of volunteer medical help, so free

Local food, fresh air, and natural remedies help to keep Italians sprightly and in good health.

help is always available. One stellar example is the Misericordia in Florence, a Catholic service that has its own clinics and ambulances, and another is the national Guardia Medica, a network of doctors who make free house calls at any time of the day or night (both can be found by looking in the local phone book). Many cities also have set up free health clinics for illegal immigrants who would otherwise not be able to pay for treatment. You can find out about these at the office of the *comune* (municipality) where you live.

How to Become Eligible
for Public Health Care

The Unità Sanitaria Locale, or USL (pronounced "oozl" by Italians), is the government agency responsible for running the vast network of the Italian health care system. USL (also known as USSL) has local branches throughout the peninsula that handle all the paperwork connected to public medical treatment. You can locate the nearest USL office by looking in the Italian phone book under "A" for "*Azienda Sanitaria Locale*" or "*Azienda USL.*" The requirements for national health coverage eligibility vary depending on your status. If you are a student, resident, or an employee of an Italian company, or are on a self-employment visa, chances are you're eligible. In order to prove eligibility, you will have to present a series of documents ranging from receipts of wages or a letter of school enrollment to the more basic *permesso di soggiorno* and *codice fiscale*. Freelancers will first have to register with the local office of the INPS (the Italian equivalent of the Social Security Administration, pronounced "eemps") and make contributions once or twice a year; these often amount to the equivalent of several thousand dollars. Once you register for the *mutuo* (coverage), you will be assigned a *medico mutualistico,* or general practitioner. If you don't earn an income in Italy (and therefore don't pay the health tax), you will have to pay an annual fee for coverage. In past years this fee has been about 800,000 lire ($500).

Private Italian Health Care and Insurance

Even though Italians must make payments to the public system, those who can afford it often take out private insurance policies as well and generally avoid the public health care system whenever possible. Some even go to other countries, such as France and the United States, to have serious operations performed; Gianni Agnelli, ex-CEO of Fiat Auto, for example, had heart surgery in Monte Carlo. The price of private insurance policies varies according to the coverage provided but generally costs about 2 million lire ($1,300) per year. In general, the biggest advantage of these policies is that they provide you with disability pay if your recovery requires that you stay home from work, which is especially important for the self-employed. If you are interested in getting a private policy, the biggest company is Istituto Nazionale delle Assicurazioni (INA), which was once public but has now been privatized. Other big ones include Sanicard, Filo Diretto, Europa Assistance, and Pronto Assistance. Addresses for local branches are listed in the Italian yellow pages under "*Assicurazioni*" ("Insurance Companies).

Finding Pharmacies, Prescriptions, and Medicine

The Italian pharmacy, or *farmacia,* can be recognized by the large green neon cross that usually hangs outside of the front door. Inside, elegant European hair and beauty products line the shelves beside locked glass cabinets of pretty combs, bottles of bubble bath, cellulite creams, and sleek hypoallergenic makeup products from northern Europe. Go knowing what you want: this is not the place to browse. The *farmacista* does not like you to take things from the shelves and prefers to wait on you just as in a clothing store. Once the pharmacist retrieves your product, you must watch him or her meticulously wrap it in paper, which in some cases can be highly embarrassing, especially for more modest Americans used to the impersonal treatment of American pharmacies (try wrapping a box of tampons or condoms with a bunch of strangers watching, and you'll get the picture).

In Italy, the pharmacy serves as a kind of miniclinic where medical advice is sought and over-the-counter treatments are tried before actually calling the family doctor. Since many medicines that are sold over the counter in Italy would require a prescription in the United States, you can actually "play doctor" on your own to a greater degree. One of the more famous local pharmacies is the Vatican pharmacy in Rome because it can fill prescriptions from some other countries (Italian pharmacies can accept prescriptions only from Italian doctors). In addition, it is known to carry a wider range of pharmaceutical products than typical pharmacies do. All pharmacies have limited opening hours and share rotating Sunday and night shifts for emergencies. You can find schedules of these shifts in any local newspaper. Every pharmacy that is closed has a poster outside with listings of the nearest open pharmacy in case you need it.

All Italian pharmacies sell some American products, such as One-a-Day vitamins, Pampers diapers, and Oral-B dental floss, and for the most part there are Italian equivalents of all products. Because many of the American pharmaceutical companies export their products, often the same medicine is sold in Europe but under a different name, such as the Italian ibuprofen product, which is called Alfogen. There is also a whole range of local products worth trying, including the tart lemon- or orange-flavored chewable vitamin C pills that taste like candy, a personal favorite.

When Italians deal with prescription medicine, they don't joke around. Most medicines come in the form of suppositories and shots, in addition to pills. It is even common for a doctor to prescribe shots and expect you to administer them yourself. In fact, in many Italian households there is at least one person skilled at doing so, and a supply of syringes is commonly found in the bathroom medicine cabinet (you can even buy syringes at the supermarket). For those weak of stomach, you can pay a small fee at one of the local clinics to have a nurse do it for you. If you take prescription medicine regularly, have your doctor in the United States write a short description of what it is or find someone at home who can take care of shipping your refills. Also, find out your medicine's generic name before you leave the United States.

Health Care for Women

Birth control, menstrual problems, and the possibility of pregnancy are serious issues made more complicated abroad because of the added difficulty of culture shock and the language barrier. One of the questions more commonly asked is if one can buy American brands of tampons (also called *"i tampon"* or *"i tampax"* in Italy), *assorbenti* (pads), and *salvaslip* (panty liners) in an Italian pharmacy. The answer is yes. However, American prescriptions for the birth control pill cannot be filled there. You should either bring a supply of your pill with you from the States or plan to see an Italian gynecologist once you arrive (to get the Italian pill, or *pillola*, you do need a prescription, as in the United States). If you are planning to stay for less than one year, the first option is preferable. A pregnancy exam is called *"un test di gravidanza,"* and an over-the-counter version can be bought in any pharmacy. For an *infezione della vescica* (bladder infection), forget searching for cranberry juice as cranberries don't exist in Italy, let alone the juice. Instead, you'll have to go to the doctor and get a prescription for medicine. This is also true if you need medicine to treat *candida* (yeast infections).

Finding Additional Help

When it comes to more delicate medical issues, being in Italy can become stressful from the linguistic mistakes commonly made (e.g., mistaking the word *preservativo*, or condom, for "preservatives") to finding out your American prescription for medicine cannot be filled in the local pharmacy. Dealing with these issues can also prove costly. The Associazione Italiana per l'Educazione Demografica (AIED) is a sort of Italian Planned Parenthood that provides a full range of medical services for men and women of all ages at inexpensive rates (a general visit costs about 70,000 lire, or $50). There are more than twenty-five cities with AIED branches, as well as a national Web site (see the end of this chapter for information).

The International Association for Medical Assistance to Travelers (IAMAT) is a nonprofit organization based in New York. It can provide you without charge a list of doctors in Italy who speak English and have been trained in the United States, Great Britain, or Canada. IAMAT recommends that you call and get this list before you leave home, but you can also request it once in Italy. If you have Internet access, one helpful local resource you may want to access is *Salute, Medicina e Internet* (www.sameint.it), an Italian health Internet site. This site has a separate section for doctors and the public. The latter takes you to databases of health articles, dictionary entries, and clinical analyses of specific problems. It has addresses of Italian health care services and even provides alphabetical listings of nonprescription medicines available in drugstores, plus their cost. However, use the information as a starting point, not for reliable advice, since some of the content may be inaccurate or outdated.

Useful Addresses

In an emergency dial 113 and ask for an *ambulanza*.

AMERICAN INSURANCE AGENCIES
OFFERING OVERSEAS COVERAGE

Travel Guard International
1145 Clark Street
Stevens Point, WI 54481
tel (715) 345-0505
tel (800) 826-1300

Travel Insured International, Inc.
52-S Oakland Avenue
P.O. Box 280568
East Hartford, CT 06128-0568
tel (800) 243-3174
fax (860) 528-8005

Travel Safe Insurance
Chester Perfetto Agency

2113 Penn Avenue
Reading, PA 19609
tel (610) 678-0373
tel (800) 523-8020

Wallach & Co.
107 West Federal Street
P.O. Box 480
Middleburg, VA 22117-0480
tel (703) 667-3166
tel (800) 237-6615
fax (703) 687-3172

HOSPITALS AND HEALTH SERVICES
CATERING TO THE ENGLISH-SPEAKING
COMMUNITY

European Hospital
Via Portuense, 696
00149 Roma
tel (06) 659759
fax (06) 65975727

International Health Center
Via San Paolo, 15
20121 Milano
tel (02) 72004080
fax (02) 865690

Rome American Hospital
Via Emilio Longoni, 69
00155 Roma
tel (06) 2255290
fax (06) 2285062

Studio di Odontoiatra Specialistica Associato
Via Gilera, 12
20043 Arcore (Milano)
tel (039) 6013004
fax (039) 617868
(orthodontists)

GENERAL ASSISTANCE

(English language not guaranteed)
AIED:

AIED (Associazione Italiana Educazione Demografica)—headquarters
Via Salaria, 58
00198 Roma
tel (06) 8840661
fax (06) 85301120
www.aied.it
info@aied.it

AIED—Florence
Via Ricasoli, 10
50122 Firenze
tel/fax (055) 215237

AIED—Padua
Via S. Chiara, 1
35123 Padova
tel (049) 8756277

AIED—Pisa
Via delle Casa Dipinte, 17
56100 Pisa
tel (050) 540676

AIED—Naples
Via Cimarosa, 186
80127 Napoli
tel/fax (081) 5567604

OTHER SOURCES OF HELP:

AVO (Associazione Volontari Ospedalieri)
Via Cartucci, 4
50123 Firenze
tel (055) 2344567
(free medical interpreting)

Eurolens
Via Venturoli, 67
40138 Bologna
tel (1670) 15480 (toll-free)
fax (051) 344600
genesis@mailbox.iunet.it
(contact lens products, 24-hour assistance and overnight shipping)

Farmacia del Vaticano
Porta Sant'Anna Entrance
00120 Città del Vaticano
tel (06) 69883422
fax (06) 69885361

IAMAT—International Association for Medical Assistance to Travelers
417 Center Street
Lewiston, NY 14092
tel (716) 754-4883
fax (519) 836-3412

Linea Verde AIDS
tel (1678) 61061
(free AIDS hotline)

Samaritans
Via San Giovanni in Laterano, 250
00184 Roma
tel (06) 70454444
(free counseling in person or by phone)

CHAPTER EIGHT

Lo Shopping

Shopping in Italy is not meant to be convenient, and that is exactly what traditionalists love about it. They consider shopping an art form and one of the main reasons they are able to attain such a high quality of life. In fact, there's no such thing as a "convenience store" in Italy— well, there was, but it didn't last very long. In the summer of 1996, Italy saw its first ever twenty-four-hour store, called Drugstore, open in Rome's main train station. The idea was great: eternal shopping in the Eternal City. Yet, from its first hour in business the Drugstore caused controversy. Newspapers warned that the "hideous stores" would spread to other parts of the country as if they were an infectious disease. One paper published an article on the kinds of people who would actually shop round the clock, describing them as "starving artists, women with ripped stockings, and sexual adventurers." Whoever dreamt up the idea of the Drugstore overlooked one huge obstacle: Italians sleep at night, they don't go shopping. A store clerk explains, "Can you imagine Romans getting into their car at two A.M., driving to the train station, parking in the deserted piazza, and coming to us with shoes that need to be resoled?" By its fourth month in business, struggling with sagging sales and unable to find employees willing to work the night shift, the Drugstore was forced into normal business hours.

The Drugstore took the fun out of Italian shopping because it made it too easy. In Italy, finding the shop that sells the items you need, negotiating the strict store hours, and remembering which stores are closed on what day makes *fare lo shopping* a time-consuming daily exercise. You are expected to wait for products; they aren't expected to wait for you on a twenty-four-hour store shelf. Finding the perfect specimen of fruit or the freshest bread takes skill, and shopping is deeply rooted in a tradition of quality, timing, and selection. You must identify which fruit vendor has the best fruit in season and wake up early to get bread when it comes out of the oven. The fruit vendor is a fruit specialist and the baker only knows bread, and they are both undisputed masters in their fields. In fact, shopping is so specialized that you might have to go to as many stores as the number of products you need. For example, in order to make an omelet for breakfast you would go to the *latteria* for milk, the *macelleria* for eggs and bacon, the *panetteria* for bread, the *fruttivendolo* for tomatoes, and the *alimentari* for cheese. In addition, shopping in Italy is considered a social activity and the Drugstore offered a very unsociable atmosphere. Italian mom-and-pop stores give personalized attention, and chances are you'll know each employee on a first-name basis and they'll know what you buy each day. Italians go faithfully to the same stores, not just to shop but to share cooking tips and gossip as well.

Knowing Where to Go for the Basics

IL BAR

Each day starts off with a visit to the bar for an *espresso* or *cappuccino,* a pastry, and a little friendly conversation with the bartender. (The American concept of anything as heavy as eggs and bacon, or even pancakes, for breakfast is unheard of in Italy.) The local bar is a social center where retirees meet to play cards and Italians of all ages crowd together to watch televised soccer matches. The bar you frequent says a lot about your lifestyle. There are posh bars with gold-colored sugar bowls, mirrored walls, and pink marble counters with standing room only for businesspeople on the run. Then there are bars with yellowed soccer posters covering walls that desperately need painting and rickety wooden chairs where you can sit for hours and read a book. Don't be misled by the myriad of so-called "American bars"—more often than not there's nothing particularly American about them, the name is used just to attract attention.

TABACCHI (TOBACCO SHOPS)

Tobacco stores are recognized by the black "T" sign hanging over their door. After Italian unification in 1861, the state had a monopoly on selling tobacco, salt, and quinine medicine for treating malaria carried by mosquitoes. Quinine hasn't been sold in more than thirty years and the stuff isn't even made anymore, but the state stubbornly holds on to its exclusive right to sell it. As for salt, it can now be purchased in other grocery stores. The only things left for *tabacchi* to sell are ice cream, bus and lottery tickets, regular postage stamps, *bolli* (tax stamps), and, of course, cigarettes. In addition to dominating the distribution and sale of tobacco, the state also produces its own brand of cigarettes—appropriately called "MS" for *Monopolio dello Stato*—which are cheaper than American brands but less sophisticated.

EDICOLE (KIOSKS)

Newspapers and magazines are distributed through state-licensed *edicole*, or newspaper kiosks. Very few Italians subscribe to newspapers, so most make a morning trip to one of these little Towers of Babel, stuffed with flyers, racy posters, and stacks of printed material. Italy lacks the tradition of the fat weekend paper, perhaps because many *edicole* are closed on Sundays. However, in big cities some newsstands carry *The New York Times* a few days late. You can also find a good selection of Italian magazines packed with free gadgets (e.g., CDs and videos), as well as American publications such as the *International Herald Tribune* and the international edition of *Newsweek*.

ALIMENTARI (GROCERY STORES)

The *alimentari* is the general grocery store, where you can buy not only bottled drinks and packaged goods but *prosciutto* and *mozzarella* delectably displayed in glass cases along with other cold cuts and cheese. You often also find curiosities there, such as *merluzzo* (dried cod) or sweet green olives in barrels on the floor. There are specialized versions of the *alimentari*, such as the *pizzicheria*, which technically only sells dried meats, and the *fornaio*, which sells bread and pasta. Some *alimentari* also serve as a *latteria* where you can buy fresh milk if you don't fancy the *latte a lunga conservazione*, or "long-life" milk, sold in cardboard boxes. When shopping at the *alimentari*, shout out your order to demand attention from the salespeople. Don't be shy if you want to be served; as with much of Italian shopping, here you must be aggressive. If you prefer more courteous shopping etiquette, you may want to consider ordering your goods by phone and having them delivered to your home. Many *alimentari* offer this service.

MERCATI (OUTDOOR MARKETS)

In the mornings some outdoor *piazze* are converted into fresh fruit and vegetable markets where you can haggle over prices and inspect fruit for ripeness and quality. (Fruit and vegetables are also sold at the *fruttivendoli,* or fruit stores.) Italians always buy produce that is in season, knowing better than to buy watermelons before July or *porcini* mushrooms anytime after November. You'll find fruits and vegetables you've never tasted before that vary from region to region as dictated by local temperatures. For example, *puntarelle,* a type of curly lettuce prepared with anchovy paste and vinegar, is a Roman specialty. Other common vegetables include *cicoria* (chicory), *broccoletti di rapa* (the leaves and tiny flowers of the broccoli plant), and yellow zucchini flowers (often stuffed with *mozzarella* and fried lightly). Watch out for "sexy" produce whose name has a double meaning in Italian, such as *piselli* (peas). Even the harmless *cavolo* (cabbage) is used by Italians as an expletive in moments of extreme frustration. In larger cities, you can often find outdoor markets that specialize in "exotic" produce and goods. For example, in Rome, African and Chinese produce stands line Piazza Vittorio near the Termini train station. The Porta Portese flea market in Trastevere on Sunday mornings carries Turkish cakes and spices from the Far East, and Jewish minimarkets can be found in the Roman Ghetto. There is even an Islamic outdoor market near the Islamic mosque on Viale della Moschea in the Parioli section of town.

Aside from produce markets, each town has its own selection of outdoor markets selling anything from clothing and leather bags to bric-a-brac and housewares. There are busy fish markets all along the seafronts, and in small towns you can find markets specializing in local products such as pottery and flowers, the most prestigious flower market being San Remo's Mercato dei Fiori, which caters to shops all over Europe. Rome's two-mile-long Porta Portese Sunday morning market is considered Italy's best flea market by many, and Florence's Mercato delle Pulci on the last Sunday of each month always attracts a good crowd as well. Then there is a wide selection of antique markets, or *mercati dell'antiquariato,* where you can find valuable furniture at rea-

Shopping for artichokes in Rome's Campo de' Fiori market.

sonable prices. One of the most famous antique markets is the one held in Arezzo's Piazza Grande on the last weekend of each month. Others include Naples's Piazza Bellini antique market and Pisa's Ponte di Mezzo market (both on the second weekend of the month), as well as Lucca's Piazza San Martino market (on the third weekend of each month). To find out more about markets in your area consult the local newspaper or the Internet sites sponsored by the town hall of your *comune* (see Chapter 10).

CHAIN STORES AND *I DISCOUNT*

There are larger American-style supermarkets (*supermercati*), such as Coop, and department stores (*grandi magazzini*), such as STANDA, UPIM, Esselunga, COIN, La Rinascente, and Metro, that are open longer hours and don't close for lunch. You'll find a map of *ipermercati*, or megamarkets, at the beginning of the Italian phone book. Recently, discount supermarkets, simply called *i discount*, have started appearing on the outskirts of Italian cities, stocking cheaper no-name products. Outside the city centers you'll also find large do-it-yourself stores (*fai da te*), gardening stores, and big discount furniture stores. The largest mall in Italy, Gigli, opened along the highway outside of Florence in 1997, complete with a huge Home Depot–like store.

OTHER TYPES OF STORES

There are also many other kinds of stores that will make your shopping more active and colorful. These include the *enoteca* (wine shop), *ferramenta* (hardware store), *macelleria* (butcher shop), *panetteria* (bread shop/bakery), *pasticceria* (pastry shop), *tipografia* (typography), *tintoria* or *lavanderia* (dry cleaner/laundromat), *paninoteca* (sandwich store), *farmacia* (pharmacy), *profumeria* (perfume shop), *cartoleria* (stationery store), *libreria* (bookstore), *gelateria* (ice cream shop), and *gioielleria* (jewelry store).

Tips for Successful Shopping

Shops are open from 9:00 A.M. to 1:30 P.M. and 3:30 or 4:00 to 7:30 or 8:00 P.M. There are variations in the schedule between north and south and according to season. The Italian day is structured around lunch, the most important daily ritual. Stores and offices shut down and streets are emptied, making it impossible for you to run errands. This three- to four-hour-long *pausa* was created to accommodate two things, eating and digesting, but the tradition of the *pausa* (or *siesta*, as it's called in other Latin countries) is slowly disappearing. An increasing number of shop owners choose not to close for the long lunch break at all but close a bit earlier in the evening to compensate. These have an *orario nonstop* or *orario continuato* (nonstop or continuous schedule). A handful of *tabacchi, farmacie,* and *benzinai* (gas stations) stay open twenty-four hours a day.

In addition to store hours, you must know which stores are closed on which days. It once was safe to assume that all stores were closed on Sunday because this was mandated by Italian law. Now laws have been relaxed, and more stores choose to stay open on the seventh day. Smaller family-owned shops often take Saturday afternoons off to get a jump start on Sundays. Many stores, such as clothing stores and shops selling

Bars are often the first stop of the day for an espresso or cappuccino.

household items, are closed Monday mornings, while *alimentari* are almost always closed one afternoon in the middle of the week, usually Wednesday or Thursday. Outdoor vegetable markets operate only in the morning and shut down before lunch. Restaurants and bars have a designated *giorno di riposo*, or rest day, each week (usually Sunday or Monday), when they are completely closed. Pretty much all businesses close for summer vacation during the week around August 15th (*ferragosto*). This also applies to most pharmacies and movie theaters. Sometimes an extra vacation day, called "*il ponte*" (literally, "the bridge") is added onto smaller holidays, and you can also count on shops being closed then.

When shopping for food, you should order what you want from the sales people behind the counter, wait for them to calculate the total amount due, then go to the *cassa* (cash register) to pay. Afterward, go back and get your purchases. This system requires a lot of running around within the store, much waiting in line, and a little getting used to. Each time you make a purchase, even a small one, make sure you get a *scontrino,* or receipt. For tax purposes it's illegal both for the shopkeeper not to give you one and for you not to ask for it. The Italian tax police (Guardia di Finanza), who watch for *scontrino* infractions, have been known to fine customers leaving stores without a receipt for as little as a can of soda. But don't be surprised if shopkeepers offer you tiny discounts, or *sconticini,* once they get to know you well. It's silently understood that you will accept the discount in exchange for not asking for a receipt. Remember that sales tax is always included in the price of the item.

FINDING SPECIALTY ITEMS

Americans living in Italy like to reminisce about particular food cravings they can't indulge in outside the United States. No matter how much you enjoy Italian risotto or *bucatini all'amatriciana,* you are destined to wake up one night to the sound of your own stomach after that first dream of a medium-rare cheeseburger and crispy dill pickle, or a piece of fluffy pita bread smothered in hummus. It happens to the best of us. Your strongest cravings for American foods will occur around Thanksgiving, Halloween, and Independence Day, when images of pumpkin pie, Reese's Peanut Butter Cups, and potato salad will dance in your head. The cravings will intensify as you dash to specialty food stores, desperately searching for these holiday goodies.

Luckily, Italian food stores today cater to the requests of their increasingly diversified clientele, though the culinary habits of the Italians themselves are changing only slowly. Stores that carry matzoh, taco shells, chocolate chips, pancake mix, and even bagels exist in many major cities. Port cities such as Genoa and southern cities such as Naples and Palermo have stores to serve those with a taste for the Middle East, carrying spices such as cumin, turmeric, and coriander. In recent years grocery stores have been opened by Chinese, Korean, Ethiopian, and Indian immigrants, offering everything from curry powders to soy sauce and bean curd. Many cities have kosher food stores, sometimes spelled with an "a" or a "c" (*kasher, casher,* or *cosher*).

In fact, you can buy just about anything in Italy today, especially if you live in one of the bigger cities. There are a few exceptions, such as American dairy products like cheddar cheese and sour cream, but these can be replaced with Italian favorites such as *caciottina dolce* or *panna.* One Tex-Mex restaurant in Rome actually flies fresh sour cream to Italy daily. (If you can't go a month without cilantro or dill, there have been occasional cilantro sightings at outdoor markets.) It's a bit more difficult to find the selection of low-fat products that is available in the United States. There are *latte scremato* (low-fat milk) and *yogurt magro* (low-fat yogurt), but nonfat dairy products are rare. There is no nonfat milk, and Lactaid drinkers will be at a loss. If you have a fancy for particular brand-name American foods, you should bring them from the United States, because you may not find them. Some exceptions include common products such as Philadelphia cream cheese, Kellogg's corn flakes, Heinz ketchup, and Campbell's soup.

But chances are the diverse and delicious tastes of the Italian cuisine will eventually make you swear off your native cooking. You'll find yourself enjoying the regional specialties with the same hungry passion as the Italians. Learning the regional differences, as well as where to find the products you need and which ones are available during certain months, are the best parts of *lo shopping:* rice and polenta (cornmeal) replace pasta as the primary food staple in some areas of the north; sugary sweets made from almond paste available in Sicily cannot be found elsewhere; and focaccia, the delicious bread of Genoa, can't be purchased south of Florence. Different regions make *castagnaccio* bread from chestnuts and pine seeds, and Ligurians eat pancakes made from chickpea flour. Calabria has a kind of spicy sausage called *nduia* that is so soft you spread it onto bread with a butter knife, and Sardinian chefs use the bitter *mirto* (myrtle) berry as a side to meat the same way we pair cranberries with turkey. The way you prepare food will also change. You'll start pouring olive oil over your food, shunning the usual American sauces and creams. You'll hardly use butter, and in general you'll eat more vegetables and less meat. Of course, you'll learn to prepare pasta hundreds of different ways, making it possible for you to eat it every night of the week without getting bored.

Shopping for Clothing and Shoes

In the United States, Americans are used to large clothing stores where you can take clothes from racks at your leisure and return purchases within thirty days without salespeople even asking you why. In Italy, all this is different. Except for in large department stores, salespeople at clothing stores don't allow you to browse, which can make the shopping experience very unpleasant. As soon as you enter the store, you have to tell them what you want and what size you wear. (Never unfold neatly stacked sweaters without asking the *commessa,* or salesperson, to do it for you, unless you want to risk getting curtly reprimanded.) If you want to try an item on, be prepared for a lack of privacy: either the dressing room curtain will cover only your midsection, or the salesperson will barge in unannounced. In addition, the problem, according to them, is never the merchandise. If shoes are too small, it must be because your feet are temporarily swollen; if they're

*Shopping in Italy involves knowing where and when to shop
and having a good eye for quality.*

too big, it's because you should wear thicker socks. No matter what,
those particular shoes are always, according to them, "this year's
hottest fashion." If you do fall victim to their pressure to buy something
and then decide to return it later, you will not get your money back. At
best—and this is rare—they'll give you store credit.

Clothing sales, or *saldi*, are a tricky game in Italy. Some sales are
downright illegal and all others are controlled by the state, prohibiting
the shopkeeper from offering the big discounts bargain hunters want.
Usually the big sales are in January and July or August. When Italians
really want to find bargains, they go to outdoor flea markets to get used
clothing, antiques, and other collectibles. You can find just about anything there from vintage World War II helmets to used leather jackets.
(For U.S.-Italian clothing and shoe size equivalencies, consult the
Appendix.)

Tax Rebate for Non–European Union Residents

As a non-EU citizen, you are entitled to a partial IVA refund on
purchases exceeding 300,000 lire when you leave the European Union,
as long as those purchases have been made at a "tax-free shop" and you
keep your receipt. These shops give you a "tax-free cheque" when you
make your purchase. When you leave the EU, go to the Dogana-Ufficio

Viaggiatori (Customs Office) at the airport, train station, or seaport you are departing from to get a validation stamp on your tax-free cheque. With one brand of cheques you can go to the nearby "tax-free counter" to collect your cash refund, although with others you have to mail in the cheque. I've tried getting an IVA refund twice but both times was disappointed by how much effort I spent for what turned out to be a small refund.

Useful Addresses: Stores Catering to Ethnic Tastes

FLORENCE:
Old England Store
Via Vecchietti, 28/r
50123 Firenze
tel (055) 211983
fax (055) 288312
(tea, cookies, desserts)
Pegna
Via dello Studio, 8
50122 Firenze
tel (055) 282701
fax (055) 2302357
(some Mexican and Chinese cooking
ingredients)
Sugar Blues
Via dei Serragli, 57/r
50127 Firenze
tel/fax (055) 268378
(natural foods)
MILAN:
Surgelati Cattaneo G.
Via Fratelli Bronzetti, 37
20123 Milano
tel (02) 741948
Tex Mex Drugstore
Via M. Quadrio, 23
20123 Milano
tel (02) 654694
(take-out fajitas, brownies, etc.)
ROME:
Castroni
Via Cola di Rienzo, 196

00193 Roma
tel (06) 6874383
Funari Alimentari—Pantheon
Via dei Pastini, 121
00186 Roma
tel (06) 6789160
(some Mexican foods)
Innocenti
Via Natale del Grande, 31
(at the corner of Piazza San Cosimato,
66, in Trastevere)
00153 Roma
tel (06) 5812725
Kasher Supermarket
Via Catalana, 5 (in the Jewish ghetto)
00186 Roma
tel (06) 70452760
(kosher foods)
Korean Market
Via Cavour, 84
00184 Roma
tel (06) 4885060
fax (06) 4885280
Oriental Store
Via Filippo Turati, 130/132
00185 Roma
tel (06) 4455631

CHAPTER NINE

Getting Around:
Transportation

In Italy, moving from point A to point B is not just a practical exercise of getting to your destination. It involves style, maximum horsepower, and the appropriate attitude. It is a macho world of revved-up engines and sound barrier–breaking speeds, where the most admired road warriors boast a cunning understanding of how to cut ahead of traffic. Once they get to the red light, many Italian drivers don't even bother to stop, claiming that the red light is a "suggestion to stop," not a command. A couple of quick glances to the left and right, and the bold sail on through the intersection. Those who do make a full halt at the light are followed by other drivers with the palm of their hand hovering over their horns, waiting to honk them out of their way the exact millisecond they see green. When the light turns, the race is on. . . .

Public Transportation:
Life in the Slow Lane

The long, narrow Italian peninsula is geographically inconvenient for those who use public transportation. There are more train connections in the north, and reaching areas of the deep south cannot be done in a single maneuver. On a local level, buses move slowly on the congested cobblestone streets. After hours of waiting for a bus, you'll find that two or three empty ones arrive at the same time, traveling in herds like migrating geese. Workers' strikes can paralyze the system at any time with virtually no prior notice. Unfortunately for the commuter, union leaders have learned that the most effective time to strike is during rush hour or on the day before a national holiday. Most departure and arrival schedules should be read with a critical eye, except for those of the trains, which generally run on time. In fact, the train company is so proud of its punctuality that it promises it will refund a portion of the price of a train ticket if the train arrives more than thirty minutes late (recently, it has also added faster trains, making this a preferred form of travel). Small commuter planes make longitudinal travel in the peninsula comfortable yet usually expensive, although prices are currently being slashed. There are 137 airports in Italy, 32 of which offer international service. Most international flights come into either Rome's Fiumicino airport (Leonardo da Vinci) or Milan's Malpensa Airport, the latter often being closed due to fog in colder months. Because of airline deregulation, some new private airlines such as AirOne have forced Alitalia, the state-owned airline, into competitive price wars that consumers can take advantage of. If you are one of the lucky few living in Venice, you can cruise your way through the canals on a *vaporetto* to reach your destination. Hydrofoils (*aliscafi*) and ferries (*traghetti*) make daily runs to the Italian islands such as Sardinia, Elba, and Sicily. Italian taxis are much more expensive and impossible to flag down, making it necessary either to call them or to get them at one of the few stations where they wait for customers. Ultimately, walking or bicycling is often the fastest mode of transportation to avoid the suffocating traffic and the confusing web of one-way streets.

THE *METROPOLITANE*

Rome, Milan, Naples, and Palermo are equipped with subway services called *metropolitane*. Metro stops are identified by an illuminated or red "M" sign. While the Milan subway is useful to people getting around within the city, the two Roman subway lines are used mostly by people going into or getting out of the center. Although building additional subway lines in other cities would surely be advantageous, builders are faced with too many obstacles buried deep below, since the ground under many cities is saturated with ancient Roman and Etruscan ruins. If you watch Federico Fellini's film *Roma*, you will never be able to ride the Italian subways without an ominous feeling of trespassing in someone else's ancient living room.

Mopeds and scooters are one of the preferred modes of transportation in Italy, numbering more than 1.5 million.

BUSES AND TRAMS

Italy has more public buses than any other European country. Many of the smaller towns do not have train stations and therefore can be reached only by car or bus (this is especially true of Tuscan hill towns and vineyards). In an effort to fight pollution, some buses are being replaced with electric trams. Bus tickets are sometimes difficult to come by because they can be purchased only at *tabacchi*, bus terminals, and some newsstands. Larger bus stops have automated ticket machines, but these are few and far between. One regular ticket, or *corso semplice*, is good for sixty to ninety minutes, depending on the city. There are also day-long *intrarete* tickets, *tessere mensili* (month-long discount passes), and additional discounts for students and the elderly that can be bought at the offices of the local bus authority. (The name of that authority changes from town to town. For example, in Florence it is called ATAF.) Ticket prices are generally the same for buses, trams, and the subway.

Despite the delays and the traffic, there is one refreshing aspect of the Italian bus system that probably makes it unique worldwide: it is based on the honor system. In fact, many people get around by bus without paying a lira. To give you an idea of the odds, I have been riding Italian public buses for about ten years and have seen the bus police only three times. If you get caught, however, you will be expected to pay a cash fine on the spot (in recent years it was 50,000 lire, or $30). Easily identifiable uniformed officers hop from one bus to the next, usually boarding at the busiest stops on a route, checking that all passengers have validated tickets (*biglietti timbrati*). Some sneaky passengers opt to stand strategically adjacent to the ticket validation machine located at the back of the bus so that they can stuff their unvalidated ticket into the machine if the ticket police board.

Bus stops are identified by a signpost on the side of the road. Only a handful of buses is listed on each sign, so if you are at a busy stop frequented by many different buses you will find yourself running back and forth among the many signs, trying to figure out which bus you want. The bus number is listed on the top of the sign with the names of each bus stop underneath and the schedule of operating buses (most city buses run about every ten minutes). There is no map, so you must know the name of the piazza or street of your stop before boarding. You can also ask the bus drivers, who are usually very willing to assist a lost traveler, or consult the local edition of *Tutto Città*, a road atlas supplement to the phone book that has a detailed map of bus routes. (Maps can also be obtained from the main bus headquarters.) The *autobus notturno*, or night bus, is listed on the bus signs with a black "N" adjacent to the bus number. Unfortunately, night service is inadequate and some buses stop running as early as 9:00 P.M. Be careful not to miss a night bus, for you might have to wait as much as an hour until the next one.

Some bus routes are famous with foreigners, and anyone who lives in Rome knows that bus 64 is like no other bus on this planet. It is the main artery connecting the heart of the Catholic world (Vatican City) to the gateway of the rest of the world (Stazione Termini, the main train station). Religious pilgrims and tourists travel by train and air to the Eternal City, but it is bus 64 that takes them to the last leg of their journey: Saint Peter's Basilica. Stepping aboard is like entering a medieval carnival with gypsies and priests, smartly dressed aristocrats, musicians, beggars, merchants, and strangers speaking in unfamiliar tongues. But don't get too caught up with watching the spectacle around you when riding bus 64—it also has the highest incidence of pickpocketing and robbery of any bus in Italy.

TRAINS

The FS, or Ferrovia dello Stato, is the national railroad company. Recently the state invested billions of lire in renovations, and new high-speed trains rivaling France's famous TGV bullet train are in the works. Now some Italian trains come equipped with outlets for laptop computers, video screens, and double beds. The Eurostar Italia is the newest arrival in the Ferrovia family, and offers commuters a speedy, elegant, and comfortable travel alternative that includes free candy and newspapers. Unlike other trains, for which you can purchase your ticket up until the moment of departure, the Eurostar Italia requires that you purchase it at least a few hours beforehand and make a seat reservation.

Regular trains generally do not cost much. The *rapido* trains are the fastest and require a 30 percent *supplemento rapido* fee on top of the price of the ticket (this is what you get back if your train is more than thirty minutes late). These include the Intercity (IC) and Eurocity (EC) trains, which travel to neighboring European countries as well. The cheaper *espresso* and *diretto* trains are not fast, contrary to what their names imply, because they stop at all smaller cities. The slowest and least expensive of the Italian trains is the *locale,* which will remind you of "The Little Engine That Could" and have you mumbling "I think I can, I think I can" throughout your journey.

In the past, to get train schedule information you had to do considerable legwork. But this is changing fast. Internet sites have been created that provide most of the information you need (see Chapter 10). If you're a traditionalist, you can call the station, but the phone lines are nearly always busy. You can also go to the train station itself (to the *biglietti ordinari e ridotti* counter) or a travel agent to find out about schedules and to buy tickets. Each train station has the daily schedule printed on a large yellow or white poster pinned up on the wall or in a glass case at the end of the tracks. Some stations also have computerized schedule terminals that can be accessed by typing in your destination, and, of course, there is also the information desk. If you plan to use Italian trains frequently, you should buy a copy of the FS train schedule, which is available at newsstands and the station.

Three words of general advice: First, there are many incidents of robbery on trains, especially night trains, so always be aware of who is sitting next to you and never leave your bags unattended. Second, remember that all train tickets must be validated by the passenger before boarding. If you forget to validate your ticket at the station, you must pay a 10,000-lire (approx. $7) fine on board. The small validation machines can be found at the entrance to each *binario,* or platform. All tickets and the *supplemento rapido* can be purchased on board for an additional fee, but it is better to buy them at the ticket counter or from a travel agency before departure. Lastly, because seat reservations are not required, many trains fill up with passengers cramming the corridors, especially on weekends or holidays. If you have the time before departure, buy a *prenotazione* (reservation).

DISCOUNT TRAVEL

In general, 50 percent discounts on Italian train rates are available to children under the age of twelve and travelers over the age of sixty-five. Americans can also purchase a Eurailpass or Eurail Flexipass for extended train travel in Europe. These passes can be bought from Council Travel in the United States (see end of this chapter for address), among other sources, and are for first-class travel only and range from about $500 to more than $1,400. For people under twenty-six, there are also the Eurail Youthpass and Eurail Youth Flexipass, which are limited to second-class travel and, like the first-class passes, last anywhere from ten days to three months. Prices range from around $350 to upward of $1,000. For two or more people traveling together, there are the Eurail Saverpass and Eurail Saver Flexipass for first-class travel only.

In Italy, students will want to make a trip to one of the many branches of the Centro Turistico Studentesco (CTS), the Italian student travel agency affiliated with Council Travel in the United States. CTS sells two discount train passes for travel within Europe: RIT (20 percent discount) and Treni BIJ (40 percent). Neither of these discounts covers the additional *supplemento rapido* charge for the faster trains. Students can apply at CTS for the *carta dello studente*, the Italian version of the International Student Identity Card. If you are not a student but under the age of twenty-six, you can apply for a *carta giovani*, which can get you some discounts on other forms of travel, especially plane fares. CTS has branches all over Italy, but if you have Internet access you can check out its Web site (www.cts.it). We have listed CTS's Rome address at the end of this chapter.

Private Transportation:
Life in the Fast Lane

Surviving the on-the-road scene is no easy feat in Italy. All the myths you have heard about Italian drivers are true. Finding a place to park your car is like fitting a square peg into a round hole: cars are double-parked, triple-parked, even quadruple-parked. I have even seen a lightweight Fiat Cinquecento being parked upside down. Once you change gears from "park" to "drive," the scenario gets worse. You will see two-wheelers, eighteen-wheelers, and even three-wheeled Ape vehicles that look like a cross between a motorbike and a minitruck. *Motorini* (mopeds) speed by you as if you were driving in a galactic meteor storm. On the *superstrade* (expressways), don't even dare to travel in the left-hand fast lane without a high-caliber engine. You can count on a big blue Alfa or BMW sliding up centimeters away from your back bumper, flashing high beams to signal that either you clear the road or you become road kill. The famous blue cars, or *"macchine blu"* (usually FIATs or Alfa Romeos), have a special reputation in Italy for being driven exclusively by people in power who somewhere along the way came to believe that speed limits and driving regulations don't apply to them. Though you might not believe it, the maximum driving speed in the cities really is 50 kilometers per hour (31 miles per hour) and 90 kph (56 mph) on rural roads. On the *superstrade* or *autostrade* (highways) speeds should technically go no higher than 130 kph (81 mph).

Driver's Licenses

Driving license agreements between Italy and the United States are reciprocal: Italians are permitted to drive in the United States for one year with their Italian license, and Americans can drive in Italy with their U.S. license for one year before having to take the Italian driver's test, though I have heard of Americans driving in Italy for as long as twenty years without obtaining an Italian license. Many foreigners in Italy opt to get the inexpensive International Driver's Permit from their local branch of the Automobile Association of America (AAA) before moving to Italy. This is no more than a translation of your U.S. license and is valid for one year.

To obtain an Italian driver's license, you must register for both the written and practical test at the nearest office of the Automobile Club d'Italia (ACI), which also offers car registration, driving lessons, and twenty-four hour roadside assistance. The actual test is taken at the Ufficio di Motorizzazione, the state Department of Motor Vehicles. It is based on European standards (including kilometers instead of miles and different driving laws) and can be taken in English if you don't speak Italian well. Several years ago, the Italian transportation minister decided that the test was too easy, so he switched to a more demanding one. Following criticism that the new test was too difficult, he decided to try it out for himself and failed. Rather than brush up on his own driving skills, he sent the new test back to make it "easier." Even so it's still hard, including questions that test your knowledge of first aid, insurance, and the length of truck axles. There is a two-hundred-page test booklet that can be bought in special bookstores or from ACI to help prepare for the exam. Because automatic transmission cars are virtually unheard of in Italy (even with rental cars), Americans should learn to master stick-shift driving. In addition to successfully passing both the written and practical exams, you must take an eye exam, provide photos, and pay an application fee. You will get a *foglio rosa* (learner's permit) first. Once you have obtained the driver's license, you must buy the expensive *marca da bollo* tax stamp each year to keep your license valid (in recent years it has cost 70,000 lire, or about $50).

ENTERING THE *CENTRO STORICO*

Because of the alarmingly high level of smog that is eroding many of Italy's most precious landmarks, almost all Italian cities have taken measures to limit the amount of traffic that enters the *centri storici*, or historic centers. In past years some cities, such as Milan, have designated *targhe alterne* days: on certain days, only cars with license plates ending in an even number can enter the center, and the odd bunch are allowed in on alternate days. Now, in some cities, there are days when only cars with a *marmitta catalitica*, or ecologically sound muffler, can drive around. Many city governments have made it illegal for any car to enter the center without a special *centro storico* pass, available only to residents and store owners with addresses in the center. The situation in Rome promises more nightmares for drivers since the city administration passed a *fascia blu* ordinance banning practically all vehicular traffic from the center. Sometimes the effort to block off the centers becomes extreme and a bit senseless. For example, legislation was recently passed banning all wedding processions with more than six cars.

RENTING A CAR

Autonoleggio, or renting a car, is expensive because you will have to pay the additional 19 percent IVA tax on top of the rental fee. It's actually a better deal to arrange the rental from the United States, pay in full there, and pick up your car in Italy. You can save up to 50 percent by doing this since one week of renting can cost more than 800,000 lire ($530). At the end of this chapter is a list of car rental agencies with branch offices all over the country and pickup/drop-off points, including, among others, Leonardo da Vinci Airport (Fiumicino), Ciampino Airport, Termini train station (Rome); Malpensa Airport, Linate Airport, and Centrale train station (Milan); Amerigo Vespucci Airport and Santa Maria Novella train station (Florence); Marco Polo Airport and Santa Lucia train station (Venice); Capodichino Airport (Naples) and Cinisi–Punta Raisi Airport (Palermo). The toll-free reservation numbers we have listed are good from any phone in Italy. The only one that does not have a toll-free number is Hertz, and you can call either the local branch listed in the phone book or the Milan office to make a reservation.

Buying a Car

If you are not a resident in Italy, you can buy a car and drive it there for up to one year without paying the 19 percent IVA tax that residents and citizens must pay. You should go to your local *comune* office and ask for an *atto sostitutivo,* in which you declare that you are not a resident of the European Union and therefore not liable for the value-added tax. Once you have achieved that special status, you can buy a car and get Escursionisti Esteri (EE) license plates, which are valid for one year. You cannot renew EE plates once the year is up. You must either sell the car or take it out of the country, paying IVA when you leave.

If you are a resident of Italy, you must register (*immatricolare*) your car like anyone else and pay the tax. You will then be given national license plates (*targhe nazionali*). Until a few years ago all Italian license plates bore the name of the city the car originated from, but legislators decided to change the plates so that you cannot tell where a car originates anymore. Now some Italians want the old plates back because they feel the roads have become too impersonal.

If you buy a used car, you must complete a transfer of ownership (*passaggio di proprietà*) and might have to wait at least a year until the registration papers (*libretto di circolazione*) are in your name. While you wait for the *libretto,* you will have to obtain a temporary one called the *foglio sostitutivo,* which must be renewed every three months at the Ufficio di Motorizzazione, or Department of Motor Vehicles. In addition, buying a car usually means inheriting the previous owner's parking and moving violation fines. All car owners must pay an annual *bollo,* or tax, determined by the size of the car's engine. It can be paid at the ACI (Automobile Club d'Italia) office by the end of January each year.

A snowbound mini Fiat in the Italian Alps.

THE PERILS OF PARKING

Parking in Italy can be a nightmare. For example, in Rome there are 300,000 public parking spaces for the city's 2 million cars, and very few Italians have private parking facilities. Pay parking spaces are marked by a blue line painted on the ground and parking meters. Any parking you find that is not paid parking is probably illegal. Be careful: the *vigili urbani* police readily give out *multe* (parking tickets) or clamp a "boot" onto your wheel, leaving you grounded. A map of legal parking lots is published in the front pages of your local telephone book. In addition, some parking lots are guarded by self-nominated "parking attendants," who will offer to "protect" your car against robbery or damage. It is a good idea to donate 1,000 lire to their efforts—neglecting to do so might cost much more if you have to repaint your car after it has been "keyed."

THE HIGH PRICE OF GASOLINE

Gas prices in Italy are high, and filling up a medium-sized tank can cost as much as 50,000 lire (approx. $35). Many cars still take the less expensive unleaded gas, which creates black exhaust fumes. Most gas stations follow the same hours of operation as retail stores, so driving around late at night looking for an open gas station is unwise. Hours are generally from 7:00 A.M. to 12:30 P.M. and 3:00 to 7:30 P.M., closed on Sundays, though highways do have twenty-four-hour service stations. There are also automatic machines at some stations that accept 10,000- and 50,000-lire bills, and these are often open late at night, though you will find that it is just as difficult to find one of these stations as it is getting the machine to accept a worn banknote.

INSURANCE

There are two basic kinds of automobile insurance in Italy. The first is the so-called *bonus-malus*. With this kind, the premium you pay varies depending on the number of accidents you cause. If you don't have any accidents in a given year, the premium is much lower, if you've had accidents in the past, the premium will automatically be higher. The second kind of insurance is called the *assicurazione con franchigia fissa ed assoluta*. In this case you have to pay a set deductible before the insurance company will cover damages. Two companies that sell insurance are RAS and Allianz Subalpina.

The *carta verde* is international road insurance, which all vehicles traveling outside of Italy must have. If you have an accident, remember to get the *numero di targa* (license plate number), *marca e tipo di macchina* (brand and model of car), *numero di patente* (driver's license number), address, and phone number of the other driver. It is also useful to make a quick sketch of the events, since it will be requested by your insurance company. If you and the other driver are able to come to a friendly agreement of what happened, you fill out a *constatazione amichevole-denuncia di sinistro*, which means that the case will be settled in court by the insurance companies without any witnesses present. You should also be aware that it is illegal to drive your car or even your moped without the *libretto di circolazione* (registration papers) and proof of insurance. Police can stop you and ask to check these even if you have not committed any infractions. Make sure to keep the originals (photocopies will not do) in your vehicle at all times. The Automobile Club d'Italia (ACI) also offers roadside assistance, which can be obtained by dialing "116" on the phone.

THE APPEAL OF *MOTORINI* AND SCOOTERS

When I was a student in a study abroad program in Padua as a junior in college, I could think of no better way to immerse myself in the Italian experience than to jet around from class to class on a *motorino*, or moped. But when I looked into buying one, I discovered that the prices were much too high for my budget . . . until one day, when I was approached by a man on the street who asked me if I wanted to buy his bright red Piaggio moped for only 50,000 lire, or about $35. How could I resist? I had the moped for seventy-two wind-in-my-hair-filled hours—zipping around, offering rides to friends, making picnic excursions to the countryside—before two police officers stopped me and charged me with possession of a stolen *motorino*. I was given a court date and appointed a lawyer. In court, my lawyer was able to convince the judge that I hadn't stolen it myself but was powerless to defend me against a more sinister charge: in Italy there is a law that makes it illegal to buy something for less than it's worth. I was obviously guilty, having bought a 500,000-lire ($300) item at little more than a tenth of its value. My lawyer tried to prove that I hadn't known the real value of the moped when I'd bought it, but this wasn't convincing in the least. My lawyer then attempted the "culturally ignorant defense" by suggesting that in America buying something for less is actually seen as a positive thing. Having rehearsed this explanation with me before the hearing, he turned to me at the opportune moment and asked in broken English why I had bought the moped, to which I answered loudly, "Bargain!" The charges against me were dropped, and my record was left pristine.

Using a moped or scooter to get around is probably the most practical solution to moving in traffic-infested city streets because they can slip between cars and are easy to park. Of course, they are potentially dangerous. Italy is home to more than 1.5 million mopeds, though if you drive frequently you'll swear you see that many in your own city every day. If you want to join the *motorino* madness, there are a few things you should remember before you buy one. First, it is technically illegal to ride double, although the police are sometimes tolerant (this seems to be more true the farther south you go). In fact, they will often make a real issue of it only if you ride double while committing other infractions. Second, it is illegal to ride without a helmet if you are under eighteen. Legislation is being debated that would force all moped drivers to wear helmets, but in any event every rider should seriously consider using one, especially in the rain, when streets are slippery and visibility is poor. Third, make sure the seller gives you the *libretto di circolazione* (registration papers) with the moped, and make sure the *numero di telaio* (serial number) on the *libretto* matches the one on the moped. *Libretti* are a hot commodity on the black market, and if you buy a moped without one, it's probably been stolen.

You are also required to have insurance on the *motorino,* at least to cover damages you could inflict on others. Purchasing insurance against theft of mopeds and scooters is not mandatory but highly recommended. You will be given a little booklet with a *numero di polizza* (insurance policy number) by the insurance company. *Targhe* (license plates) are *nominativi,* meaning they are issued in your name. If you sell your moped or scooter later, you should take off the plate and stick it on your new vehicle. You can apply for a plate at the Ufficio di Motorizzazione or go to one of the special agencies that will do the paperwork for you. There is an annual tax due in the first months of the year that keeps your plate valid. If you are caught driving a moped or scooter without a license plate or insurance, the fine can be as high as 1 million lire ($700). Remember that some models take *miscella*—a mixture of gasoline and oil—rather than pure gasoline, and if you don't put it in, you could cause serious damage to your engine.

Useful Addresses

AUTOMOBILE CLUB D'ITALIA (ACI)

24-hour road emergency assistance: dial 116.
www.aci.it
info@aci.it
FLORENCE:
Viale Amendola, 36
50121 Firenze
tel (055) 24861
fax (055) 2343257
MILAN:
Corso Venezia, 43
20121 Milano
tel (02) 77451
fax (02) 781844
NAPLES:
Piazzale Tecchio, 49/D
80125 Napoli
tel (081) 2394511
fax (081) 5933644
ROME:
Via Marsala, 8
00185 Roma
tel (06) 49981
fax (06) 49982234

CAR RENTAL AGENCIES
(NATIONAL NUMBERS)
Avis
tel (1678) 63063
www.avis.com
Dollaro Express
tel (1678) 65110
dollaro@uni.net
www.dollaroexpress.it
Hertz
tel (02) 67746
Maggiore (Budget)
tel (1478) 67067
COUNCIL TRAVEL
Council Travel
National Reservation Center
1030 Massachusetts Avenue, Suite 200
Cambridge, MA 02138
tel (800) 226-8624
Council Travel
205 East 42nd Street
New York, NY 10017-5706
tel (212) 822-2700
(Or call (800) 2COUNCIL toll-free for the office nearest you)

CTS

Via Genova, 16
00184 Roma
tel (06) 46791
www.cts.it
cta@ciee.org

NATIONAL INSURANCE PROVIDERS
FOR CARS AND MOPEDS

Allianz Subalpina
Via Alfieri, 22

10123 Torino
tel (011) 5161111
fax (011) 5161255
RAS
Riunione Adriatica di Sicurità
Piazza San Silvestro, 12
00186 Roma
tel (06) 67681

CHAPTER TEN

La Virtual Vita:
Italian Cyberspace

One of the favorite pastimes of American expatriates is complaining about the difficulty of obtaining information in Italy. They tell stories about waiting in lines at public offices for hours to get specific information, only to be greeted with blank stares and the usual response: "No written information exists." Yet, these expatriates are missing out on a basic fact: while daily life may be muddled by a distinct lack of technology, the Internet is making many of their complaints about a lack of written information archaic. You can now access Italian databases and archives on line that are unavailable even if you go in person to consult them. In fact, many of the best-organized and most informative Italian Web sites are those sponsored by the government.

But that's not all the Italian Net is good for. With a personal computer, modem, and Internet access, you can find the sensuous pleasures of Italian wine, art, literature, and music at the touch of a few quick keystrokes. You can learn about local politics and culture, read the national Constitution, or find out the movie schedule at the cinema around the corner. Even train and plane schedules are at your disposal to download and print. If you need to look up the phone number of an Italian company and don't have the yellow pages handy, you can often find the number on the Web. Can't remember when street-cleaning day is? Just check the Web site of your town hall. Want to find a cycling club you can join? Just a quick "http://www" and you're on your way.

Even with technological breakthroughs, many Italians still prefer the old-fashioned way of communicating.

With an on-line Italian presence that is expanding at an average rate of 350 percent per year, there's plenty of *cyberinformazioni* to keep you busy.

This section represents many hours of on-line research to find what we consider the best sites on the Italian Net (of course, due to the nature of the Internet, these sites can be accessed from anywhere in the world). For those readers who don't speak much Italian, you'll find that many of the sites listed feature English-language text, too, though this is not to say they have been translated well. In addition, you'll notice that there's some overlap from one site to the next, as the frantic competition for "who has the best links" rages on. Even if you don't find what you're looking for on our list, chances are that it is out there somewhere, floating around in cyberspace, and can be found by using popular search engines such as Yahoo! or Alta Vista.

Setting Up an Account

Many Americans opt to open an account with CompuServe or America On Line before leaving the United States because of their wide selection of local access numbers in Italy. Payment is made by using an American credit card, which means making sure you pay your bill in the United States on time every month so the service is not cut off. It also generally means paying an additional fee to use the foreign access number, which can be as much as six dollars more per month. Also, if you have an Internet account with an American provider, you will probably have to call France or England for technical assistance (for example, as of now this is true of CompuServe). If you're planning to stay long-term, getting a local server might be an easier option. You will find that most Italian servers require you to pay a lump annual sum rather than monthly installments (the cost is usually somewhere between 150,000 and 400,000 lire, or $100 and $260, per year). We have listed addresses of major Italian servers at the end of this chapter.

Italian Government Sites: Making Daily Life Easier

LOCAL GOVERNMENT ON LINE

Before 1915, foreigners could come to Italy without a passport. All they needed was a pack on the back, a letter of recommendation from an official, and a satchelful of money. No government officials could follow their movements, no customs officers could track them down. Today, things are not so simple, but the Internet is freeing up the bureaucracy. In order to make the enormous amount of bureaucratic information out there more accessible, many Italian *comuni* (municipalities), *regioni* (regions), and *province* (provinces) have created *reti civiche*, or online civic networks. In particular, the *communi* provide information about mundane but essential things worth knowing such as garbage collection days and local property taxes. They also provide information about local art, culture, and history. They include

---

Vocabolario Virtuale

Before you can surf the Italian Net, you have to learn some jargon. Many of the words Italians use to refer to computers and the Internet are in English, even when an Italian equivalent exists. For example, they always say "computer," "modem," and "Internet" but use *"tastiera"* for "keyboard" and *"schermo"* for "screen." You'll also notice that most of the Italian Net addresses end with ".it" instead of ".com". Here are some of the Italian terms you need to know:

English	Italian
@	chiocciolina; chiocciola
_ (underline)	linetta in basso
- (hyphen)	il meno, trattino
. (dot)	punto
:	due punti
/	slash che parte da destra; slash; barra
\	slash che parte da sinistra; backslash
//	doppia slash; doppia barra

---

addresses of local government offices, schools, universities, associations, museums, and libraries that cannot be found anywhere else on the Italian Net. They also have listings of conferences, exhibitions, trade shows, *sagre* (festivals), and folklore. You should look for areas marked *servizi* (services), *servizi al cittadino* (citizens' services), or *ufficio informazioni* (information bureau). Anything labeled "*stranieri*" (foreigners) or "*cittadini extracomunitari*" (non-EU citizens) is for you.

For example, one of the most extensive sites is the *Rete Civica di Milano* (http://wrcm.usr.dsi.unimi.it/), which includes the *comune, regione,* and *provincia.* When you go to the Milan home page, you can choose *I Servizi di Milano,* which leads to information about: *Dove alloggiare* (Where to stay), *Cosa Vedere* (What to see), *Come orientarsi* (How to orient yourself), *Dove divertirsi* (Where to have fun), *Come fare gli affari* (How to do business), and *Calcio a Milano* (Soccer in Milan). Things to look for include street and subway maps, museums and theater listings, cinema schedules, and hotel addresses. If you choose the *Comune di Milano,* you get to the Palazzo Marino site, one of the best in the country. Its *Ufficio Informazioni* is divided into various sectors:

Vocabolario Virtuale

English	Italian
browse	*sfogliare*
database	*banche dati*
decode	*deciffrare*
delete	*cancellare*
e-mail	*posta elettronica; e-mail*
e-mail address	*indirizzo elettronico; indirizzo e-mail*
multimedia	*multimediale*
network	*rete*
on-line	*in rete; on-line*
select	*selezionare*
user	*utente*
www	*vu vu vu; doppia vu tre volte*

- *casa* (home)
- *circolazione e trasporti* (circulation and transportation)
- *cultura* (culture)
- *istruzione* (education)
- *lavoro* (work)
- *persona* (people)
- *sanità e assistenza* (health and social services)
- *servizi zonali* (neighborhood services)
- *sport, turismo e tempo libero* (sports, tourism, and free time)
- *strutture cittadine* (citizen centers)

Each of these sectors has dozens of articles about how to get things done in Italy. For example, the sector *Persona* includes information about getting married, obtaining a *carta d'identità,* and changing residency. The *Lavoro* page has more than 120 different work-related topics to choose from, including information about work authorization, permits, taxes, and professional associations.

Some places to search for links to these government sites include the *Osservatorio Reti,* or "Networks Observatory" of the *Città Invisibile* site (www.citinv.it), *Turismo* (www.turismo.it), and *Le Nostre Reti Civiche,* or "Our Civic Networks" (www.logical.it/civica/). You can sometimes find them by typing www.comune.[name of the city in Italian].it:80/ (for example, Rome's site is www.comune.roma.it:80/). This will definitely work for the following cities: Bologna, Firenze, Livorno, Lucca, Messina, Modena, Pisa, Prato, Roma, Siena, and Torino. Sometimes this formula works for *province* and *regioni,* too. For example, the *provincia* of Turin is provincia.torino.it, that of Asti is provincia.asti.it, and the *regione* of Piedmont is regione.piemonte.it.

ITALIAN EMBASSIES ON LINE

In Chapter 2 we mentioned that the Italian Embassy in Washington, D.C., is now on line (www.italyemb.nw.dc.us:80/italy). Other Italian Embassies are also on line, a favorite being the embassy in Tokyo, Japan (http://sunsite.sut.ac.jp/embitaly). Aside from information about visas and Italian events in the cities where they are located, these embassies offer cultural and practical information about Italy for any English-speaker anywhere in the world. They have sections on frequently asked questions (called "FAQs"), "tips for travellers," statistical data, a virtual newsstand, and the Italian national anthem, which plays aloud while you surf. They also have links to all of the major national Italian government offices on line. For a list of other Italian Embassies, try *Electronic Embassy* (www.embassy.org); choose first "foreign embassies," then "Italy."

ON-LINE GOVERNMENT DATABASES

AIPA (www.aipa.it) is a large site sponsored by the Enti della Pubblica Amministrazione, or Central Public Administration Agencies. These agencies include, among others, the Ministries of Finance, Foreign Trade, and Industry. The site contains the names and addresses of ministries and public nonprofit organizations. With increasing privatization, the issue of antitrust has become paramount in Italy in recent years, and the Autorità Garante della Concorrenza e del Mercato (www.agcm.it), also known as the "Italian Competition Authority," offers press releases, weekly bulletins, and publications on line in English. If you have questions about antitrust, you can even try e-mailing it at antitrust@agcm.it. The state mint, or Istituto Poligrafico e Zecca dello Stato (www.ipzs.it), has its own on-line database called "Ispolitel-Giuritel" that you can subscribe to by sending a request for information to the e-mail address on the *IPZS* site. This database includes more than twelve different sections that address legal, commercial, and fiscal issues, among others.

Major Italian Research Institutes On Line

CNR, or the Milan Research Area of the National Research Council (www.mi.cnr.it), has two useful databases on its site. The first, called *The Italian General Subject Tree*, contains more than seventy different topics to choose from with links to thousands of Italian sites on anything from résumés and geology to on-line Italian Star Trek clubs (unfortunately, within each topic the entries are arranged in random order, which can get messy). The second, called *Windows on Italy* (access it by typing www.mi.cnr.it/WOI), includes information about the history of the country, its regions, nightlife, itineraries, a miniencyclopedia of Italian culture called "Cultural Tidbits," and even the Italian National Constitution.

CRS4 is the site of the Center for Advanced Studies, Research, and Development in Sardinia (www.crs4.it). It sponsors *Search in Italy*, a search engine connected to an archive of more than 100,000 files and linked to hundreds of servers. For example, when I typed "Napoli" it came up with 3,341 files that included links to the University of Naples, a Naples Internet Club, and local hotels. If you click on *Web Initiatives* you will get a list of CRS4's Net projects, including *Virtual Sardinia*, a three-dimensional trip through the island of Sardinia, and the *Italian Solidarity Home Page*, which has information about all of the major nonprofit organizations in Italy. *Sections of Italian Literature in HTML Format* has an abbreviated literary anthology with excerpts from all genres and periods, plus a history of the Italian language.

Commercial Web Sites

There are thousands of Italian commercial Web sites, all overshadowed by the two biggest ones, Italia On Line and Telecom Italia Net, known by locals as IOL and TIN (the latter was recently formed as a merger of two competitors, Telecom On Line and Video On Line). But, large or small, they all tend to offer the same kinds of topics under slightly different names: *Media* (news), *Arte e Spettacolo* (art and performing arts), *Cultura* (culture), *Cucina* (cooking), *Musica* (music), *Turismo* (tourism), *Moda* (fashion), *Politica* (politics), and so on. Most of them provide information in English, too, and each offers some unique attractions. There are also many foreign sites that provide excellent information about the country, such as *Dolce Vita* (www.dolcevita.com), which has information about Italian design, fashion, travel, and food in English. It includes an "agenda" and a "finder" for fashion and design that lists events and addresses. To get an archive of short descriptions of Italian sites and links to them, check out *What's New in Italy,* sponsored by *Itnet* (www.it.net). The Web addresses of the links are actually written underneath the descriptions, making it easy to print them for future consultation. Here are some of the best Italian commercial sites.

ITALIA ON LINE

Italia On Line (IOL) (www.iol.it), offers a search engine for information about Italian cities called *In Città*. When I picked *Roma,* it came up with seventeen entries, including hotels, the Rome city hall site, and local cycling information. It also hosts Touring Club Italiano (TCI), a leading Italian travel association and tour guide publisher. It even has, among other things, the full text of Pellegrino Artusi's famous cookbook *La scienza in cucina e l'arte di mangiar bene,* the definitive Tuscan gastronomical guide written by this Tuscan master in 1891.

TELECOM ITALIA NET

Telecom Italia Net (www.tin.it), offers *Movie Online,* sponsored by a professional Italian filmmaking magazine, with the latest news about film festivals and awards, an international film database with more than 40,000 titles from 1928 to the present (updated daily), and the filmmaking magazine itself. The section on the home page called *Canali VOL* features the travel magazine *Gente e Viaggi,* the Venetian theater

La Fenice, and Cinecittà, Italy's Hollywood. Cinecittà's site includes trailers of Italian films, information about the industry, and even a place to post your résumé. TIN also includes *Medweb,* an Italian on-line health newspaper with articles and databases galore.

NETTUNO

Another favorite is *Nettuno* (www.nettuno.it), based in Bologna. It hosts *Antique On Line,* a gold mine of information that includes a *mercatino* (market), where buyers in search of specific items can post their requests, and a list of exhibitions. The main attraction is a *galleria* organized by type and ranging from dolls and books to mosaics and fountain pens. Nettuno also has a large section for children called *Ragazzi,* which includes things such as children's events throughout Italy.

DADANET

Dadanet (www.dada.it) has a great section called *Italy* that leads to links all over the country. When I picked *Trentino,* it came up with almost 15 sites ranging from local speleology to wine tasting. From the home page you can also pick "ARS," which has a section called *Musei e Gallerie* (Museums and Galleries), including everything from the Leonardo da Vinci museum in Vinci and the Museo Morandi in Bologna to the Louvre in Paris and the Whitney Museum of American Art in New York City.

LA CITTÀ INVISIBILE

Finally, *La Città Invisibile,* or "The Invisible City" (www.citinv.it), is a large nonprofit Italian site that provides information you won't easily find in other places, such as publications related to volunteering, world peace, animal rights, politics, and newsletters of nonprofit organizations. Its *Osservatorio Reti* links to the Italian *reti civiche* and other networks all over the world.

NEWS AND POLITICS

Up until a few years ago, Italians could only buy the print version of publications at the local newsstand, subscriptions being virtually unheard of. Now you can find almost all of them on line. Virtual newsstands can be found on most of the major commercial sites, but two personal favorites are *L'Edicola* (www.rirr.cnuce.cnr.it/edicola.html) and *Editoria* on the *Fiera* part of the *Nettuno* site (www.nettuno.it), which include both Italian and American publications. Some of the larger Italian newspapers on line include *La Repubblica* (www .repubblica.it), *La Stampa* (www.lastampa.it), and *Corriere della Sera* (www.globnet.rcs.it).

Ansa (www.ansa.it) and *Asca* (www.asca.it) are two Italian news agencies that offer daily news in both Italian and English. *Ansa* also offers *Who's Who of the Presidency,* with biographical information in English about all of the *ministri* (ministers), as well as the phone and fax numbers of the press office directors for each one. *Asca* includes *Il "Chi è" del Parlamento* ("The Who's Who of the Parliament") and *Il "Chi è" del Governo* ("The Who's Who of the Government"), which provide titles and names of all the Italian ministers, their undersecretaries, and in-depth biographical information. For information about specific political parties, try the *Agora* site (www.agora.it).

SPORTS

It won't take long before you'll realize how important it is to have some understanding of *calcio* (soccer), the Italian national pastime. *Datasport News* (www.datasport.it) has almost everything you need to know, including the latest scores on all major sports, TV listings, clubs, and sports sites worldwide. *Sport* (www.sport.it) connects with all of the national Italian sports federations, the Olympic Committee (CONI), and smaller associations all over the peninsula. Bike enthusiasts will enjoy *Cycling in Italy* (www.cycling.it/) and will surely find the *Trento Bike Pages* site (www-math.science.unitn.it/Bike/Countries/ Italy/) more than sufficient. It includes information about races, newsletters, books, maps, and clubs, plus it provides trail descriptions and tour reports from the most adventurous enthusiasts. If you're looking for the smell of hay and the sound of virtual horse hooves, or simply want to find places to go horseback riding, try *Cavallo Web* (www .cavalloweb.it). For sailing information, including Italian sailing schools and charters, try *Velanet* (www.velanet.it).

ALPnet (www.alpcom.it) has one of the best sports sections around, including great information on anything from Alpine skiing and Italian volleyball to the international baseball association and the Italian Swim Web. It is often hard to connect with because it's so popular in the Alpine region—maybe because of its *Meteo* (weather) section with continual updates on the weather and ski conditions (also check out its *Panoramica del Teatro Italiano,* which provides reviews of current theater productions all over the country). For additional in-depth ski information, including snow and road conditions, schools, and lodges, try *The Snow-Linker* under *Associazioni Sportive* on the *Fileita* site (www.fileita.it).

MUSIC AND THEATER

You won't want to miss the site of La Scala (www.lascala.milano.it), the famous Milanese opera house. It contains information about the history of the theater, the current season's events, and general theater news. You can also go directly to its archive in English which has detailed information about artists, performers, and shows both at La Scala and elsewhere, and you can search for data by subject, place, date, or keyword. For schedules of concerts and ticket information about the ancient Roman amphitheater the Arena di Verona, go to the *Così* site (www.cosi.it/verona). *Musica Classica Italia* (www.musica.it) has information about Italian classical music festivals, concerts, and composers, as well as listings of musical associations, competitions, orchestras, and groups. *Opera* (www.opera.it) has details on opera seasons worldwide, information about singers and operas, and reviews.

WINE AND FOOD

If you're a wine connoisseur, *The Italian Internet Winery* (www.wine.it) offers a staggering quantity of information. Not only can you "Select a wine varietal and press Go!" to find out about any kind of Italian wine you please, you can search the database of the Movimento del Turismo del Vino and pick from more than three hundred Italian wineries catering to tourists. You can even order wine on line (too bad the Net doesn't include downloadable samples of products). The *Veronafiere* site (www.veronafiere.it) also has a section called *Slow Food Guide to the Wines of the World Catalogue,* which allows you to search for wine by vineyard or name. *Winetel Italy* (www.winetel-Italy.com) is designed more for someone in the wine business, with its archive of wine statistics, the latest wine news, and a link to the Young Italian Wine Entrepreneurs Association. If you're looking for culinary information instead, try the *Cuisine* section of *Dolce Vita* (www.dolcevita.com). It has articles by Marcella Hazan and a great pasta dictionary with names, illustrations, and recipes. Or, you can look at *Italian Cuisine* (www.italcuisine.it) to find Italian culinary history and recipes, as well as recipes from all over the world.

TRANSPORTATION, TRAVEL, AND TOURISM

The Centro Turistico Studentesco e Giovanile (CTS) (www.cts.it) is the most popular youth/student travel agency around. Its site includes information for both young and old on discount air fares, train prices, and hotel rates, as well as *Parchi On Line,* a database of Italian parks (for another great listing of parks, reserves, and wetlands in Italy and the EU, see *Parks in Italy* at www.comunic.it). *Travel Italy* (www.travel .it) has information on all aspects of vacationing in Italy, including hotels, youth hostels, and houses for rent. It also has information on trekking, thermal spas, and cruises. *Doit* (www.doit.it) has information on planes, trains, subways, and ships, plus it offers *Italy Net,* which has hotel and camping information, as well as excellent travel-related links. When it comes to information about history, culture, and daily events in local cities and regions, the options are overwhelming. *Turismo* (www.turismo.it) has everything on museums, monuments, and places to visit. *Citynet* (www.city.net/countries/Italy) has links to more than one hundred Italian cities and regions in alphabetical order. Many of the Italian Internet servers also have a button on their home page that links to databases about places and events in their area. Some of the best of these sites are:

* **Alto Adige, Veneto, and the Dolomites:** *Altea* (www.altea.it); *Sunrise* (www.sunrise.it); *Dolomiti* (www.dolomiti.it)
* **Capri:** *Capri* (www.capri.it)
* **Emilia-Romagna, including Bologna, Parma, Padova, and Verona:** *Nettuno* (www.nettuno.it); *DSNet* (www.dsnet.it); *Immagica* (www.immagica.it)
* **Florence:** *Firenze by Net* (www.mega.it); *Firenzenet* (www .firenze.net); *Firenze On Line* (www.fionline.it); *Florence On-Line* (www.fol.it/); *Florence-Italy* (www.alba.fi.it); *Dada* (www .dada.it)
* **Friuli–Venezia Giulia, including Trieste and Udine:** *Spin* (www.spin.it)
* **Genoa and Liguria:** Take the *Doit* (www.doit.it) home page to the *Turismo* section
* **Ischia:** *Ischia On Line* (www.ischiaonline.it)
* **Lake Garda:** *Gardanet* (www.gardanet.it)
* **Milan:** *Informazioni Generali su Milano* (www.polimi.it/It/ ALT/Italia/Milano/)

* **Padua:** *Padova* (www.iperv.it/IPER-V/PADOVA/intro.html)
* **Rome:** *Roma 2000* (www.roma2000.it); CTS's *Vivi Roma* (www.cts.it); *Giada InfoCenter Rome* (http://giada.nexus.it)
* **Sardinia:** *Sardegna and Cagliari* (www.sardegna.com); *crs4* (www.crs4.it)
* **Sicily:** *Sicily* (www.sicily.infcom.it)
* **Turin:** *Servizio Telematico Pubblico della Città* (http://csi2000.csi.it)
* **Tuscany:** *Etrurianet* (www.etrurianet.it); *Versilia* (www.versilia .toscana.it)
* **Val d'Aosta:** *Vallee d'Aosta* (www.valleedaoste.com)
* **Venice:** *Venetia* (www.venetia.it)

RELIGIOUS AND ETHNIC SITES

The year 2000 is rapidly approaching, and so are the Jubilee celebrations. For news about the Città del Vaticano in English, check out the home page of the Holy See (www.vatican.va/) or the site of *Christus Rex* (www.christusrex.org), which includes news, articles, and even photos of sacred places. For the Jubilee in particular, you can go right to the organizers of the Eternal City's events at the Agenzia Romana per la Preparazione del Giubileo (www.romagiubileo.it). You can also go to the more commercial *Giubileo* (www.giubileo.com), which offers detailed information in English about the city and events leading up to the anniversary. For information on the Italian Jewish Network, try the *Network dell'Ebraismo Italiano* on the *Inrete* site (www.inrete.it). It has information about the Jewish community and events it sponsors, plus more than five hundred links to local and international Jewish groups.

Business and Financial Help On Line

FINDING GENERAL INFORMATION

Two of the most indispensable resources for business on the Italian Net are the *Pagine Gialle On Line* (www.paginegialle.it), the Italian yellow pages (also check out *Europages* at www.europages.com for all of Europe), and *The Italian Stock Exchange* (www.borsaitalia.it) with up-to-date, official information in English. Main sections on the site include market data, listed companies, intermediaries, and options. Another is the Istituto Nazionale di Statistica (ISTAT), (www.istat.it), the National Bureau of Statistics. This is useful if you need to make a marketing presentation or business proposal since you can find its annual report, including information about the Italian economy, trade, population, and more, on line. If you're looking for legal information, try the Istituto per la Documentazione Giuridica del CNR (www .idg.fi.cnr.it). It includes links to the Corte Suprema di Cassazione, the Camera dei Deputati, and the Senato della Repubblica. It also connects to Italian law libraries on line and provides a general guide to finding legal information on the Net.

More commercial business sites include *Business International* (www.business-Italy.it/), which includes detailed information on national and regional conferences, investing, the economy, currency, and resource costs. *Business International* also sponsors Business Italy Group, a network of Italian divisions of foreign multinationals based in Rome, Business Italy On Line, which has information especially useful for investors, and The Benchmarking Club, whose on-line information includes schedules of seminars, networking contacts, a bulletin board service, and a newsletter. Some companies that belong to the club include American Express, Colgate, and Fiat Auto. Another private business association is The Italian Business Institute (http://business. institutes.wmw.com/IT/), which offers on-line services such as a database of company contacts, industry and market reports, a list of trade fairs, and a directory of members. (It has a monthly subscription fee.) *TrADE-Net Italy* (www.tradenet.it) includes an Italian industry directory in English where you can find companies selling everything from armchairs to zinc. It also has a directory of hotels and events all over the country. Or, if you are interested in fashion, the Camera Nazionale della Moda Italiana, or National Chamber of Italian Fashion (www .Italycollections.it), is the official national organization that coordinates and promotes fashion shows and events in Italy. Its site is in both English and Italian and includes a calendar of shows and information about designers.

Larger general sites with good business sections include *Eureka* (www.eureka.it), which has a section on its home page called *Affari* with links to things such as Italian MBA programs, personnel agencies, financial databases, and the New York Stock Exchange. *Nettuno* (www.nettuno.it), which was mentioned earlier in the chapter, has a section on its site called *Netfiera* that is divided into four main sections: *Aziende* (Companies), *Associazioni* (Associations), *Pubblica Amminis-*

trazione (Public Administration), and *Istruzione e Formazione* (Education and Training). Under associations, for example, you can find the Italian multimedia computing association, the industrial association of the Bologna province, and local branches of the Lion's Club. *Telecom Italia Net* (www.tin.it), another site mentioned earlier, has a great *Economia e Finanza* database as part of its *Canali Video OnLine* section. It includes *Lawnet*, with legal news, and *World and Business*, with links to international sites such as Moody's and Bloomberg. TIN's *Vetrina Aziende* also has more than thirty-five categories of companies to peruse.

ACCESSING FINANCIAL PUBLICATIONS

Il Sole 24 Ore (www.ilsole24ore.it) is Italy's main financial newspaper. In addition to articles, the site links to other sites related to Italian economy, taxes, and law. It also has a database of corporations and associations and includes a word search feature. *Operazione Trasparenza* is its on-line publication of annual reports of many Italian companies and banks. You can e-mail the staff with questions (info @sole2). *Milano Finanza* (www.milanofinanza.it) is an Italian finance magazine that has international stock market information, plus articles on various topics such as trading systems, emerging markets, and foreign investing in Italy. In order to access the information, you must register on line, which is free.

Electronic Bulletin Board Services, Newsgroups, Mailing Lists, and Chat Rooms

To get in touch directly with Italians via the Internet, there are a few local sites you may want to try. Two of the most popular international Italian newsgroups are *soc.culture.italian* and *it.cultura*. *Cilea* (www .cilea.it/maillist/) has *Mailing Lists Italiane*, which gives descriptions of hundreds of lists and provides forms for getting subscriptions, and *Italian Newsgroups* has descriptions of newsgroups and links to them. *Pantheon* (www.pantheon.it/mailgate/) is another newsgroups gateway. If you want to write to expatriates in Italy and have membership in CompuServe, try its *CompuServe's Italian Forum*, located in the *Travel* file.

Anticipating Possible Obstacles

Even with more than two hundred local Italian Internet servers, it would be an exaggeration at this stage to say that the Internet has fully invaded Italy. Some members of the older generation are technophobic and find cyberspace intimidating. For others, the concept of surfing the Net is simply too cold, and they reject the concept of chat rooms and e-mail, saying that a copper wire could never replace a warm kiss on each cheek. Unfortunately, at the center of Italian cyberlife is *il telefono,* or the telephone, which doesn't help. Recently, Telecom Italia has been making an effort to improve its standards, including installing new toll-free assistance lines and offering ISDN Internet access service for the home or office. However, if you're going to be on the Net for hours, every minute will cost you dearly since you are paying for a *chiamata urbana,* which costs about 150 lire ($0.10) every two to six minutes. When the European Telecommunications Commission ordered that Telecom Italia change its rates in early 1996, it caused an uproar with Italian Internet users. Because the changes included an increase in the cost of local calls, they were afraid it might threaten their existence. For now, *cybervita* keeps on truckin'.

Aside from the quirky telephone system itself, the American computer user may run into a few obstacles when it comes to setting up shop in Italy, such as problems with software, hardware, and on-line access. The more you can anticipate before leaving the States, the better off you will be. Here are some of the most common problems.

HARDWARE AND SOFTWARE

Italian keyboards have more keys than American keyboards do, and the familiar keys are located in different places. This can cause problems especially when trying to locate symbols if you're using U.S.A.-formatted software programs. Some older Italian computers don't even have the @ or the ~ sign, vital for Internet usage. If you plan to buy a computer in Italy, be aware that it is difficult and expensive to get an American keyboard for it. When shipping hardware from the United States, you will have to pay Italian customs tax on the value of the equipment shipped (when I shipped a computer valued at $1,000, I had to pay 300,000 lire, or about $200, tax when I received it). This value is generally determined by the amount you declare on the insurance form. Make sure to state that the equipment is used and is not for resale if you want to lower this tax amount.

When it comes to software, you may not like using your favorite American software program translated into Italian since it can be annoying to follow Italian commands such as *"riavviare"* instead of "restart." Luckily, even if you buy a computer in Italy with Italian system software, you can still use your English-language program with no problem. However, it's useful to find a good software supplier at home before leaving. Call some of the American mail-order companies, and ask about their overseas services. You can find the numbers of such companies in the back of any of the most popular computer magazines. If you're looking for Italian stores that sell multimedia products, *Freemedia* (www .freemedia.com/negozi/) has a "multimedia yellow pages" on line.

ON-LINE ACCESS

The most serious problem for on-line access is that Italy has slower baud rates and even local calls are expensive. Buy the fastest modem possible, set it at its maximum potential, and keep your fingers crossed. When trying to go on line in Italy, you may also find that many older homes and offices do not have the RJ11-style American phone jack but use a large three-pronged jack instead. To connect your modem to the phone line, you will have to buy a three-pronged-to-RJ11 converter at any electrical supply store for about 3,000 lire ($2). Or you can hook up your modem by removing the RJ11 plug from the back of the phone apparatus and connecting it to your modem. One word of caution: make sure the phone system you're using is not a PBX (private branch exchange) system, as is the case in some hotel rooms. The voltage in this system is different, and you risk ruining your modem.

Another big problem Americans face when going on line in Italy is trying to get their American modem (including most standard modems, such as Hayes modems) to "ignore" the Italian dial tone. The Italian dial tone sounds different from the American one, and you have to "teach" your modem to ignore it or to do what is called "make a blind dial." To do so, add "X3" after the "AT" on your modem's initialization string, the correct command to make a blind dial. If there is an "&F" in your initialization string, add the "X3" after that.

Useful Addresses:
Major Italian Internet Servers

Agorà Telematica
(Torre Argentina Società di Servizi)
tel (06) 6991742
fax (06) 69920123
s.agora@agora.stm.it
www.agora.stm.it/address.html
**Associazione Italiana Internet
Providers (AIIP)**
tel (02) 26821182
fax (02) 26821311
info@aiip.it
www.aiip.it
Cineca/Nettuno
tel (051) 6599411
fax (051) 6592581
consul@cineca.it
www.nettuno.it
Dadanet
tel (055) 245083
fax (055) 2345082
segreteria@dada.it
www.dada.it
Dinonet
tel (055) 6531770
fax (055) 6532115
posta@dinonet.it
www.dinonet.it
Galactica
tel (02) 29006150
fax (02) 29006153
staff@galactica.it
www.galactica.it
I.Net
tel (02) 26162258
fax (02) 26821311
info@inet.it
www.inet.it

IT.net
tel (010) 6503641
fax (010) 6503781
info@IT.net
www.it.net
Italia.Com
(A national consortium of providers, telephone numbers of affiliated companies
can be found on the site.)
www.italia.com
Italia On Line
tel (02) 48201110
fax (02) 48201121
pr@iol.it
www.iol.it
Iunet
tel (02) 48366671
fax (02) 48366672
iunet@iunet.it
www.iunet.it
McLink (Technimedia)
tel (06) 418921
fax (06) 41732169
mc0001@mclink.it
www.mclink.it
Telecom Italia Net (TIN)
tel (167) 018787 (accounts)
tel (167) 070707 (technical assistance)
webmaster@how.tin.it
www.tin.it
Telnetwork
(A national network)
tel (0382) 529751
fax (0382) 528074
info@telnetwork.it
www2.telnetwork.it

Studying

Students admire the view of Siena.

CHAPTER ELEVEN

Student Life

Studying abroad means more than just transporting your studies to a new geographic location. It means learning not only about a new place and new subjects, but about yourself and your ability to take care of yourself far from home. Your senses will be overloaded with new sounds, tastes, and sights that no textbook or lecture can replicate. You will compare two entirely different ways of life and discover things you like more about your new country and things you like less. It is this insight that will bring a richer understanding of who you are and can be a crucial element in your personal growth. One of the things you will have to decide early on in the application process is how long to go for, and your choice will hinge on many things, depending on your situation back home. If you are enrolled in a college in the United States, you will have to see whether a semester or year abroad can fit in with your requirements for graduation and major. For some students, a year or even a semester is too long, and they opt to go on a summer program instead. For others, a semester is just not enough to do all the things they want to do.

Choosing Where to Go

Where you choose to study can fundamentally affect your entire study abroad experience, since schools tend to gear courses to the local surroundings and since location, as well as the concentration of other students and foreigners present, can contribute to your own feelings of culture shock. Factors to take into account include the size of the city or town, its relative position within Italy, the concentration of other students, and local resources such as art and architecture. Here is a general overview of what to expect from some of the most popular places in Italy.

ROME

Rome, the capital city, has great numbers of American students, as well as students from all corners of the globe. They are attracted to the city's ancient ruins, international scene, active nightlife, and religious attractions such as the Vatican. Rome is where the Italian government is based and where many international organizations such as the United Nations have large-scale operations. It is also a center of Italian film, media, and fashion. One thing that students often find overwhelming in Rome is the large size and the dense traffic, and for some the problems of assimilating into a metropolis are too much. As a result, many choose to hang out in the bohemian Trastevere area of the city because it feels more like a small town with accessible dimensions. Of course, Rome's size and opportunities are also its biggest assets for an adventurous student ready to take on the challenge of Italy's largest city.

FLORENCE

Florence is a center of Renaissance art and architecture, as well as modern-day Italian craftsmanship. It is especially popular with students interested in art history and fine arts. It is also near the Chianti wine region, which makes it an ideal location for wine-tasting classes. The city is small enough that you can easily get around by bicycle, making it a popular choice for foreigners. In fact, so many American students choose Florence each year that it has become the largest American study abroad location in the world. This can be both positive and negative. The positive side is that because of the many local American university programs, students may find it easier to make the transition abroad. The negative side is that many students complain there are too many Americans, making it difficult to avoid hearing English spoken in the streets. If you are committed to learning Italian and to meeting Italians, it can be done, but you will have to make a concerted effort to integrate with local culture.

MILAN AND TURIN

Milan and Turin are large cities located in northern Italy, both of which play vital roles in the nation's economy. Turin, in Piedmont, is home to the Fiat Auto car company and hence is a bustling industrial city. Milan is Italy's financial capital, where many major Italian and international banks are headquartered. It is a center of advertising but mainly one of the world's top centers of high fashion. Milan is full of businesspeople and tourists, who come mainly to attend the city's constant flow of trade fairs and runway shows. Most of the students interested in these topics come here to study, and many of the country's best M.B.A. programs are based here (see Chapter 13).

UNIVERSITY TOWNS

Some smaller Italian towns are known locally as "university towns" because of their high concentration of students. These include Bologna, Perugia, Siena, Urbino, and Padua. Each has a large public Italian university, and the overall student-to-local-population ratio is high. A foreign student in these settings will find more organized events for young people and more of a collegiate atmosphere, though not in the American sense of the word since Italian universities don't have real "campuses." Bologna and Padua, for example, are home to two of Italy's oldest universities. Bologna is also known historically for its political liberalism and its avant-garde music scene, and it houses several year-long American university programs, including the Johns Hopkins master's program. Padua also houses two important American study abroad centers, Boston University and the University of California. Nevertheless, both towns have limited numbers of American students and many Italians.

Siena, Urbino, and Perugia are where Italy's three famous Università per Stranieri (Universities for Foreigners) are located and therefore have a more diverse student body. Because the towns are geared toward foreigners, they also make it easier for American students to adapt more quickly. Perugia, located in Umbria, is small and isolated, and while you see numerous Americans wandering through the crowded streets (as well as many other foreign influences, such as Irish pubs), Perugia has maintained its own Italian identity. Siena, on the other hand, is also a popular Tuscan tourist destination, which means it fills up with foreigners in high season. Urbino is located near the eastern, Adriatic coast of Italy, close to the Republic of San Marino. Set

The piazza at San Gimignano, a popular hangout for Americans.

atop a hill, the town is surrounded by sixteenth-century walls and hosts several American university programs in addition to the University for Foreigners.

VENICE

Venice's maze of narrow walkways darkened by the shadows of humid palaces searching for solid ground make it a fascinating, mysterious place to study. You can listen to these buildings crack and squeak as they shift their weight from side to side, and to the sounds of waves licking up around them as you stroll about in the evening after class. In the past, Venice attracted many American painters and writers, though today there are few American programs based in Venice, perhaps because it is so far to the north. The city is, however, home to the prestigious Peggy Guggenheim Collection, which attracts art history students as well as architecture students who come to examine this "floating city." Students who live in Venice complain about the lack of nightlife, as very few bars stay open late.

SOUTHERN LOCATIONS

Big cities in the south, such as Naples and Palermo, tend to attract few American students because there are few American study abroad centers located there. Naples is, however, home to a large American military base, which makes the local American presence significant though generally removed from city life. Adventurous students who want to immerse themselves completely in the rich Italian culture with fewer foreign influences might want to head south. Keep in mind, though, that because there are fewer Americans overall you will tend to stick out much more than in places such as Florence or Rome. If you want to attend an Italian university, there are programs in Bari and Calabria as well.

Housing

If you are attending an American university program or a large Italian-language school, your program will most likely take care of arranging housing for you. If you are attending an Italian university, there will be an office to help you find housing, but you will generally be responsible for arranging it on your own. No matter what your situation, though, in some cases when you arrive in Italy housing may not be available yet. When I first went to Italy, I arrived a week early, hoping to become acquainted with my new surroundings before the semester began. But when I got to the administrative offices at the school, I found they were already closed for the day. Using my then-limited knowledge of Italian, I discovered that the youth hostels were full and the only hotels available were well out of my price range. Ultimately, after much searching, I found a convent that rented rooms. You can always find some kind of last-minute arrangement if need be, but anticipating potential problems will help make the initial transition a lot easier.

Dormitory Living

An Italian dorm is often a *pensione* (small hotel) or villa that has been converted into student housing. Sometimes you have the option of living in an Italian university dorm, or *casa dello studente*, that is inhabited mainly by out-of-town Italian students. However, there are few such dorms in Italy since most students attend their hometown university and live at home with their parents. Also, Italian dorms normally provide just a place to sleep and don't include the commissary, student center, or organized social activities usually found in American dorms. In Italy fraternities and sororities are virtually nonexistent, so don't count on them for housing.

LIFE WITH A HOST FAMILY

Living with an Italian host family is one of the most authentic ways for foreign students to become immersed in local culture, especially in a country that places so much emphasis on home life. It also means adapting to an entirely new structure of interaction and accepting house rules and codes of conduct. Often host parents will provide more than just a place to sleep and one meal a day, extending their hospitality to two or three daily meals with the family, the loan of a bicycle or moped, and even weekend trips to nearby towns. In fact, one of the biggest complaints by American students who live with Italian families is that the families expect them to participate in their activities too much. Americans who aren't used to the attention sometimes feel that they are being treated like children, even obliged to meet curfews never imposed back home. Others enjoy the experience immensely and say they feel as though they have a second family away from home. Some maintain contact with the family for years after they leave, forming a lifelong bond. Ultimately, the quality of your experience all depends on the availability and expectations of your host parents, the presence of host siblings, and your own attitude.

It is important to explore options for changing families if the one you are assigned to doesn't work out. Most university programs are able to switch students into other families after a few weeks if both parties agree the arrangement isn't working. The best way to handle possible problems with an Italian family is, first, to be patient with and understanding of their differences and habits; then, if the problems persist, discuss them with someone in the student office of your program. By no means stay with a family if there are serious problems that don't seem to be getting better. Let your program adviser explain the situation to the family for you.

SHARING AN APARTMENT WITH OTHER STUDENTS

Living in an apartment with other American students from your program is a common option in the larger study abroad centers such as Florence and Rome, where there are whole networks of landlords who rent to the schools on a regular basis. In these cities, there are also university bulletin boards full of ads from American and other foreign students seeking roommates. If you attend an American program, chances are the school will already have an apartment lined up for you when you arrive. The advantage is that if anything goes wrong, the school will help you select a new house or find other housing alternatives. However, in exchange for the service, you are generally charged quite a bit more by the school than if you found the apartment on your own. With this type of arrangement, as in a dormitory, you are assigned housemates, which means you have no say as to whom you will live with. Another disadvantage is that you will probably hear English being spoken around you all the time at home. When you're feeling homesick or are experiencing culture shock, this can be a great source of comfort. If your goal is to learn Italian well, this can be an interference or even a hindrance.

Living with Italian students is, on the other hand, one of the best ways to get to know the Italian culture up close. Yet because there isn't an Italian tradition of leaving home to attend university, the number of Italian university students you can live with is relatively small. Nevertheless, there are some Italians who attend universities away from home because the one in their own hometown doesn't offer the degree or specialization they are seeking. In bigger cities you should have little difficulty finding Italian housemates by combing through ads on university bulletin boards or through the local student housing office. One great advantage of this housing arrangement is that you can speak and hear Italian continuously, in both a conversational and a practical way (e.g., from writing grocery lists to negotiating cleaning duties), make friends with Italians, and learn the culture well. A big difference from living with American students is that here there is no American adviser overseeing your housing problems and payments. You are responsible for calling the landlord yourself when there's no heat and going to the phone company in person to complain about billing problems.

Using Your Free Time Productively

LEARNING THE LANGUAGE

From signing up for an additional language course to organizing sessions with an Italian language exchange partner, learning as much Italian as possible should be considered a full-time extracurricular activity from the moment you arrive. Although you might not normally watch television, making a habit of watching the nightly news is a good way to become familiar with basic grammar, vocabulary, and idioms, as well as important Italian current events. Start off with American shows and movies dubbed in Italian, as they are generally easier to understand. Then move on to Italian shows and films, as they are the best way to become familiar with different local dialects and slang. To develop your reading skills, buy an Italian newspaper each morning, perhaps a national one with a more informal writing style such as *La Repubblica* or a local paper from the town where you are studying. In addition, try reading Italian literature, starting out with children's books and moving on to adult literature as you improve. I found that reading Italian translations of American books I'd already read in English was good for starters.

MAKING THE MOST OF YOUR PROGRAM

To make the most out of your study abroad program, the first thing you should do is decide why you have chosen to study in Italy in particular and how to coordinate your study abroad with possible academic requirements back home. Perhaps you have to take certain courses in order to meet graduation requirements, or perhaps you are thinking about changing majors or beginning a minor at your school back home. This is a good time to explore new options. Even if you are not planning to explore new subjects, take some classes you wouldn't normally take at home. These can include organized supplementary classes such as cooking or pottery, or attending guest lectures about art history. In addition, whenever possible try to schedule classes so that you have Friday afternoons free for travel. Making the most of your studies also means spending time away from the program and the other students in it. Make Italian friends outside of it by looking into activities not directly related to the school, such as clubs sponsored by the local city (for some ideas, see Chapter 3).

CREATING EXTRACURRICULAR ACTIVITIES FOR YOURSELF

Many people opt to participate in sporting activities during their free time. Italian gyms are usually very expensive, but there are clubs and teams sponsored by local communities at low cost or even free. Each town has its soccer fields, swimming pools, and tennis courts that are open to the public, and many offer kayaking and rowing along Italy's many rivers. Of, if you are in the north, you can go skiing or rock climbing. You can find out about these opportunities by contacting your local town hall or by looking in the phone book under *"Associazioni Sportive."* Jogging is not popular the way it is in the States, and you may get stared at if you go jogging through the streets. However, each town has parks or hills where enthusiasts go (if you study in Tuscany, "jogs" are often hill workouts). It is important to understand that different Italian standards of dress also apply to jogging: men don't normally jog in public without a shirt on, and women do not wear skimpy tank tops and short shorts.

There is no shortage of artistic and cultural extracurricular activities in Italy. From painting classes to photography lessons, from volunteering to internships, you will never run out of possibilities (for more information on the last two, see Chapter 22). Where you study will also determine these activities, since each town has its own specialties. In Florence, you can learn Florentine papermaking from local masters. In Naples, you can study how coral jewelry is made. In Rome, you can go on endless walking tours of the famous locations where American expatriates have stayed in the past.

TRAVELING

A big advantage of studying in Italy is its small size and relative vicinity to many of Europe's most important cities. Italy is slightly larger than the state of Arizona, and you can travel between the major cities by taking train rides that last just a few hours to experience incredible variations in local cuisine, lifestyle, and dialects. For example, Naples is only two hours from Rome, while Florence is another two and a half hours to the north. Because the differences between the north and south are so strong, if you study in one area you should definitely plan a trip to the other. Also, don't forget the islands of Sicily, Elba, and Sardinia, which offer their own distinct cultures, cuisine, and wildlife. Because Italy is small, it is also accessible and welcoming, and you should consider traveling to nearby destinations, perhaps even alone. Many study abroad students decide to pack their bags and spend the weekend exploring a town by themselves and taking pictures. Even if you travel by yourself, the animated and warm nature of Italians is constant company, and you will never really feel alone.

When it comes to visiting the rest of Europe, you can purchase a Eurailpass or rent a car and visit places as different as England and Norway. The French Riviera and the Cannes Film Festival in the spring are only a night train away, and the Alpine slopes of Switzerland and Austria are just a few hours from Turin. You could take a boat from Bari or Brindisi and visit Greece for a bit of preseason tanning in the spring, or even board a ship for nearby Tunisia from Naples or Sicily. The beaches in Croatia are some of Europe's best and lie just a few hours outside the Trieste border, while Munich's Oktoberfest beer festival in the fall is always a favorite with college students.

SOCIALIZING

Italians are famous for being extremely social by nature. It is evident not just in their personalities but in their architecture, urban planning, and eating habits. All Italian cities are constructed around *piazze*, or town squares. In the evenings when the weather is warmer, both young and old take strolls along the boulevards to see and be seen. This time is reserved for meeting friends, making friends, and being social. Many Italian buildings are built around a courtyard, which offers tenants a common meeting place. Italian meals are traditionally composed of multiple courses that often last for more than two hours. All of these details in Italian life are meant to strengthen a sense of comradery and community.

Discotheques and nightclubs, though often expensive (entrance generally costs 19,000–30,000 lire, or $7–$20), are frequented with the same passion in Italy as in the United States, and during summer months beach towns such as Rimini make dancing an all-night party. But in winter many young Italians prefer to go to the local bar to play cards and share a drink, or have friends over for dinner and conversation. In Italy, you can also hang out at *centri sociali*, or social centers, which are often located in old warehouses that have been taken over by students and hippies. They are often connected to left-wing associations or political parties that throw parties with dancing, live music, and sometimes free food. The *centri sociali* are recognizable by Communist banners hanging outside or colorful graffiti sprayed all over the building's exterior, including the word *"Occupato"* ("Occupied") to let you know the building's become the (illegal) property of the partygoers.

Summers in Italy are full of outdoor nightlife, much more than in the States. Most cities have an annual Festa dell'Unità, sponsored by the Communist Party, which includes outdoor food stands, book stalls, and concerts. Ancient amphitheaters are regularly turned into outdoor concert halls that attract some of Italy's best performers, who play for free. All cities have outdoor film screenings in local *piazze*, and stadiums. Individual cities also have their own special annual summer events. For example, Rome has a series of events and concerts during June and July called "Estate Romana."

Dealing with Stress Abroad

When you study abroad, there are stresses that you would never encounter at home, and not being able to understand what's being said around you is definitely nerve-racking. It is important to recognize the symptoms of stress and try to do something about them before they get out of hand. It is also important to identify exactly what is stressing you out, since it's easy to blame your stress on "Italy" when it may actually be caused by a specific run-in with an impatient shopkeeper. One thing you can do on a regular basis to alleviate stress is to keep a journal, recording all your discoveries and frustrations. It will help you gain more perspective on your experience. If you ever find that the stress becomes too much for you to deal with on your own, talk to a counselor or adviser at your study abroad program. There are also American psychiatrists and therapists practicing in Italy if you would like to seek outside help.

HOMESICKNESS

When I first went to Italy to study, I had to call home from a pay phone down the street since my student apartment didn't have a phone. That was back when Italian calling cards didn't exist and you couldn't connect automatically to an American operator. Between trying to communicate in Italian that I wanted to make a collect call and the horrible static on the line, I got a sudden, unexpected dose of homesickness. If you've been away at college for a while, dealing with separation from your family probably will not be difficult, though the pangs of nostalgia will hit you at times. This is especially true if you have left a boyfriend or girlfriend behind. You may find yourself afraid that the other person will not wait for your return and will find someone else in the meantime. You may also be afraid of your own desire to meet other people in Italy. Sometimes just being overseas can bring out issues that already existed before you left—but then they must be dealt with through long-distance phone calls and letters, not in person. When I was on my study abroad program, two students missed their boyfriends so much they actually dropped out and flew back to the States. Ultimately, it seemed, they just weren't ready to make the transition. Other friends found new love abroad and then had to deal with the pain of separation when the semester ended.

Resisting Temptation

One of the most common complaints among American students in Italy is that they can't help but gain five to ten pounds from all the delicious bread, pasta, and pastries around. Italians tend to eat what they want but in moderation, therefore generally remaining trim. Italians also apply this moderation to drinking alcohol, having started drinking wine in small quantities as children. Since wine is seen as a healthy part of the meal, teenagers and adults don't tend to use drinking as a social activity in and of itself. Therefore, it is uncommon to see Italians drunk. Many American college students, on the other hand, are used to heavy drinking parties back in the States. Since good Italian wine is so inexpensive, they often tend to exaggerate and become drunk, much to the disapproval of Italians. But aside from the disapproval, getting drunk in a foreign country is even more risky than at home, since you are less able to judge local customs or the potential dangers around you.

Two other temptations that are often hard to resist are Italian coffee and cigarettes. Between cappuccinos, espressos, and caffe lattes, Americans tend to make their stay in Italy a caffeine fest. Moderate American smokers also tend to increase their daily intake since smoking is more common than it is back home. For nonsmokers intolerant of smoke, being surrounded by smokers can be a real problem.

Using Common Sense

Being abroad means gaining a kind of independence you may never have had in your life, not even at college back home, since overseas you have near-total freedom with fewer social restraints. You feel less inhibited about being who you want and doing what you like. Because many study abroad programs are less academically rigorous than their American counterparts, you also have more free time to use as you like. As a result, many American students go wild and do things they would never do at home—potentially dangerous things such as experimenting with drugs or hitchhiking. In fact, one of the most common problems among American students in Italy is that they don't apply the same rules of safety they would at home, especially in smaller Italian cities such as Padua and Florence, which seem crime-free but are actually not. American women sometimes do things such as walking alone late at night or accepting rides from strangers. Remember that it is important to act with exactly the same sense of precaution you would normally use in the States.

CHAPTER TWELVE

American Universities

There are more than ninety American study abroad programs in sixteen different locations around the country. Of these, more than forty are in Florence and twenty-five in Rome. In fact, Florence is the largest American study abroad center in the world. Since one of the most important factors in your decision is location (as discussed in Chapter 11), the list at the end of this chapter is organized by city. Other factors you should consider include cost, the availability of transfer credit, courses, and "perks" such as field trips to local sites and guest lectures. The program I participated in gave us keys to the school facilities so that we could work on our art projects over the weekend and at night; it also provided us with a video membership card at a nearby video movie rental store and a VCR so that we could watch Italian movies at the student center.

Choosing a Program

From New York University to the University of California at Los Angeles, almost all major American universities organize study abroad programs in Italy for juniors and seniors. If your school does not have a program, or if it offers one but you would prefer to attend another, contact your academic adviser or the study abroad office to inquire about transfer credit policies. At least some—and sometimes all—credit earned abroad can usually be applied toward your degree. The universities listed at the end of this chapter have programs in Italy that are open to students from other schools, not just their own (we have also listed the University of California programs because of their size, although they accept students only from the nine UC schools.) Most of the Italy programs last one semester, one summer, or one year and do not result in a degree at the end. If you are interested in receiving a degree or graduate credit, it can be done through some schools with degree programs based in Italy. In general, most classes are taught in English, except for Italian-language courses and courses taken at local Italian universities. Some programs, such as the Middlebury program in Florence, teach their courses exclusively in Italian.

COURSES OFFERED

The vast majority of programs offer courses in Italian language and literature, history, and art history. However, many also offer film, business, economics, social sciences, and political science courses. Of course, whatever the topic, the classes normally have an Italian or European focus, making the learning a hands-on experience. Which city you study in will also determine the types of courses you will take. If you attend Pitzer College's program in Parma, for example, you can take a course tailored to local history and culture. Some programs offer field research courses and organized internship programs at local businesses. For instance, the Lexia program in Venice offers semester-long field research projects on topics such as the Italian Jewish ghetto and the maintenance of Venice's waterways.

A few schools specialize in fine arts and have developed large art studios in which students can work. The Pratt Institute, famous for its New York–based program, offers architecture, design, and applied arts at its Pratt Studios in Italy. The enrollment is limited to about twenty students (sophomore to graduate students), courses last one term, and most instruction is in English. Studio Arts Centers International (SACI) has a large studio in Florence that is connected with local jewelry-making, batik, and photography studios. The University of Georgia's program in Cortona gives classes in printmaking, illustration, papermaking, and book arts, among others. It says that each year 90 percent of the students on its program are art majors. The Sarah Lawrence College program offers fine arts courses through Il Bisonte Studio and music through the Scuola di Musica di Sesto Fiorentino

Two American students take a pause from their studies to admire the Ponte Vecchio and the Arno River in Florence.

(most of the college's courses are taught in Italian). If you're interested in architecture, you may want to consider the University of Florida (connected with the Vicenza Institute of Architecture), Syracuse University, and New York University.

For business courses, Gonzaga University's Florence program has courses in business administration, management, marketing, and finance. The University Studies Abroad Consortium offers two programs in Turin, one of which is the Business Studies Program. The program is connected with the Scuola di Amministrazione Aziendale, one of Italy's most prestigious business schools, part of the University of

Turin. The maximum enrollment is forty students, and aside from taking courses such as "International Marketing" and "Comparative Management," you go on tours of local corporations to get a taste of the Italian business world. Many other programs offer business-related courses as part of their curriculum, too.

AMERICAN PROGRAMS HOSTED BY ITALIAN UNIVERSITIES

When American programs are hosted by Italian universities, it means that students in the program can take courses at the Italian schools and often can live in local university housing. They may also be able to use the university's libraries, cafeterias, and other facilities. The benefit of enrolling in one of these programs over directly enrolling in an Italian university is that here you have the American school staff guiding you through the process. It also means that there are American professors teaching courses. In some cases, the "hosting" by the public university simply means a coordination between the two schools, and you can attend the American program but not take any Italian university courses if you prefer. Some of the Italian university "hosts" include the University of Florence (hosts Middlebury College, Rutgers University, Sarah Lawrence College, Smith College, Syracuse University, University of Connecticut, Wells College); University of L'Aquila (University of Miami); University of Padua (Boston University); University of Rome "La Sapienza" (SUNY at Stony Brook); University of Venice (Lexia); University of Siena (SUNY Buffalo); University of Parma (Pitzer College); University of Bologna (Brown University and Dickinson College); and the University of Urbino (University of Central Florida and SUNY at New Paltz). The University for Foreigners in Siena hosts the University of Delaware and the University of Massachusetts at Amherst and provides the orientation for students in the American Institute for Foreign Study (AIFS) program in Florence. Another Italy-based university that hosts American study abroad programs is the American University of Rome, which is connected directly with the World Capitals Program of American University in Washington, D.C. It hosts the College Consortium for International Studies, Saint John's University, and Whitworth College.

SCHOOLS WITH CAMPUSES

Many of the American programs in Italy are small enough that they don't have their own campus but hold classes in the classrooms of a local school, often the popular Dante Alighieri or the Lorenzo de' Medici language schools. However, a few are large enough to have their own campus, which usually consists of a renovated Italian palace where classes are held and where students sometimes live. Many of these are located in or near Florence, such as Florida State University's Palazzo Alessandri, New York University's Villa La Pietra, and the University of Michigan's Villa Corsi Salviati in Sesto Fiorentino. One of the most luxurious campuses is Georgetown University's Villa Le Balze, a Renaissance mansion in Fiesole, a small town on the hills overlooking Florence. Each summer's enrollment is generally limited to about twenty students, who roam the villa's three acres and olive groves freely and attend literature and writing classes in the library, gardens, and classrooms.

DEGREE PROGRAMS AND GRADUATE CREDIT

If you want to spend more than just one semester or a year in Italy, or if you are seeking graduate credit, there are schools in Italy that offer graduate credit courses and degree programs. A partial list includes the Fashion Institute of Technology in Florence, Middlebury College, New York University (art and architecture), Studio Arts Centers International, and Syracuse University (fine arts and architecture). Some programs award bachelor's and master's degrees, are accredited by the Accrediting Council for Independent Colleges and Schools in the United States, and are affiliated with major American institutions. John Cabot University in Rome offers a Bachelor in Business Administration for those who complete the necessary four years of study there. It also offers B.A.'s in Art History and even English Literature, as well as two-year associate's degrees. The American University of Rome has four-year degree programs, including a Bachelor of Business Administration in International Business degrees and B.A.'s in International Relations, Italian Studies, and Interdisciplinary Studies. It also offers two-year Associate degrees in Liberal Arts and International Business programs. St. John's University in Rome, accredited with the American Assembly of Collegiate Schools of Business (AACSB), has an M.B.A. program, as does the European School of Economics, with branches in Rome, Vicenza, and Lucca. Florence is home to the European University Institute (EUI) for postgraduate studies in history, civilization, economics, law, political science, and social science. EUI was established by the member states of the European Union for doctoral studies and is one of the most prestigious institutions of its kind, with a multinational student body, professors from all over the world, and a slew of fellowships and grants available. Graduate credit can also be earned at Johns Hopkins University's Paul Nitze School of Advanced International Studies program in Bologna as part of its master's program. In addition, both Johns Hopkins's Villa Spelman and Harvard University's Villa "I Tatti" in Florence host graduate students doing research.

Tuition and Expenses

Tuition for the Italy programs varies as much as tuition in the United States. If you attend the overseas program of your own college, usually you pay the regular price of tuition, as if you were going to stay on the American campus, plus some additional fee. Sometimes you can actually save money by studying overseas, especially if you attend a more expensive American college and opt for an overseas program sponsored by a less expensive American school (e.g., a state school). In this case you would normally pay that school's tuition and apply for transfer credit. Just to give you a sense of the range of prices for Italy programs, in 1997 Dickinson College's program in Bologna cost $25,700 for the year, while the Pratt Institute's program cost $7,500 for one term. Brown University's program in Bologna cost about $21,500 for the year but included housing costs. The University of Central Florida's summer program in Urbino cost $2,100, plus credit fee and air travel. Some schools have two costs of tuition, one for residents of the home college's state, the other for out-of-state residents. For example, one term at Lock Haven's program in Cassino cost $3,800 for in-state students, $6,500 for out-of-state ones. In addition to tuition, there are also fees for overseas health insurance (often as low as $100), airfare (approximately $800), and utilities (about $400 for the year).

People often think that Italy is cheap and are then surprised to discover it's actually quite expensive. Aside from the basic living expenses, you should anticipate spending money on studio fees and art supplies if you take art classes; museums and health clubs; shopping and nightlife. Schools often organize field trips to nearby towns, and usually these trips are not included in the price of tuition. Often a semester in Italy is supplemented by weekend travel or preceded or followed by a one-month Eurailpass trip around the European continent (see Chapter 9). So plan your finances accordingly.

FELLOWSHIPS, SCHOLARSHIPS, AND GRANTS

Some of the programs in Italy do offer loans, grants, and scholarships, but generally speaking you must apply for financial aid through your home college. There are, however, some private foundations that offer aid for study abroad, and you can find books with information on others in the reference rooms of public libraries or in your university's research/career center.

FULBRIGHT GRANTS The Institute of International Education (IIE) administers the highly competitive, government-funded, one-year-long Fulbright Grants. These grants are considered among the best both because of the monetary value (approximately $15,000 per year) and the freedom recipients are given. Most people use them to work on independent study projects. One Fulbright scholar, for example, spent a year studying Italian film in Rome. If you win a grant, you will have to arrange for an adviser in Italy before you go. Essentially, if you get one of these, you are free to spend a year doing what you please, provided you stick to your original idea. In 1997, approximately twenty-five students won grants to go to Italy.

There are different levels of Fulbright grants. The lowest level is designed for graduating seniors, who can apply during their senior year but cannot use the grant until they have already received their bachelor's degree. The second level is for graduate students who have not yet completed their Ph.D. The third level is for people who have already completed their Ph.D. and would like to go to Italy to lecture in their field. In recent years the application deadline has been set at the end of October. However, if you are enrolled in a school the deadline will be earlier, since you will have to complete in-house interviews (if you are not enrolled in a school, you will apply directly through IIE and there will be no interview). One of the application requirements is proficiency in Italian, or a minimum of one or two years of college-level Italian, depending on your field of interest.

THE AMERICAN ACADEMY IN ROME If you're a postgraduate student in fine arts, classical studies, or humanities, you can't miss the Rome Prize fellowship opportunities with the American Academy in Rome. The academy is considered by many the leading American overseas center for advanced research in the fine arts and humanities, as well as independent study. The academy was founded in 1894 by architect Charles McKim, partner in the firm of McKim, Mead, and

White. He wanted to create a center where not only architects but people of all different professions could meet and learn from Italy firsthand. Both McKim and his partner Stanford White were Italophiles, as evidenced by the fact that so many of their American projects stemmed directly from Italian styles (the firm used Bernini's colonnade before St. Peter's in Rome as a model for Pennsylvania Station in New York City, the Colosseum for the stadium at Harvard University, and Ghiberti's doors in the duomo of Florence for the doors of the Boston Public Library). When White was in Italy, he had a ship anchored off the coast of Livorno, waiting to receive the mantelpieces, frescoes, and cloth that he would buy for American houses he was designing.

In the past, fellows at the academy have included authors such as Nadine Gordimer, Joseph Brodsky, and Ralph Ellison, as well as painter Frank Stella and architect Robert Venturi. Fellowships include stipend, room, and board at the academy's magnificent villa overlooking the Eternal City (many believe it has the best view of Rome), with sprawling landscaped gardens and lofty white gallery space for fellows who want to exhibit their work. Fellows can also take advantage of the academy's extensive library collection, European tours, and famous guest lecturers stopping by on their way through Italy. The fellowships application is due in November each year, but competition is tough as they are among the most prestigious in the world.

Useful Addresses

FELLOWSHIPS AND GRANTS

American Academy in Rome
7 East 60th Street
New York, NY 10022
tel (212) 751-7200
fax (212) 751-7220

American Academy in Rome
Via Angelo Masina, 5
00153 Roma
tel (06) 58461
fax (06) 5810788

**Institute of International Education
(IIE)—Fulbright Grants**
U.S. Student Programs Division
809 United Nations Plaza
New York, NY 10017

tel (212) 883-8200
fax (212) 984-5452
www.iie.org

AMERICAN UNIVERSITIES WITH PROGRAMS
IN ITALY

BOLOGNA:
Brown University
Office of International Programs
P.O. Box 1973
Providence, RI 02912-1973
tel (401) 863-3555
fax (401) 863-3311
oip_office@brown.edu

Dickinson College
Off-Campus Studies

P.O. Box 1773
Carlisle, PA 17013-2896
ocs@dickinson.edu
tel (717) 245-1341
fax (717) 245-1668
Indiana University
Overseas Studies Office
303 Franklin Hall
Bloomington, IN 47405
tel (812) 855-9304
fax (812) 855-6452
overseas@indiana.edu
Johns Hopkins University
Paul H. Nitze School of Advanced
International Studies
Admissions Office
1740 Massachusetts Avenue, N.W.
Washington, DC 20036-1983
tel (202) 663-5600
fax (202) 663-5615
For all University of California students:
Universitywide Office of EAP
Hollister Research Center
University of California
Santa Barbara, CA 93106-1140
tel (805) 893-4762
fax (805) 893-2583
www.uoeap.ucsb.edu
CASSINO:
Lock Haven University
Institute for International Studies
Lock Haven, PA 17745-2390
tel (717) 893-2140
fax (717) 893-2537
CASTELFRANCO:
University of Florida (see Rome)
CORTONA:
University of Georgia
Lamar Dodd School of Art
Visual Arts Building
Athens, GA 30602-4102
cortona@uga.cc.uga.edu
tel (706) 542-7011
fax (706) 542-2467
FLORENCE:
**Accent International Consortium for
Academic Programs Abroad**
425 Market Street, 2nd Floor

San Francisco, CA 94105
tel (415) 904-7756
fax (415) 904-7759
sfaccent@aol.com
**American Institute for Foreign Study
(AIFS)**
Richmond College Program
102 Greenwich Avenue
Greenwich, CT 06830
tel (800) 727-2437
fax (203) 869-9615
info@aifs.org
www.aifs.org
Associated Colleges of the Midwest
205 West Wacker Drive, Suite 1300
Chicago, IL 60606
tel (312) 263-5000
fax (312) 263-5879
City College of San Francisco
50 Phelan Avenue, Box A-71
San Francisco, CA 94112
tel (415) 239-3582
fax (415) 239-3804
Coast Community College District
International Education Office
1370 Adams Avenue
Costa Mesa, CA 92626
tel (714) 438-4704
fax (714) 438-4891
**College Consortium for International
Studies**
2000 P Street, N.W., Suite 503
Washington, DC 20036
tel (800) 453-6956
tel (202) 223-0330
fax (202) 223-0999
ccis@intr.net
College of William and Mary
Reves Center for International Studies
Program Abroad
P.O. Box 8795
Williamsburg, VA 23187-8795
tel (757) 221-3594
fax (757) 221-3597
DePaul University
Foreign Study Office
2320 North Kenmore, SAC 530
Chicago, IL 60614-3298

tel (773) 325-7450
fax (773) 325-7452
wrldinfo@wppost.depaul.edu
Drake University
Institute of Italian Studies
2507 University Avenue
Des Moines, IA 50311
tel (515) 271-2084
fax (515) 271-4588
European University Institute
Badia Fiesolana
Via dei Roccettini, 9
50016 San Domenico di Fiesole (FI)
tel (055) 4685373
fax (055) 4685444
applyres@datacomm.iue.it
www.iue.it
Fairfield University
Dolan House
Fairfield, CT 06430-7524
tel (203) 254-4220
fax (203) 254-4106
Fashion Institute of Technology
International Programs
A Building, Suite 605
Seventh Avenue at 27th Street
New York, NY 10001-5992
tel (212) 760-7601
fax (212) 594-9413
Florida State University
Study Abroad Programs
Tallahassee, FL 32306-4046
tel (800) 374-8581
tel (904) 644-3272
fax (904) 644-8817
fsuabroad@admin.fsu.edu
Georgetown University (in Fiesole)
Villa Le Balze Program
School for Summer and Continuing
Education
Box 571006
Washington, DC 20057-1006
tel (202) 687-5624
fax (202) 687-8954
http://guweb.georgetown.edu/ssce
Gonzaga University
East 502 Boone Avenue
Spokane, WA 99228-0001

tel (800) 523-9712
fax (509) 324-5987
Harding University
900 East Center Street, Box 754
Searcy, AR 72149
tel (501) 279-4529
fax (501) 279-4042
Harvard University
Villa I Tatti
University Place
124 Mt. Auburn Street
Cambridge, MA 02138-5762
tel (617) 495-8042
fax (617) 495-8041
James Madison University
Office of International Education
Paul Street House
Harrisonburg, VA 22807
tel (540) 568-6419
fax (540) 568-3310
Johns Hopkins University
Villa Spelman
The Charles S. Singleton Center
Via San Leonardo, 13
50125 Firenze
tel (055) 221615
Los Angeles Community Colleges
International Education Program
770 Wilshire Blvd.
Los Angeles, CA 90029
tel (213) 891-2282
fax (213) 891-2150
Middlebury College
Study Abroad
Middlebury, VT 05753-6131
tel (802) 443-5000 ext. 5543
fax (802) 443-2075
**National Registration Center for Study
Abroad/Scuola Leonardo da Vinci**
823 North Second Street, Room 206
Milwaukee, WI 53203
tel (414) 278-0631
fax (414) 271-8884
quest@nrcsa.com
New York University
International Study Office
100 Washington Square East, Room
908B

New York, NY 10003-6688
tel (212) 998-8677
fax (212) 995-4833
Nicholls State University
Box 2080
Thibodaux, LA 70310
tel (504) 448-4440
fax (504) 449-7028
Northern Arizona University
Office of International Studies
P.O. Box 5598
Flagstaff, AZ 86011-5598
tel (520) 523-2409
fax (520) 523-9489
**Rockland Community College Center
for International Studies (SUNY)**
145 College Road
Suffern, NY 10901
tel (914) 574-4205
fax (914) 574-4423
Rutgers Study Abroad
Milledoler Hall
New Brunswick, NJ 08903
tel (908) 932-7787
fax (908) 932-8659
Sarah Lawrence College
Office of International Programs
1 Mead Way
Bronxville, NY 10708
tel (800) 873-4752
fax (914) 395-2666
Smith College
College Hall 23
Northampton, MA 01063
tel (413) 585-4905
fax (413) 585-4906
intlstudy@ais.smith.edu
**Studio Art Centers International
Florence (SACI)**
809 United Nations Plaza
New York, NY 10017-3580
tel (800) 344-9186
tel (212) 984-5548
fax (212) 984-5325
Syracuse University
International Programs Abroad
119 Euclid Avenue
Syracuse, NY 13244-4170

tel (800) 235-3472
tel (315) 443-3471
fax (315) 443-4593
University of Arizona
Harvill Building, Room 147, Box 11
Tucson, AZ 85721
tel (520) 621-4819
fax (520) 621-2757
University of Connecticut
Study Abroad Programs U-207
843 Bolton Road
Storrs, CT 06269
tel (860) 486-5022
fax (860) 486-2976
**University of Michigan/University of
Wisconsin**
Office of International Programs
G513 Michigan Union
530 South State Street
Ann Arbor, MI 48109-1349
tel (313) 764-4311
fax (313) 764-3229
oip@umich.edu
**University of North Carolina at Chapel
Hill**
Study Abroad
Caldwell Hall
Campus Box 3130
UNC-CH
Chapel Hill, NC 27599
tel (919) 962-7001
fax (919) 962-2262
abroad@unc.edu
www.unc.edu/depts/abroad
Wells College
Off-Campus Programs
Aurora, NY 13026
tel (315) 364-3288
fax (315) 364-3257
L'AQUILA:
University of Miami
International Education and Exchange
Programs
P.O. Box 248005
Coral Gables, FL 33124-1610
tel (800) 557-5421
tel (305) 284-3434
fax (305) 284-6629

MILAN:
Academic Year Abroad
P.O. Box 733
Stone Ridge, NY 12484-0733
tel/fax (914) 687-2470
Institute of European Studies
223 West Ohio Street
Chicago, IL 60610
tel (800) 995-2300
tel (312) 944-1750
fax (312) 944-1448
iesiascr@mcs.net
For all University of California students:
Universitywide Office of EAP (see
Bologna)
PADUA:
Boston University
Division of International Programs
232 Bay State Road, 5th Floor
Boston, MA 02215
tel (617) 353-9888
fax (617) 353-5402
abroad@bu.edu
For all University of California students:
Universitywide Office of EAP (see
Bologna)
PARMA:
Pitzer College
External Studies
1050 North Mills Avenue
Claremont, CA 91711-6110
tel (909) 621-8104
fax (909) 621-0518
PERUGIA:
Lake Erie College
391 West Washington Street
Painesville, OH 44077
tel (216) 639-7854
fax (216) 352-3533
PISA:
For all University of California students:
Universitywide Office of EAP (see
Bologna)
ROME:
American University
World Capitals Program
Tenley Campus
Constitution Building

Washington, DC 20016
tel (202) 895-4900
fax (202) 895-4960
American University of Rome
Via Pietro Roselli, 4
00153 Roma
tel (06) 58330919
fax (06) 58330992
**College Consortium for International
Studies (see Florence)**
Cornell University
International Programs
474 Uris Hall
Ithaca, NY 14853-7601
tel (607) 255-6807
fax (607) 255-8476
Dartmouth College (see Florence)
DePaul University (see Florence)
Drake University (see Florence)
European School of Economics
Large del Nazareno, 15
00187 Roma
tel (06) 6780503
fax (06) 6780293
ese.rome@flashnet.it
John Cabot University
Office of Admissions
Via della Lungara, 233
00165 Roma
tel (06) 6878881
fax (06) 6832088
Loyola University Chicago
Rome Center Office
6525 North Sheridan Road
Chicago, IL 60626
tel (800) 344-7662
tel (773) 508-2760
fax (773) 508-8797
**National Registration Center for Study
Abroad (see Florence)**
Pratt Institute
School of Architecture
200 Willoughby Avenue
Brooklyn, NY 11205
tel (718) 399-4306
tel (718) 636-3433
fax (718) 399-4332

Rockland Community College (see Florence)
St. John's University
Study Abroad Office
8000 Utopia Parkway
Jamaica, NY 11439
tel (718) 990-6104
fax (718) 380-8934
St. John's University
(Graduate Center in Rome)
Via S. Maria Mediatrice, 24
00165 Roma
tel (06) 636937
fax (06) 6372337
Saint Mary's College
Rome Program
145A Regina Hall
Notre Dame, IN 46556
tel (219) 284-4586
fax (219) 284-4716
State University of New York at Stony Brook (SUNY)
E54340 Melville Library
Stony Brook, NY 11794-3397
tel (516) 632-7030
fax (516) 632-6544
Temple University
International Programs
Conwell Hall, Fifth Floor
Philadelphia, PA 19122
tel (215) 204-4684
fax (215) 204-5735
Trinity College
International Programs Office
300 Summit Street
Hartford, CT 06106-3100
tel (860) 297-2436
beustis@trincoll.com
University of Florida
Overseas Studies
123 Tigert Hall
Gainesville, FL 32611-3225
tel (352) 392-5380
fax (352) 392-5575
University of Washington
Office of International Programs and Exchanges
Box 355815

Seattle, WA 98195-5815
tel (206) 543-9272
fax (206) 685-3511
Whitworth College
Center for International Education
300 West Hawthorne Road
Spokane, WA 99251-2702
tel (509) 466-3797
fax (509) 466-3723
SIENA:
Academic Year Abroad (see Milan)
National Registration Center for Study Abroad (see Florence)
School for International Training
Kipling Road
Brattleboro, VT 05301
tel (800) 336-1616
tel (802) 257-7751
fax (802) 258-3500
State University of New York College at Buffalo
1300 Elmwood Avenue
Buffalo, NY 14222
tel (716) 878-4620
fax (716) 878-3054
Study Abroad Coordinator
Department of Foreign Languages and Literatures
University of Delaware
326 Smith Hall
Newark, DE 19716
tel (302) 831-6458
fax (302) 831-6459
University of Massachusetts Amherst
International Programs
W. S. Clark International Center
Amherst, MA 01003
tel (413) 545-2710
fax (413) 545-1201
For all University of California students:
Universitywide Office of EAP (see Bologna)
TURIN:
University Studies Abroad Consortium/323
University of Nevada Reno
Reno, NV 89557-0093
tel (702) 784-6569

fax (702) 784-6010
scs@unr.edu
www.scs.unr.edu/~usac

URBINO:

College of William and Mary (see Florence)

State University of New York at New Paltz (SUNY)
Office of International Education, HAB 33
New Paltz, NY 12561-2499
tel (914) 257-3125
fax (914) 257-3129

University of Central Florida
UCF Urbino Program
Department of Foreign Languages and Literatures

Box 161348
Orlando, FL 32816-1348
tel (407) 823-2470
fax (407) 823-5156

VENICE:

LEXIA Exchange International
378 Cambridge Avenue
Palo Alto, CA 94306-1554
tel (415) 327-9191
fax (415) 327-9192
lexia@lexiaintl.org
www.lexiaintl.org

For all University of California students:
Universitywide Office of EAP (see Bologna)

VICENZA:

University of Florida (see Rome)

CHAPTER THIRTEEN

Italian Universities

The University of Bologna is the oldest university in the world, founded sometime between the year 1000 and 1158. It built its *domus,* one of the world's first dormitories, as early as the fourteenth century. The University of Padua, founded in 1222, counted Galileo Galilei, Nicolaus Copernicus, and Francesco Petrarch among its teachers. Even Dante Alighieri taught there during a three-day seminar. But Bologna and Padua are not alone in providing a long history of tradition, antiquity, and excellence— all Italian universities do. Furthermore, the quality of Italian university education is superior, students graduating with a high level of specialization and knowledge. But attending an Italian university will also appeal to your more practical sense because it costs so little. A state university student pays on average 1,300,000 lire per year, or about $1,000. Because you cannot pay "per credit" as you do in the United States, taking a single course costs the same as enrolling full-time.

There are, of course, drawbacks. At an Italian university the bureaucratic chaos, lack of guidance, and difficulty of oral exams can be daunting, even to Italians. In fact, of the 65 percent of Italian high school graduates who enroll in the universities, only one-third ever make it to graduation. Another problem at the universities is overcrowding. Between 1951 and 1971, the number of graduating university students tripled, and by 1993 it had increased again by half. Then the inevitable happened: the schools ran out of room. Now La

Sapienza in Rome is trying to fit 150,000 bodies into classrooms designed for 20,000. The Law Department at the Statale di Milano has only one professor per 330 students. To compensate, there are *lettori* (lecturers), who are responsible for smaller discussion groups, but they, too, are often overwhelmed by the numbers. On a daily basis, this translates into a mad rush to the classrooms to try to get a seat. Some students get there as early as six o'clock to line up outside the building. Latecomers must be content with sitting on the floor near the lectern or at the back beyond hearing range. Some, fed up with the hassle, find friends to record the lectures and cram professors' podiums with tape recorders, while many just decide not to attend class and show up only during exams. Others, outraged and frustrated with the university system, literally take to the streets and protest. Because of these problems, most Italian students don't graduate before the age of twenty-six.

As you read about the complicated enrollment procedures and rigorous academic schedule, you may start to wonder if any American before you has attempted such a feat. The universities are difficult for Italians, which means they'll be even more difficult for you. But remember that many Americans before you have tried and succeeded. They've taken single courses and also gotten Italian degrees with top honors. If you are up to the challenge of studying at an Italian university, when you complete your courses you will be more than just proficient in your field of study: you can confidently claim to being proficient in Italian bureaucracy and part of the Italian academic elite.

General Enrollment Procedures

As an American you have the same enrollment choices as an Italian student, but the requirements differ. The simplest route is to take *corsi singoli*, or single courses. In order to take these, you must be already enrolled in an American university, and the courses count as "outside credit." If you are not, you can apply to a Università per Stranieri (University for Foreigners), such as in Siena or Perugia, the special program for foreigners at the University of Florence, or one of the private Italian universities (each private university has its own enrollment procedures and should be contacted directly for the application package). There is also a wide selection of local public music conservatories and art institutes as well.

The most difficult route at the public university is that of the *corso di laurea* (degree track), which lasts a minimum of four years and leads to the *laurea* degree, considered by many Italians equivalent to the American master's degree (the American bachelor's degree is generally considered inferior to the *laurea*), and the title of *dottore* (doctor). Between these two choices there are other levels of degrees that require more or less of a commitment. The *diploma universitario* (university diploma), also known as the *laurea breve*, or short degree, lasts two years and is similar to the American junior college degree. The *corso di perfezionamento* ("perfection" course) lasts one year and provides students with the opportunity to study in-depth topics related to their field of study or profession, while the *scuola di specializzazione* (specialization school) is for people who already have the *laurea* and need extra professional training. Since 1969, Italian universities have offered a degree higher than the *laurea,* called the *dottorato di ricerca* (research doctorate), similar to the American Ph.D. degree, which takes approximately four years to complete.

How to Enroll in a Public University

There are two Italian authorities in the United States involved in the application process. The first is the Ufficio Studenti of the Italian Cultural Institute (see end of this chapter for addresses). It has all of the information you need about application requirements, specific universities, and current costs. You should check with it each year because the requirements and deadlines for Americans change. The second is the Ufficio Studenti of the Italian Consulate (see Chapter 3 for addresses), which handles the legal part, including the issuance of visas, certification of degrees, and authentication of translated transcripts. When you start researching which university you'd like to apply to, also start collecting original copies of your high school and college diplomas, a course catalog from your university, and an official copy of your transcript and birth certificate. Eventually all documents, including descriptions of the courses you took, will have to be translated into Italian. You will send the application directly to the university yourself, and it will instruct you how to make payment. Once you receive a receipt for that payment, you must take it to the Italian Consulate, where you will complete the necessary paperwork for the study visa.

If you want to apply for the *corso di laurea* or other degree program, you must complete the preregistration and registration processes in the United States, as well as qualifying examinations in Italy. During the preregistration process, you must prove that you can speak and write Italian and that you have completed some college-level studies in the United States. You may not apply straight out of high school. For single courses, contact the Italian Cultural Institute after mid-May for updates. If you are interested in enrolling in a degree track program, contact the Italian Cultural Institute around mid-February.

If you have been a legal resident of Italy for more than one year and have a valid *permesso di soggiorno,* you can apply directly to the university through the Ufficio Studenti Stranieri (Foreign Student Office) at the university. If you have been a resident for less time, you must complete the application process via mail through the Italian Consulate that presides over the American city or town where you still have residency.

TUITION

Tuition, called the *tassa scolastica* or *tassa universitaria,* is not technically "tuition" at all but an education tax determined by the government. Students either pick up the tuition bill at the *segreteria,* the main administrative office of the department, or arrange to have the bill sent home. Either way, the university bill must be paid at the post office like any housing bill. A student can pay it off all at once or in *rate* (installments). The receipt is then presented at the *segreteria,* where a record of payment is stamped in your *libretto universitario,* a small booklet that contains your photo and a record of all the exams you have taken with the grades you received.

TRANSFERRING CREDITS BACK HOME

Sometimes American students have problems transferring Italian university credits to their schools back in the United States. Before you decide to enroll in an Italian program, check with your study abroad adviser about transfer credit policies. Some American schools will not accept transfer credit because their own departments offer the same or similar courses; others with smaller Italian departments are happy to accept them. If the credits will not be accepted, you might want to enroll in the study abroad program of an American university that offers Italian university courses as part of its curriculum. You will pay more than if you enrolled directly at the Italian school, but you will not lose time or money later making up missing credits.

Understanding the Italian
University System

Italian universities are divided into various *facoltà*, or departments. Each *facoltà* has its own administration and functions as a separate school from the others within the university. Transferring from one department to another is as complicated as transferring schools in the United States. Some of the biggest *facoltà* include *Lettere* (Humanities), *Medicina* (Medicine), *Ingegneria* (Engineering), *Giurisprudenza* (Law), *Architettura* (Architecture), *Agraria* (Agrarian Sciences), *Veterinaria* (Veterinary Sciences), *Scienze Politiche* (Political Science), and *Economia Commercio* (Economics).

The universities have alternating periods of classes and exams. Some departments use the semester system, and some are on yearly course schedules. Most students find out about their schedules on October 1 each fall. By November a student's schedule should be definite. Universities work around the following general schedule:

Primo semestre (first semester)	October to December, maybe a bit into January
Sessione d'esame invernale (winter exams)	January and February
Secondo semestre (second semester)	March to early June
Sessione d'esame estiva (summer exams)	June, July, and September (closed during August)

COURSES

The average course at an Italian university meets twice a week for one to one and a half hours per session. It lasts a total of one semester or one year. In a *corso obbligatorio*, or required course, a student usually has no choice as to meeting time or professor. *Corsi opzionali* or *corsi facoltativi*—what we call "electives" in the United States—may be taken by students as long as they stay within their *indirizzo* (major). A *corso a numero chiuso* is a limited-enrollment course. If a course is *chiuso* (closed) after 100 students, for example, those left over must wait either until another student drops out or until the following academic year. Available courses are normally listed by computer printout on the main bulletin board of the department. Consult the board right away, since students begin lining up early in the morning and places fill up quickly.

EXAMS

At Italian universities you often have to pass both a written and an oral exam for each course in order to get credit for it. Certain majors also require practical exams (e.g., in the laboratory) or essays. Sometimes students study for an exam for months, only to discover the day before that the professor has decided to cancel and reschedule for one to four months later. In courses that require a written exam, you have to pass the written part before you are admitted to the oral part. The grade you receive on the exams is the combined grade you receive for the course. The highest grade you can get on an exam is *trenta con lode* (30 with honors); the lowest passing grade is *diciotto* (18).

Italian university exams are excruciatingly difficult, and the fact that all exams are open to the public only makes for additional stress. To protect against students being judged unfairly, by law there must be more than one professor present during the oral exam. Therefore, you will have to get used to facing a panel of professors. Sometimes, when only one is present, another person (even someone who is not a professor) will be called to serve as a witness. If students don't pass an exam or if they get a grade they don't like, they can choose to refuse the grade and have the opportunity to try again later. But trying again can be more difficult, since students are often viewed poorly once they have failed and their chances of passing are thus even lower. Because of this, many students prefer to study for years for a single exam until they are sure of passing it. It's not uncommon for a student who took a course in a given year to take the final exam, or *dare l'esame*, two years after the completion of the course. You will find Italian university students studying for exams without being enrolled in any courses at all. The average full-time student takes about four to six exams per year. Exams are so important that Italians don't ask students what year they are in but how many exams they have completed, to judge how far along in their studies they are. Exams are also how students determine seniority among themselves. The universities have strict graduation requirements that insist that students pass between twenty and thirty-five exams. If they don't keep up, students become *fuori corso*, or "off track," sometimes to the point that they are enrolled in university for upward of seven years.

THE THESIS AND GRADUATION

In order to graduate with the *laurea*, almost all Italian students must write a *tesi* (thesis) of approximately 85 to 300 pages, the length varying according to department. Generally, the topic of the thesis is suggested by the student but ultimately decided on by the thesis adviser. It usually takes a student approximately one to two years to research and write the thesis. There are normally six periods during the year when students can defend their thesis for the degree and six different periods when they can take graduation examinations. The final moment of the Italian university student's career is the oral defense of the thesis in an auditorium full of people (the defense is always open to the public). The board of eleven professors interrogates the student about the research he or she has done, looks at the student's school record, and makes the *proclamazione* (declaration) by awarding a final grade. Each professor can award a maximum of ten points, and they can collectively agree to award you honors; hence the best grade is *centodieci con lode* (110 with honors). If you get this, in some schools everyone in the room stands up to honor you.

After the thesis defense, students often go for a fancy dinner or have a small *festa di laurea* (graduation party) on the weekend. There is no collective graduation ceremony, but each city has different traditions. For example, in Padua in May the university walls are covered with hand-painted posters called *papiri*. These bear cartoons and caricatures of graduating students, designed by their friends and family, and often have comic poems to accompany them. The students wear pointed dunce hats around town all day, and each *facoltà* has a different-colored hat. Everyone stops to greet the graduates and congratulate them. They are often undressed in public by friends, sprayed with shaving cream, or dunked into fountains.

Italian M.B.A. and Master's Programs

Many public universities, including the DAMS programs in Bologna and Rome, are now offering master's degrees in fields such as arts and humanities. In recent years the Master in Business Administration has also become popular in Italy. The Associazione per la Formazione alla Direzione Aziendale (ASFOR) accredits M.B.A. programs based on a series of criteria that the schools must meet, including class size, which is usually small. These programs are offered at both public and private universities, and the tuition ranges from 1.5 million lire ($1,000) to 30 million lire ($20,000). The most famous is the Bocconi in Milan. Three of the programs—Istituto G. Tagliacarne, SOGEA, and STOÀ—are actually free. A few well-recognized schools offer master's degrees that are not ASFOR-accredited. For example, Centro Internazionale di Studi Economici Turistici (CISET) is the International Center of Studies on the Tourist Economy at the University of Venice Cà Foscari. The Istituto Formazione Operatori Aziendali (IFOA) is part of the chamber of commerce of Emilia-Romagna. If you want to apply to any of the M.B.A. or master's programs, you can contact them directly using the addresses provided at the end of this chapter.

Scholarship Opportunities

The Rotary International Foundation offers approximately 1,200 privately funded Ambassadorial Scholarships each year (maximum award $22,000) for people who want to study abroad for three months, six months, one year, or several years. Of those scholarships, one-third are for American students. In 1997, about forty students were sent to Italy and enrolled in Italian universities. They studied international business, architecture, speech pathology, elementary education, and linguistics, among other subjects. The requirements are fairly flexible, but remember that you must have completed at least two years of college before you leave and that you must enroll in an academic program (there is discussion of enlarging the program to include internships abroad as well). The scholarships are open to people of all ages. In fact, the scholarships are called "Ambassadorial" because recipients are expected to act as "ambassadors of goodwill." Part of the requirements once you are in Italy is to speak to local Rotary Clubs about American culture and the experience of living abroad. You must also submit reports about your experience at midyear and after you have finished. If you do want to apply, you must start the application process eighteen months to two years before you wish to leave.

Useful Addresses

Because many public Italian universities don't have admissions offices the way American schools do, the following fax numbers are for the office of the university's president or the student office. Most schools don't have brochures ready to distribute to interested students, so you should always call first and ask for specific information. You will rarely receive information via fax, and if you send a fax asking for general admissions requirements, most likely you will not receive an answer. The best way to get information is to contact a branch of the Italian Cultural Institute in the United States.

ITALIAN CULTURAL INSTITUTES
IN THE UNITED STATES

CHICAGO:
Istituto Italiano di Cultura
500 North Michigan Avenue, Suite 1450
Chicago, IL 60611
tel (312) 822-9545/822-0928
fax (312) 822-9622
iicch@mcs.com
www.mcs.com/~iicch
LOS ANGELES:
Istituto Italiano di Cultura
1023 Hilgard Avenue
Los Angeles, CA 90024
tel (310) 443-3250
fax (310) 443-3254
iic-la@konix-int.com
http://konix-int.com/IIC/
NEW YORK:
Istituto Italiano di Cultura
686 Park Avenue
New York, NY 10021
tel (212) 879-4242
fax (212) 861-4018
segr@italcultny.org
www.italcultny.org
SAN FRANCISCO:
Istituto Italiano di Cultura
425 Bush Street, Suite 301
San Francisco, CA 94108
tel (415) 788-7142
fax (415) 788-6389
istituto@sfiic.org
www.sfiic.org
WASHINGTON, D.C.:
Istituto Italiano di Cultura
1717 Massachusetts Avenue, N.W.,
Suite 104
Washington, DC 20036
tel (202) 328-3840

fax (202) 745-0364
italcult@ix.netcom.com

SCHOLARSHIPS
Rotary International Foundation
1 Rotary Center
1560 Sherman Avenue
Evanston, IL 60201
tel (847) 866-3000
fax (847) 866-0934
www.rotary.org

PUBLIC ITALIAN UNIVERSITIES
BARI:
Università degli Studi di Bari
Piazza Umberto, 1
70121 Bari
tel (080) 5711111
fax (080) 5714641
BOLOGNA:
Università degli Studi di Bologna
Via Zamboni, 33
40126 Bologna
tel (051) 259032
fax (051) 259034
www.unibo.it
CAGLIARI:
Università degli Studi di Cagliari
Via Università, 40
09124 Cagliari
tel (070) 6751
fax (070) 669425
www.unica.it
CALABRIA:
Università della Calabria
Arcavacata di Rende
87036 Rende (CS)
tel (0984) 4911
fax (0984) 493616

FLORENCE:
Università degli Studi di Firenze
Piazza San Marco, 4
50121 Firenze
tel (055) 27571
fax (055) 264194
www.unifi.it

MACERATA:
Università degli Studi di Macerata
Piaggia dell'Università, 2
62100 Macerata
tel (0733) 2581
fax (0733) 235869

MILAN:
Politecnico di Milano
Piazza Leonardo da Vinci, 32
20133 Milano
tel (02) 23991
fax (02) 23992199
www.polimi.it
Università Cattolica del Sacro Cuore
Largo Gemelli, 1
20123 Milano
tel (02) 72341
fax (02) 72342210
Università degli Studi di Milano
Via Festa del Perdono, 7
20122 Milano
tel (02) 58351
fax (02) 58302641
www.unimi.it

NAPLES:
Università degli Studi di Napoli Federico II
Corso Umberto, 1
80138 Napoli
tel (081) 5477111
fax (081) 5477234
www.unina.it

PADUA:
Università degli Studi di Padova
Via 8 Febbraio, 2
Palazzo Central "Il Bo"
35122 Padova
tel (049) 8273111
fax (049) 8273009
www.unipd.it

PALERMO:
Università degli Studi di Palermo
Piazza Marina, 61
90133 Palermo
tel (091) 334139
fax (091) 6110448
www.unipa.it

PARMA:
Università degli Studi di Parma
Via Università, 12
43100 Parma
tel (0521) 2041
fax (0521) 204357

PISA:
Università degli Studi di Pisa
Lungarno Pacinotti, 44
56100 Pisa
tel (050) 920111
fax (050) 42446

ROME:
Università degli Studi di Roma "La Sapienza"
Piazzale Aldo Moro, 5
00185 Roma
tel (06) 4959388
fax (06) 49912400

TURIN:
Università degli Studi di Torino
Via Verdi, 8
10124 Torino
tel (011) 6702200
fax (011) 6702218
www.unito.it

VENICE:
Università degli Studi di Venezia Cà Foscari
Dorsoduro 3246
30123 Venezia
tel (041) 2578237
fax (041) 2578351
www.unive.it

ITALIAN M.B.A. PROGRAMS

ASFOR (for general information about programs)
Via Tabacchi, 56
20136 Milano

tel (02) 8376293
fax (02) 8373561
www.asfor.it
asfor@mi.nettuno.it

BARI:

Scuola di Perfezionamento di Gestione Aziendale (SPEGEA)
Strada Provinciale per Casamassima km. 3
70010 Valenzano (Bari)
tel (080) 8770270
fax (080) 8770273
(management and company development)

BOLOGNA:

Profingest
Via Buon Pastore, 2
40141 Bologna
tel (051) 474782
fax (051) 482297
profingest@profingest.dsnet.it
(management)

GENOA:

Scuola di Formazione Aziendale (SOGEA)
Via Interiano, 1
16124 Genova
tel (010) 5531005
fax (010) 532607
www.sogea.interbusiness.it
(management)

MILAN:

Consorzio Universitario MIP—Politecnico di Milano
Via Rombon, 11
20134 Milano
tel (02) 2151500
fax (02) 2152309
postmaster@mailer.mip.polimi.it
(engineering for company management)

Publitalia '80
Master in Communicazione e Marketing
Viale Fulvio Testi, 223
20162 Milano
tel (02) 66100512

fax (02) 66100610
www-master.publitalia.it
master@publitalia.it
(communications and marketing)

SDA Bocconi
Divisione Master
Via Balilla, 16/18
20136 Milano
tel (02) 58366638
fax (02) 58363275
mba@ccmail.uni-bocconi.it
www.sda.uni-bocconi.it
(business administration)

NAPLES:

STOÀ—Istituto di Studi per la Direzione e Gestione di Impresa
Villa Campolieto—Corso Resina, 283
80056 Ercolano (Napoli)
tel (081) 7882111
fax (081) 7772688
stoa.bs@agora.stm.it
(business administration)

PALERMO:

Istituto Superiore per Imprenditori e Dirigenti di Azienda (ISIDA)
Sede della Segreteria
Via Ugo La Malfa, 169
90146 Palmero
tel (091) 6886805
fax (091) 6886812
isida@mbox.vol.it
(business administration)

REGGIO EMILIA:

CIS—Scuola Aziendale di Formazione Superiore
Via Picard, 18
42100 Reggio Emilia
tel (0522) 307445
(business studies)

ROME:

Istituto Guglielmo Tagliacarne
Via Appia Pignatelli, 62
00178 Roma
tel (06) 780521
fax (06) 7842136
www.eureka.it/tagliacarne
(economic development)

Scuola di Management LUISS Guido Carli
Via Cosimo de Giorgi, 8
00158 Roma
tel (06) 4510337/4182135
fax (06) 4512863
(business administration)

SALERNO:
Scuola Direzione Organizzazione Aziendale (SDOA)
Via G. Pellegrino, 19
84019 Vietri sul Mare (SA)
tel (089) 761166
fax (089) 210002
fagsdoa@mbox.vol.it
(management)

TRIESTE:
Consorzio MIB
Via Edoardo Weiss, 15
34127 Trieste
tel (040) 5708021
fax (040) 5708031
(international business)

TURIN:
SAA Scuola di Amministrazione Aziendale dell'Università degli Studi di Torino
Via Ventimiglia, 115
10123 Torino
tel (011) 6399217
fax (011) 6637722
www.saa.unito.it
(business administration)

VICENZA:
Consorzio Universitario degli Studi di Organizzazione Aziendale (CUOA)

Villa Valmarana Morosini
Altavilla Vicentina (Vicenza)
tel (0444) 572499
fax (0444) 574474
cuoa@g.net.it
(banking and company management)

ITALIAN MASTER'S PROGRAMS

MILAN:
Centro CEFRIEL
Via Emanueli, 15
20126 Milano
tel (02) 661611
fax (02) 66100448
www.cefriel.it
(information technologies)

REGGIO EMILIA:
Istituto Formazione Operatori Aziendali Ufficio Informazioni (IFOA)
Via G. D'Arezzo, 6
42100 Reggio Emilia
tel (0522) 329111
fax (0522) 284708
(management, engineering, and foreign trade)

VENICE:
Centro Internazionale di Studi Economici Turistici (CISET)
Villa Mocenigo, Riviera San Pietro, 83
30030 Oriago di Mira (Venezia)
tel (041) 5630924
fax (041) 5630620
ciset@unive.it
(economy and tourism management)

CHAPTER FOURTEEN

Language Schools

*I know a few Italian words and several phrases, and along at first I
used to keep them bright and fresh by whetting them on Angelo; but
he partly couldn't understand and partly didn't want to, so I have
been obliged to withdraw them from the market for the present. But
this is only temporary. I am practicing. I am preparing. Some day I
shall be ready for him, and not in ineffectual French but in his native
tongue.*

—Mark Twain, *Autobiography*, 1892

The Italian language has seduced nonspeakers for centuries, with its
tender vowels, which brush past the listener's ear, and its natural
melody, which softens even the angriest words. When you listen closely,
you realize that the language is as varied as the people who speak it, for
standard Italian has evolved not only over time but across geographic
and class borders. In the early 1300s, Dante Alighieri became the first
to propose his own Florentine dialect as the basis for "standard" Italian
by writing *The Divine Comedy* in his native tongue rather than in Latin,
making it the first widely publicized work in the new language. But regional dialects are still used despite the modern-day influence of television, which has done much to homogenize the language. Every region
has its own dialect with its own pronunciation, cadence, vocabulary,
spelling, and sometimes even sentence structure. In fact, the differences are so great that often people living within a few hundred miles of
each other literally cannot understand one another (for example, when
Mount Etna on Sicily erupted, Italian TV provided translations in standard Italian of what the Sicilian witnesses were saying). Modern Italian
can be divided into at least six sublanguages, including "Gallo-Italian,"
spoken in the north; "Venetian," spoken in the Veneto region; "Tuscan,"
in central Italy; the dialects of Rome and surrounding regions such as
Umbria and Le Marche; the language of the region around Naples; and
the collection of varied dialects in both the Calabrian and Sicilian re-

gions (see Appendix). On top of this, there is the centuries-old influence of foreign tongues: citizens of northern border towns speak French and German, southerners use Spanish and Arab words, and almost everyone uses catchy American phrases and vocabulary to pepper their speech.

Like Mark Twain, you'll find Italian a pleasurable challenge, both to understand and to speak. Most things about learning it are easy: the grammar's not bad—especially if you know French or Spanish—and the pronunciation is easy once you learn the vowels because the language is phonetic. If the French have earned a reputation for being unkind to foreigners struggling to speak their language, Italians have earned just the opposite: they will be not only impressed by your efforts to communicate but enthusiastic about helping to correct your mistakes. In fact, some expatriates believe in never hitting the grammar books at all and learn the basics just by walking around and talking to people. This is not to say they all master it: there are many who communicate in pidgin Italian even after twenty years of living in Italy, while others become fluent in the most obscure street slang but have no idea how to put it down on paper.

If you want to be sure of your Italian usage and grammar, your best bet is to enroll in one of the many language schools scattered throughout the country. There are oodles to choose from, from the tiny northern town of Feltre to the Sicilian city of Catania, from the island of Elba to the Alps. Aside from the basic considerations of course duration, price, size, and location, there are some less obvious ones to take into account when choosing a school. For example, you should consider whether you want to receive a diploma at the end of the course or whether you need to learn Italian tailored to a special need, such as business, science, medicine, or law (if you're an opera singer, there are even courses to help you sing *Rigoletto* with an authentic accent). No matter which school you enroll in, classes should be used as a supplement to what you learn in daily life.

University Study Centers

When it comes to Italian universities, there are large programs for foreigners sponsored by the public universities in Siena, Florence, Bologna, Bergamo, Genoa, Parma, Trento, Urbino, Perugia, and Rome. In addition, there are three Università per Stranieri, or Universities for Foreigners, which are sponsored by the state and usually cheaper than smaller private schools. These are also recognized as the most prestigious of all, considered superior in terms of education. The Università per Stranieri di Perugia and the Università per Stranieri di Siena offer intensive three-month "full-immersion" courses year round, which include students living on campus, while the Università per Stranieri di Urbino offers courses for foreigners only in August. Siena even has special preparatory language courses for Americans who plan to enroll in Italian universities afterward. Because these programs have a campus life, there are fewer outside distractions and more organized student activities, such as field trips to nearby villages and sights. In recent years, full-immersion courses at the Università per Stranieri in Perugia cost from 450,000 lire ($300) for one month to 800,000 lire ($530) for three, Siena cost about 100,000 lire ($70) more for three months, and Urbino cost 600,000 lire ($400) for one month. None of these figures includes housing, which can cost as much as 100,000 ($70) lire per person per week. Most schools can help you arrange housing if you need it.

Language Schools

Each Italian city offers a different selection of schools than the next city. However, there are some schools with branches in different parts of the country, including the Leonardo da Vinci, Galileo Galilei, Dante Alighieri (sponsored by the state), and Torre di Babele. In terms of cost, prices vary depending on whether you enroll in intensive or regular courses, group classes, or individual lessons. For example, the Istituto Zambler in Venice charges 900,000 lire ($600) for 80 hours of group instruction, while LinguaDue in Milan charges 980,000 lire ($650) for 67 hours of intensive group instruction and 1,400,000 lire ($930) for 17 hours of intensive individual lessons. The Società Dante Alighieri in Rome asks for a onetime 70,000-lire ($50) registration fee, plus 200,000 lire ($130) per 8 hours of classes.

About one-third of the language schools in Italy are members of the Associazione Scuole di Italiano come Lingua Seconda (ASILS, or Association of Italian as a Second Language Schools). This association guarantees that its member schools have met certain criteria, such as clean and modern teaching facilities, by sending inspectors every two years. In addition, all ASILS language instructors are required to have a university degree or five years of teaching experience. Most importantly, ASILS makes sure its schools keep the number of students per class

Italian students in Rome, with the dome of St. Peter's Basilica in the background.

below fifteen. However, this doesn't necessarily mean that if a particular school is not a member you should avoid it. In fact, many reputable schools are not members of ASILS, such as the Istituto Michelangelo, which is considered one of the best Italian-language schools in Florence. The Università per Stranieri in Siena and Perugia are also members of ASILS, as are most of the schools listed at the end of this chapter.

One-on-One Private Instruction

Many schools offer one-on-one private instruction, which usually costs twice as much as group lessons, or 30,000 to 50,000 lire ($20–$35) per hour. You can also find personal language instructors outside the language schools by checking bulletin boards at the English-language bookstores or the Italian universities. If you have the time and patience to organize a language exchange between yourself and an Italian friend you'll save a bundle—this is the only real way to learn the language for free within a structured learning program. To do this, you must first find a partner who wants to learn English; then you can organize one hour of Italian conversation followed by an hour of English at an outdoor café, for example, or an "English-speaking day" one week followed by an "Italian-speaking day" the next. Many language exchange partners meet through university bulletin boards, classified ads in English-language publications, or mutual friends. Some American university programs in Italy organize exchanges, too. I know of one enterprising American woman who rounded up all her Italian friends each week for a matinee movie screening in English followed by a few hours of conversation about the film afterward. In exchange, she got one hour of free Italian lessons from each of them.

Certificates and Language Diplomas

In Italy, there is no equivalent of the American TOEFL exam, which tests foreigners' ability to speak, write, and understand English. For that matter, there isn't any Italian-language certificate or diploma recognized nationally as official proof of proficiency or fluency. Due to this lack of a national standard, many schools offer their own "diploma of fluency" to graduating students. You should approach these diplomas with a critical eye, as many amount to no more than a certificate of attendance with the school's name and the name of the course you completed printed on it. If having a language diploma is important to you, select a school based on its reputation since its diploma may be more highly regarded. One of the most prestigious diplomas of all is the Certificate of Italian as a Second Language (CILS), which was created by the University of Siena but is issued by a handful of schools around the country. There are four levels of the CILS: *principiante* (beginning), two levels of *intermedio* (intermediate), and *avanzato* (advanced).

Finding More Information

If you'd like to get brochures of language schools in Italy, you can write directly to the schools or check with a branch of the Italian Cultural Institute in the United States (see Chapter 13), which often has many on file. The institutes also sometimes offer language scholarships that cover the cost of tuition. If you're already in Italy, you can consult the *English Yellow Pages* or the Italian yellow pages under *"Scuole di Lingue."* Or, if you have Internet access, check out the Italian-language schools on line. There are three sites that publish descriptions of Italian-language schools for foreigners: *Worldwide Classroom* (www.worldwide.edu), *Study Abroad* (www.studyabroad.com), and the *BW Line* Web site, which hosts ASILS (www.bwline.com/itschools/).

Useful Addresses

UNIVERSITIES FOR FOREIGNERS

Università degli Studi di Urbino
Centro Lingustico
Via dei Fornari, 15
61029 Urbino (PS)
tel (0722) 328597
fax (0722) 328597

Università per Stranieri di Perugia
Palazzo Gallenga
Piazza Fortebraccio, 4
06122 Perugia
tel (075) 57461
fax (075) 5746213
infpost@ipqcuic.bitnet

Università per Stranieri di Siena
Via Pantaneto, 45
53100 Siena
tel (0577) 240111
fax (0577) 283163

SELECT LANGUAGE SCHOOLS

BOLOGNA:

Centro Cultura Italiana
Via Castiglione, 4
40124 Bologna
tel (051) 228003
fax (051) 227675
vil0889@iperbole.bologna.it

Società Dante Alighieri
Via Pignattari, 1
40124 Bologna
tel (051) 226658
fax (051) 226658

FLORENCE:

ABC Centro di Lingua e Cultura Italiana
Via dei Rustici, 7
50122 Firenze
tel (055) 212001
fax (055) 212112
arca@fe.pisoft.it
www.pisoft.it/abc/

The British Institute of Florence
Piazza Strozzi, 2
50123 Firenze
tel (055) 284031
fax (055) 287056
british@foLit

Centro di Lingua Italiana Calvino
Viale Fratelli Rosselli, 74
50123 Firenze
tel (055) 288081
fax (055) 288125
clic@trident.nettuno.it

Centro Fiorenza
Via S. Spirito, 14
50125 Firenze
tel (055) 2398274
fax (055) 287148
fiorence@mbox.vol.it

Centro Koine
Via Pandolfini, 27
50122 Firenze
tel (055) 213881
fax (055) 216949

Centro Lingustico Italiano Dante Alighieri
Via dei Bardi, 12
50125 Firenze
tel (055) 2342984
fax (055) 2342766
dante_fi@saatel.shiny.it

Centro Pontevecchio
Piazza del Mercato Nuovo, 1
50123 Firenze
tel (055) 294511
fax (055) 2396887

Europass
Via S. Egidio, 12
50122 Firenze
tel (055) 2345802
fax (055) 2479995

Galileo Galilei
Via degli Alfani, 68
50121 Firenze
tel (055) 294680
fax (055) 283481
info@galilei.it
www.galilei.it

Istituto Michelangelo
Via Ghibellina, 88
50123 Firenze
tel (055) 240975
fax (055) 240997

Linguaviva
Via Fiume, 17
50123 Firenze
tel (055) 294359
fax (055) 283667
lvivapi@mbox.vol.it

Machiavelli
Piazza Santo Spirito, 4
50125 Firenze
tel (055) 2396966
fax (055) 280800
machiavelli.firenze@agora.stm.it

Scuola Leonardo da Vinci
Via Brunelleschi, 4
50123 Firenze
tel (055) 280203
fax (055) 294820
scuolaleonardo@trident.nettuno.it
www.trident.nettuno.it/Mall/leonardo

Scuola Lorenzo de' Medici
Via Faenza, 43
50125 Firenze
tel (055) 287360
fax (055) 2398920
ldm@dada.it

MILAN:

Berlitz
Via Larga, 8
20122 Milano
tel (02) 8690814
fax (02) 809395

Centro Lingua e Cultura Italiana
Viale Vittorio Veneto, 10
20124 Milano
tel (02) 29512905
fax (02) 29401972
il.centro@bbs.infosquare.it

Istituto Dante Alighieri
Via Spartaco, 8
20135 Milano
tel (02) 5510249
fax (02) 55013657

Linguadue
Corso Buenos Aires, 43
20124 Milano
tel (02) 29519972
fax (02) 29519973
linduepi@mbox.vol.it

NAPLES:

L'Italiano
Centro di Lingua e Cultura
Vico Santa Maria dell'Aiuto, 17
80134 Napoli
tel (081) 5524331
fax (081) 5523023
l.italiano@mbox.netway.it

ROME:

DILIT International House
Via Marghera, 22
00185 Roma
tel (06) 4462592
fax (06) 4440888

Istituto Italiano
Via Merulana, 139
00185 Roma
tel (06) 70452138
fax (06) 70085122
istital@uni.net
Italiaidea
Piazza della Cancelleria, 85
00186 Roma
tel (06) 68307620
fax (06) 6892997
italiaidea@mail.nexus.it
Scuola Leonardo da Vinci
Corso Vittorio Emanuele, 39
00186 Roma
tel (06) 6798896
fax (06) 6795185
scuolaleonardo@trident.nettuno.it
Società Dante Alighieri
Piazza Firenze, 27
00186 Roma
tel (06) 6873722
fax (06) 6873691
Torre di Babele
Via Bixio, 74
00185 Roma
tel (06) 7008434
fax (06) 70497150
babele@flashnet.it
www.nube.com/babele

VENICE:
Istituto Zambler
Cannaregio 3764
30121 Venezia
tel (041) 5224331
fax (041) 5285628
zambler@mbox.vol.it
Società Dante Alighieri
Ponte del Purgatorio, Arsenale
30122 Venezia
tel (041) 5289127
fax (041) 5230857

OTHER SOURCES OF INFORMATION

Association of Language Schools of Italian as a Foreign Language (ASILS)
Corso Vittorio Emanuele, 39
00186 Roma
tel (06) 6798896
fax (06) 6795185
www.bwline.com/itschools/
WorldWide Classroom
Box 1166
Milwaukee, WI 53201-1166
tel (414) 224-3476
fax (414) 224-3477
www.worldwide.edu
study@worldwide.edu

CHAPTER FIFTEEN

Bookstores, Libraries, and Research

Doing research in Italy is like playing with a metal detector on the beach: you have the sense that if you keep looking you will surely find something priceless that has been hidden for centuries. When I did research at the national archives in Florence, not only did I come across a letter from an American president of the early 1800s to a member of the Tuscan nobility, but I located the origins of a Florentine palace that has long since crumbled. I even found Medici family shopping lists and saw what groceries they'd bought one October. At the Gabinetto Vieusseux I looked at volumes still caked with mud from the flooding of the Arno in 1966. From the color-coded access cards to the faded documents scrawled in brown fountain-pen ink, doing historical and literary research in Italy is a thrill. If you know where to go and how to gain access, it is also not as difficult as it might appear.

English-Language Bookstores and Libraries

Every major Italian city has at least one English-language bookstore, and larger ones, particularly Rome, have many (see end of this chapter for addresses). Two of the largest are the Economy Book and Video Center and the Anglo-American Bookshop, which has two locations and more than 40,000 titles in stock. The majority, however, are generally on the small side, their staff members more than willing to help you locate and order a book they don't have in stock. These stores are also great informational resources for expatriates looking for work, housing, and social company. Some of them, such as the Paperback Exchange in Florence, make a point of buying and selling used books; some, such as the Remainders' Center in Milan, sell new American and British books at 50 percent off of the list price. Others, including the British Bookshop in Rome, rent and sell videos in English and sell magazine subscriptions.

Feltrinelli, Italy's largest chain of bookstores, has opened a series of international branches called Feltrinelli International in Rome, Bologna, and Florence. The regular Feltrinelli branches in other cities also have some books in English. They stock classics in English and often carry an excellent selection of textbooks and videos for English teachers as well. Most new Italian paperbacks start at 18,000 lire ($12). However, there has been a recent rise in *mille lire libri*, or books that cost 1,000 lire ($.60), as well as *libri economici* (literally, "inexpensive books"), which usually cost less than 10,000 lire ($6.50). These are usually reprinted classics, not recent releases. Like most Italian bookstores, Feltrinelli rarely offers discounts or sales. Check your local phone book for addresses.

Most English libraries can be found in Florence and Rome. Aside from those we have listed at the end of this chapter, many American universities and English-language churches have their own collections and you can often consult books in their reading room. Some, such as the British Institute's Harold Acton Library in Florence (one of the largest English-language collections in all of Europe), has open stacks and the annual membership fee permits you to borrow books. Others, such as the Biblioteca di Storia e Letteratura Nordamericana (North American History and Literature Library), which once belonged to the American Consulate but is now housed by the University of Florence, require a passport, a letter from a professor stating why you need to do research, and sometimes a couple of photos. Some, including the three library branches of the British Council in Milan, Bologna, and Rome, have formed interlibrary loan systems. A few of the libraries specialize in certain topics or periods, such as the American Academy in Rome's collection of architecture, archeology and art history volumes (to access this collection, you must have a letter of presentation from a professor). The American Embassy Library is available by appointment only. The Keats-Shelley Memorial Association is one of Rome's most precious Anglo sites and has a collection of poetry from the Romantic period, not to be missed by anyone interested in verse. The museum is also located alongside the Spanish Steps and near two of Rome's best coffeehouses: Babington's English Tearoom and the famous Caffè Greco, where expatriates have gathered for years.

Italian Libraries and Research Institutes

I once went to an Italian villa in the countryside for dinner and was promptly given a tour of the house. At one point the owner stopped before a dusty bookcase and proclaimed, "Here is the best part of the house—the antique books. We had them appraised, and they are worth more than everything else we own." When I asked if he'd actually read any of them, he was not only surprised but offended. "They're not meant to be read, they're meant to be collected!" he said.

Most Italian books are printed on high-quality paper that stays white over time and is free of the wood pulp that freckles cheap American editions. Italians are proud of their collections and take good care of their books. For the researcher this means one thing: primary sources. Aside from the libraries, which are bursting with antique manuscripts, there are bookstores all over the country that specialize in collecting, trading, and restoring original texts. Antique markets have stand after stand of the most beautiful leather-bound editions imaginable, complete with gold trimming. Public high schools offer courses in bookbinding, papermaking, calligraphy, and book restoration.

ARCHIVES AND INSTITUTES

There is no better place in Italy to find primary sources than the archives, and this is especially true of the national state archives where the catalog system is so confusing that it is often necessary to solicit the help of one of the *bibliotecari* (librarians). At the Archivio di Stato in Florence you can examine things such as original diaries of famous Tuscans or Renaissance *catasti* (zoning maps), while the Archivio Storico del Comune di Roma provides documents, books, and periodicals about Rome, including government papers dating back to the sixteenth century. If you're looking for statistical information, contact Censis, ISTAT, and Nielsen, the three leading statistical research foun-

dations. They are used by all Italian newspapers for data and research and can supply information concerning anything from the number of supermarkets in Italy to the unemployment figures for each Italian region. If you need to do business or economic research, you can subscribe to the Centro Documentazione Economica per Giornalisti, a clipping service of major Italian newspapers that specializes in economic news. Or you can call the *archivio* (archive) of any large Italian newspaper for old articles, although you will usually be asked to wait a few days for material.

ITALIAN LIBRARIES

There is at least one large state-owned library per city, and many participate in a system of *prestito interbibliotecario* (interlibrary loan).

Every book published in Italy must be registered at the Rome or Florence branch of the Biblioteca Nazionale Centrale, so chances are they have what you need. Borrowing is virtually nonexistent, and service is generally slow at both branches. It is not unusual to have to return on two or three different days before getting what you request. There are also many small library collections in each city that wealthy families once owned before donating them to the local government. Many other libraries are directly connected to the state universities, such as La Sapienza in Rome; others are affiliated with local museums. Access to museum libraries is often limited to historians and doctoral students.

Some libraries are connected to political parties. For example, the Istituto Gramsci has an extensive selection of materials related to the Italian Communist Party, including historic wartime documents and diaries of partisans. Others, such as the Istituto Luce, one of the country's leading cinematographic institutes, are related to professional fields. Founded by Mussolini in 1924 and now part of the Cinecittà film studios in Rome, Istituto Luce has the best archive of film news footage and still photographs starting with the Fascist period and continuing up to the early 1970s. The RAI archive in Rome is another big archive with up-to-date film footage and video. A favorite library for foreigners is the Gabinetto Scientifico Letterario G. P. Vieusseux in Florence, founded in 1819 by a Swiss merchant. It's a treasure trove for students of eighteenth- and nineteenth-century literature and includes volumes by famous English and American authors of the past that you can't easily find in the United States. For art historians, the Kunst Library in Florence and the Vatican Library in Rome are two major hunting grounds.

GAINING ACCESS   While in the United States you "become a member" of a library, in Italy you "gain access" to it. The extent of your access depends largely on the project you are working on and whether you have a well-known professor or university backing you up. In general you must go to the Ufficio Orientamento and present a passport, driver's license, or official photo ID card; then you'll be given a *permesso di entrata* (entrance pass) or a *tessera/tesserino* (membership card) that lasts a day or a year, depending on the extent of your research. Some require you bring passport-sized photos as well. If you want access to *manoscritti* (manuscripts) and rare books, you will need to present a letter from a professor overseeing your project. If you're not affiliated with a university in Italy, get a general letter from a professor in the United States on university letterhead describing your project and stating why you have to do research in Italy. Make several copies, and address each one to individual libraries you want to use once you arrive.

LOCATING BOOKS Most of the libraries in Italy don't have a computerized card catalog system, and many of the *schede* (cards) in the catalog are handwritten. The handwriting on the older cards is often in antique cursive, and recognizing individual letters can take longer than you might suspect (using a magnifying glass may come in handy). Some libraries have only bound volumes with handwritten pages that function as catalogs, making the whole system even more mysterious. In general, catalogs are organized *per autore* (by author), *per soggetto* (by subject), or *per titolo* (by title), as you would expect.

Only librarians have access to the *magazzino/deposito librario* (stacks), making haphazard browsing impossible. When you want to look at a book, you must fill out a *modulo* on which you indicate the *collocazione* (call number), *titolo* (title), and *luogo e data di edizione* (publication place and date). In certain cases you may have to indicate the *opuscolo* (pamphlet) or *periodico/rivista/giornale/quotidiano* (magazine, journal, or newspaper), as well as the *fascicolo* (issue). You must then present the *modulo* to one of the librarians, who will give you a *scontrino* (receipt) and then make you wait while he or she gets it, which can take a few hours or sometimes several days. Often you will hear that a book is already *in prestito* (on loan), *in legatoria* or *dal legatore* (being bound), *smarrito* (lost), *alluvionato* (damaged by flooding), or simply *irreperibile* (impossible to find). Students just waiting to receive their books fill the *sale di lettura* (reading rooms) and the *sale di consultazione* (reference rooms).

Doing Genealogical Research

If you are Italian-American, searching for your roots in Italy is best done when you are already proficient in the language or you have someone who is proficient helping you. The bureaucracy involved is not as complicated as you may suspect, but it does require writing letters to various government offices to request permission to consult archives. The ease of finding information largely depends on how detailed the information is that you already have; the more birth dates and places, the easier it will be. For example, if you are told that your relative was from Naples, try to find out where exactly; many "Neapolitan" immigrants were actually from one of the dozens of tiny towns on the outskirts of the city, each with a different town hall. Because Italy used to be made up of independent city-states, the further back in history you search the more complex the archives become.

There are four Italian entities you will primarily deal with when doing your research: the Sovrintendenza Archivistica (the office regulating all of the state archives); the local *anagrafe* (census bureau), which has more modern records; the Archivio di Stato (State Archive), which has records usually dating before 1815; and the *chiesa* (church) which regulated the registering of births, deaths, and marriages in the past. However, unless you know exactly where your relatives came from and which church they attended, this resource is difficult to use. In certain cases (e.g., if your relatives were part of the Italian military) you may also deal with other sources. Each of these entities has different records and different procedures for consulting them, and their rules vary from town to town.

General Suggestions

If you can't find reference books such as *The Writer's Market* and GMAT study books in Italy, buy them from home and have them shipped by sea to save money. Or find out about overseas shipping policies from your favorite American bookstores. Once in Italy, plan your trips to libraries well; their odd hours can often lead to whole days being wasted. Take a warm sweater when you go—those old stone palaces can get cold. Also, whenever possible, do any necessary photocopying at a self-service shop to save money. If you have Internet access, check out the *rete civica,* or on-line civic network, of your town for information about local resources (see Chapter 10), as well as *Alice* (www.alice.it) for general information about the Italian publishing world, libraries, and bookstores.

Useful Addresses

BOOKSTORES SPECIALIZING
IN ENGLISH-LANGUAGE BOOKS

FLORENCE:
After Dark
Via de' Ginori, 47/r
50123 Firenze

tel/fax (055) 294203
BM Bookshop
Borgo Ognissanti, 4/r
50123 Firenze
tel/fax (055) 294575
bmbookshop@dada.it

Le Monnier
Via S. Gallo, 53/r
50129 Firenze
tel. (055) 483215
fax (055) 470209
Paperback Exchange
Via Fiesolana, 31/r
50122 Firenze
tel (055) 2478154
fax (055) 2478856
papex@dada.it
Seeber International
Via Tornabuoni, 70/r
50123 Firenze
tel (055) 215697
fax (055) 288340
MILAN:
American Bookstore
Via Camperio, 16
20123 Milano
tel (02) 878920
fax (02) 72020030
The English Bookshop
Via Mascheroni, 12
20145 Milano
tel (02) 4694468
fax (02) 48009693
Libreria Internazionale
Via Ozanam, 11
20129 Milano
tel (02) 2049022
fax (02) 29516896
Remainders' Center
Galleria Vittorio Emanuele, 17
20121 Milano
tel (02) 86464008
fax (02) 8690960
NAPLES:
Universal Books
Rione Sirignano, 1
80121 Napoli
tel/fax (081) 663217
ROME:
Ancora Bookshop
Via della Conciliazione, 63
00193 Roma
tel (06) 6868820
fax (06) 6833050
mc2720@mclink.it

Anglo-American Bookshop
Via della Vite, 102
00187 Roma
tel (06) 6795222
fax (06) 6797636
www.aab.it
Anglo-American Bookshop
via della Vite, 27 int. 4
00187 Roma
tel (06) 6784347 (magazines)
tel (06) 6789657 (technical books)
fax (06) 6783890
The British Bookshop
(2 locations)
Via Ripetta, 248
00187 Roma
tel (06) 3225837
fax (06) 3224727
The Corner Bookshop
Via del Moro, 48
00153 Roma
tel/fax (06) 5836942
The Economy Book and Video Center
Via Torino, 136
00184 Roma
tel (06) 4746877
fax (06) 483661
Libreria IV Fontane
Via Quattro Fontane, 20A
00184 Roma
tel (06) 4814484
fax (06) 4814722
Lion Bookshop
Via dei Greci, 33/36
00187 Roma
tel (06) 32654007
fax (06) 32650437
The Open Door Bookshop
Via della Lungaretta, 25
00153 Roma
tel/fax (06) 5896478

LIBRARIES, ARCHIVES, & RESEARCH
FOUNDATIONS

BOLOGNA:
**Biblioteca Centrale del Comune di
Bologna**
Via Galliera, 8
40121 Bologna

tel (051) 230800
fax (051) 222081
Biblioteca del Centro di
Documentazione delle Donne
Via Galliera, 8
40121 Bologna
tel (051) 233863
fax (051) 263460
www.orlando.women.it
Biblioteca dell'Archiginnasio
Piazza Luigi Galvani, 1
40124 Bologna
tel (051) 236488
fax (051) 261160
British Council
Corte Isolani, 8
Strada Maggiore, 19
40125 Bologna
tel (051) 225142
fax (051) 224238
FLORENCE:
Archivio di Stato
Viale Giovane Italia, 6
50012 Firenze
tel (055) 2340875
fax (055) 2341159
La Biblioteca di Storia e Letteratura
Nordamericana
Via San Gallo, 10
50129 Firenze
tel (055) 2757940
fax (055) 2757952
La Biblioteca Nazionale Centrale
Piazza di Cavallegeri, 1
50122 Firenze
tel (055) 249191
fax (055) 2342482
British Institute Harold Acton Library
Palazzo Lanfredi
Lungarno Guicciardini, 9
50125 Firenze
tel (055) 284032
fax (055) 289557
The European University Institute
The Library
Badia Fiesolana
Via dei Roccettini, 9
San Domenico di Fiesole (FI)
50016 Firenze

www.iue.it/LIB/Welcome.html
euilib@datacomm.iue.it
tel (055) 4685358
fax (055) 4685283
Il Gabinetto Scientifico Letterario G. P.
Vieusseux
Palazzo Strozzi
Piazza Strozzi
50123 Firenze
tel (055) 288342
fax (055) 2396743
The Kunst Library
Via Giuseppe Giusti, 44
50121 Firenze
tel (055) 249111
fax (055) 2491155
GENOA:
Associazione Italo Britannica
The British Library
Piazza Vittoria, 15
16121 Genova
tel (010) 591605
fax (010) 532573
Biblioteca Universitaria
Via Balbi, 3
16126 Genova
tel (010) 201719
fax (010) 205220
MILAN:
British Council Library
Via Manzoni, 38
20121 Milano
tel (02) 772221
fax (02) 781119
www.britcoun.org/italy
Centro di Studi sugli Stati Uniti
Piazza Sant'Alessandro, 1
20123 Milano
tel (02) 86339451
fax (02) 86339452
cssu@imiucca.csi.unimi.it
Nielsen
Via G. di Vittorio, 10
20094 Corsico (Milano)
tel (02) 451971
fax (02) 45866235
ROME:
American Academy Library
Via Angelo Masina, 5

00153 Roma
tel (06) 58461
fax (06) 5810788
American Embassy Library
Via Veneto, 119/a
00187 Roma
tel (06) 46742481
fax (06) 46742701
American Studies Center
Via Michelangelo Caetani, 32
00186 Roma
tel (06) 68801613
fax (06) 68307256
Archivio Storico del Comune di Roma
Piazza della Chiesa Nuova, 18
00186 Roma
tel (06) 68806241
fax (06) 68806639
Biblioteca Alessandrina
Piazzale Aldo Moro, 5
00155 Roma
tel (06) 4456820
fax (06) 491209
Biblioteca Nazionale Centrale Vittorio Emanuele II
Via Castro Pretorio, 105
00185 Roma
tel (06) 4989
fax (06) 4457635
www.sbn.it/opac
British Council Library
Via Quattro Fontane, 20
00184 Roma
tel (06) 478141
fax (06) 4814296
Censis
Fondazione Centro Studi Investimenti Sociali
Piazza di Novella, 2
00199 Roma
tel (06) 860911
fax (06) 86211367

Centro Documentazione Economica per Giornalisti
Via Cicerone, 28
00193 Roma
tel (06) 3226541
fax (06) 3226542
Istituto Nazionale di Statistica (ISTAT)
Via Cesare Balbo, 16
00184 Roma
tel (06) 46731
fax (06) 46732375
Istituto Gramsci
Via Portuense, 95
00153 Roma
tel (06) 5896025
fax (06) 5897167
Istituto Luce
Via Tuscolana, 1055
00173 Roma
tel (06) 729921
fax (06) 7221127
Keats-Shelley Memorial Association Library
Piazza di Spagna, 26
00187 Roma
tel (06) 6784235
fax (06) 6784167
Santa Susanna Library
Via XX Settembre, 15
00187 Roma
tel (06) 4827510
The Vatican Library
Biblioteca del Vaticano
00120 Città del Vaticano
tel (06) 6982
VENICE:
La Biblioteca Marciana di Venezia
Piazzetta San Marco, 7
30135 Venezia
tel (041) 5208788
fax (041) 5238803

Working

In smaller cities, teachers often commute to their lessons by bicycle.

CHAPTER SIXTEEN

Getting the Job

The main difference between looking for work in Italy and the United States is that in Italy there are many fewer jobs available. Unemployment figures have been high for a long time, and the nation currently suffers from about 12 percent unemployment (in some areas of the south, that figure reaches 50 percent). Recent university graduates wait on average one year before finding their first job, as fewer part-time positions and temporary jobs are available to keep them busy while looking for full-time work. This means that Italians enter the workforce at a much older age, and those who do find full-time positions don't give them up easily. Furthermore, negotiating a work contract is often so complicated and tiresome for both employer and employee that many people turn to illegal work, or *lavoro al nero* (almost one-fourth of all Italians are employed illegally in one way or another). This illegal employment takes many forms: employers paying part of a salary legally and the other part "under the table"; second jobs whose earnings are never declared to the Italian tax authorities. Many foreigners are employed entirely *al nero* and as a result have no job security or employee benefits; these include Americans who are fluent in Italian and highly skilled but unable to obtain work permits.

For young people, there is an additional obstacle: in Italy, it is assumed that younger people do not have the experience and qualifications necessary for meeting hiring requirements. This is often true, given the fact that few Italians graduate from university with any professional experience at all. Italians who want practical job experience before the age of thirty attend vocational high schools or specialized programs after high school. In addition, the concepts of internships and summer jobs are only just beginning to be put into practice. As a result, twenty-something professionals often are not given the same respect as their American peers are given in the United States. Americans in Italy, however unfair it might be, have some key advantages over Italians because they speak English, a much sought skill, and have more professional training behind them.

The best advice for getting a job is to solicit one aggressively through networking. Italians place enormous emphasis on who you know, and connections are considered vital to finding employment. Also, don't limit your search to what's available but create the opportunities for yourself. The success of the mom-and-pop stores in the north demonstrates that in Italy it is the enterprising entrepreneur, one who uncovers an overlooked gap in the market, who succeeds. Take into account that there are great opportunities for freelancing and part-time work but that it is much more difficult to land a full-time, contracted position. Be sensitive to the problems the nation faces, and avoid being a direct competitor with the large numbers of Italians looking for work by fine-tuning qualities that will distinguish you from them. Arrive equipped with language skills, an open mind, patience, an independent attitude, and a global perspective.

Job Hunting

How to Find Job Listings

Italian newspapers are good places to look for job listings with Italian companies, especially the national newspapers. *Il Sole 24 Ore,* the daily financial newspaper, publishes "Cercolavoro Giovani" each Monday for college graduates looking for their first jobs. It lists openings available in every sector imaginable and publishes a calendar of job fairs. *Corriere della Sera,* Italy's largest-circulation newspaper, publishes "Corriere Lavoro" each Friday, in which it claims to list more than 1,500 job openings for people of all ages. There are also many more regional publications that run want ads, and you should ask at your neighborhood *edicola* (newspaper kiosk) about them.

If you're looking for a position with an American company or a multinational, get used to scanning the "International Classified" and

"International Recruitment" ads in the *International Herald Tribune* or the *Financial Times*. However, don't expect much: of the few ads each day, you're lucky to even find one for Italy. But if you get into the habit of looking, you're bound to get a few leads and maybe even that prized "golden opportunity," such as a managerial position in a multinational firm with branches in Italy, as well as a position as a financial analyst, fund manager, or marketing specialist. Also, get into the habit of scanning want ads in English-language publications such as *Wanted in Rome*. You'd be surprised what you can find there. Recently, the Rome bureaus of both *Newsweek* and the *Los Angeles Times* advertised jobs through want ads—jobs that any young journalist would normally only dream of finding.

If you have Internet access, there are two sites you should check out. *Firenze On Line* (www.fionline.it) has one of the best Italian job-hunting sites in its *Lavoro* section. It offers weekly updates of thousands of ads, places to post your résumé, and a list of *concorsi*, or competitions. *Telecom Italia Net* (www.tin.it) has a great *Economia e Finanza* section under "Canali di Video On Line" that includes *Job On-line*, a great Italian career cyberdatabase with places to post your résumé and read about current openings.

MAKING COLD CALLS

Making "cold calls" to companies to inquire about job openings is not as commonly practiced in Italy as in the United States. You'll have to explain exactly why you're calling, perhaps saying *"Telefono per candidarmi ad un posto di lavoro nella vostra azienda"* (I'm calling to apply for a job with your company) and describing your qualifications, emphasizing your international background. Always make sure you get the company's fax number and the name of the head of personnel (*capo del personale*) or the name of a *dirigente* (manager) to whom you can send your résumé.

The Italy-America Chamber of Commerce in the United States and the American Chambers of Commerce in Milan (see Chapter 21) publish phone book–sized trade directories each year with a complete list of all the American companies that do business in Italy and Italian companies with branches in the United States. They can be used to supplement the list provided at the end of this chapter because they include smaller U.S. companies, such as *pecorino* cheese exporters and textile importers, that you might not have heard of. Be forewarned that many of the listings in the chambers' directories have only U.S. addresses. If you use the books while in Italy, you will probably have to mail your résumé back to the United States and deal with the companies' home personnel office.

NETWORKING

Italy is famous for its own kind of networking, which often resembles what we call "nepotism" or "favoritism." Italians often complain that without being *raccomandati* for a job (sponsored by someone with influence), it is almost impossible to find one. Nonetheless, in Italy being *raccomandato* does not have the same negative connotation it has in the United States. It's not applauded, but it is a widespread reality of the Italian work world. When I first came to Italy, I was approached by friends who offered to make calls on my behalf, but I rejected their help because I believed that would be taking the easy way out. Only when I dropped this attitude did I find work. If you have work connections, by all means use them.

ENTERING JOB COMPETITIONS

Italians compete for some jobs through a candidate evaluation process/competition known as a *concorso*. The openings are usually for jobs in public administration, and you can count on there being more candidates than positions available. One record *concorso* a few years ago had 36,000 candidates competing for 200 openings in a government ministry. The *concorso* usually consists of a written exam and interview to test the candidate's skills and background, and the process can last several days. Many Italians feel frustrated by the *concorsi* because it's well known that the people who are *raccomandati* have a better chance of making the final cut. American citizens who are residents of Italy may not participate in the *concorsi* in general, except in a few cases, such as the *concorso* for university *lettori* (lecturers).

Presenting Yourself

PREPARING A RÉSUMÉ

American and Italian résumés differ in length and content. In the United States we are taught that a proper résumé, except for the fields of academics and entertainment, should never exceed a single page. In Italy, the longer the *curriculum vitae* the better, since speaking highly of yourself at length is considered the best way of making a good impression. Rather than putting rapid-fire "bullet points" with the essential keywords needed to describe their professional experience, Italians write lofty paragraphs describing their aspirations, goals, hobbies, family background, and life experience. I saw one Italian *curriculum* in which the candidate wrote half a page of text describing his noble roots and explaining the importance his family name had in high-society circles. He didn't limit himself to describing his own professional training but included descriptions of what his ancestors had accomplished. He got the job he was after.

Italians also include information such as age, marital status, whether or not they have children, and a description of their physical appearance. It is common to attach a passport-sized photo to an Italian *curriculum* even if the job entails spending long, lonely shifts in a photographic darkroom, where looks are of little significance. In addition, the *curriculum* is usually arranged in chronological order, starting with a candidate's high school education, continuing with university degrees earned, and ending with work experience. Many times it won't include anything but academic background, as college graduates rarely have any professional experience to speak of, and because Italians put such priority on university degrees that they alone can win a candidate the job. As a result, an American-style single-page résumé with abundant internships and brief positions with different employers is somewhat of an oddity in Italy. But this can work in your favor, for it might win you praise for experience and professionalism. It is not essential for you to reformat your American-style résumé into the Italian style, but it *is* important that you translate it into Italian.

Writing the Cover Letter

The rules for writing a cover letter are the same as in the United States: keep the letter short, and avoid repeating everything you've said on your résumé. This is your opportunity to ask formally for an interview, or *colloquio*, and it's crucial that you use the formal *Lei* verb tense. Remember that when writing the *Lei* form, you should capitalize the pronouns *Lei* and *Le*. To start the letter, use *"Egregio Signore"* or *"Gentile Signore"* (when addressing a man), *"Gentilissima Signora"* (when addressing a woman), and *"Spettabile Ditta"* (when addressing a company, much like "To Whom It May Concern"). These can be abbreviated as "Egr. Sig.," "Gent.ma Sig.a," and "Spett.le Ditta." You should also note that the first letter of the first word of the paragraph that follows the salutation is never capitalized (see following example). To end it, write *"Distinti Saluti"* or *"Cordiali Saluti"* before your signature. In case you don't want anyone else to read it, make sure to write *"Riservata personale"* on the envelope or, if you don't have a name to address your letter to, you might write *"Alla cortese attenzione del Capo del Personale* ("To the Head of Human Resources"). The following is an example of a standard cover letter to include with your résumé:

Date

Address of the company you are writing to

Alla cortese attenzione del Capo del Personale, Egregio Signore, or Gentile Signore/Signora (add a name if you have it):

sono un laureato(a)/diplomato(a) in _____ (title of your diploma or area of expertise) e sono alla ricerca di un lavoro. Ho appreso che presso la Vostra azienda/ditta/studio/negozio ci sarebbe la possibilità di avere un impiego/posto e vi scrivo per porre la mia candidatura.

La laurea/il diploma e le mie precedenti esperienze internazionali mi fanno sperare di poter ottenere un impiego/un posto che corrisponda meglio alle mie aspirazioni. Sono di madre lingua inglese e conosco perfettamente anche l'italiano.

Allego il mio curriculum sperando che il mio interesse per il lavoro nella Vostra azienda venga ricambiato e che possa esserci per me l'occasione di un colloquio che mi permetterebbe di illustrare le mie qualifiche.

Distinti saluti,

(Your signature)

Translated into English:

To the Head of Human Resources/To Whom It May Concern/Dear Mr./Dear Ms.:

I am a graduate in _____, and I am looking for employment. I have heard that there might be an opening at your agency/company/office/shop and would like to apply for it.

I am looking for a job/position that corresponds to my degree/diploma and my previous international experiences. My native language is English, and I also know Italian fluently.

I have attached my résumé and hope that we can arrange an interview so that I may better explain my qualifications.

Best regards,

(Your signature)

INTERVIEWING

There is no formula for interviewing in Italy. The interview can be anything from extremely casual to formal and intimidating but generally is an awkward mix of the two. More often than not, *colloqui* are held at outdoor restaurants or bars over a glass of wine. The main objective often does not seem to be discussing professional credentials, but checking each other out and testing each other's *simpatia*, or compatibility. Therefore, don't be put off if you're asked about personal things such as whether or not you are married and what your age is. However, don't be misled into thinking that this more relaxed approach signifies less formality. You should be respectful and use the formal *Lei* tense with your interviewer unless he or she indicates otherwise. You should also be especially well groomed and elegantly dressed. Don't use first names, but do use professional titles (*dottore, professore, ingegnere, avvocato,* etc.).

The best way to project a *bella figura*, or good image, is to let your international background and education shine through. Italians are attracted to intelligent, well-read, cultured people. They are impressed with foreigners who make an effort to follow Italian current events. Read a few days' worth of newspapers before going to the interview to get ideas for conversation and to show your intellectual curiosity. You'll likely be asked about the United States even if you haven't been home in years. It is important to be prepared.

Sending a brief, polite thank-you note after the interview might just win you the job you're after. The tradition of the thank-you note is not common practice in Italy, and employers might be persuaded to take a second look at your résumé if you surprise them with one.

Negotiating the Offer

Don't be surprised if a somewhat vague job offer is made to you during a job interview or following it, before the terms, salary, and benefits have been discussed. Even if the offer is official, it's best to thank the employer and say you will take a few days to think it over. Too much enthusiasm may be interpreted as an acceptance. Before you accept, make sure you have answers to the following questions, some of which are addressed later in this chapter:

♦ Will you have a work contract, or is the offer *al nero* (under the table)?
♦ Will your contract be for a fixed or unlimited term?
♦ Will you be considered an autonomous worker or a *dipendente* (full-contract employee)?
♦ What will your exact salary be?
♦ Will the 19 percent IVA tax be paid by you or your employer?
♦ Are you entitled to health insurance, vacation days, and paid sick days?
♦ Are you entitled to a *tredicesima* (one-month bonus), *quattordicesima* (two-month bonus), or other bonuses?
♦ Is there a *tirocinio,* or training period, involved, and what will your salary be during it?

CONTRACTS

Unlike in the U.S. where most jobs are given without a written contract, in Italy a written contract always accompanies a new position, unless it is made under the table. There are two types of contracts used when hiring *dipendenti* (employees): *a contratto a termine* or *a tempo determinato* (fixed-duration contract) and *a contratto a tempo indeterminato* (unlimited-duration contract). Children under the age of sixteen may not work in Italy, and all others must get a *nulla osta* document (see Chapter 4) from the local town hall before they can be considered for a job. Generally, Italian employees are hired with an unlimited-duration contract, meaning they can keep their position for as long as they like. The only time fixed-duration contracts (which specify the starting and ending dates of an employee's service) are used is when the work is seasonal or when employees are hired for specific short-term tasks. A fixed-duration contract may be renewed once; if the employer renews it twice, it automatically becomes an unlimited-duration contract. Make sure your contract is in writing, and make sure it addresses issues such as vacation days and salary. If your employer doesn't have a contract ready for you to sign, you can bring in your own, following the standard business contracts given below:

UNLIMITED-DURATION CONTRACT

Egr. Sig. _____:

con riferimento agli accordi verbali intercorsi, con la presente Le comunichiamo che a partire dal giorno _____ Lei è assunto alle nostre dipendenze con lo stipendio mensile di Lire _____ [put the amount in lire in both numeric and spelled-out form] e con la qualifica di _____ nello stabilimento di _____, dove svolgerà le relative mansioni. La invitiamo a volerci rimettere l'unita copia della presente da Lei sottoscritta per accettazione.

(data, firma)

Dear Mr./Ms. _____:

In reference to the verbal agreements made, we communicate with this letter that starting from the date _____ you will be hired by us with the monthly salary of _____ lire and with the title of _____ in the location _____, where you will perform the related tasks. We request that you sign and date the attached copy of this letter to indicate your acceptance of the position.

(date, signature)

FIXED-DURATION CONTACT

Egr. sig. _____:

con riferimento agli accordi verbali intercorsi Le comunichiamo che a partire dal giorno _____ Lei è assunto alle nostre dipendenze con le funzioni di _____ per il periodo di _____ e con la retribuzione mensile di Lire _____ [put the amount in lire in both numeric and spelled-out form] per tredici mensilità. Lei sarà tenuto ad osservare il seguente orario di lavoro: _____. Il contratto s'intenderà rinnovato alle medesime condizioni per altri _____ mesi e così successivamente, se non ne verrà data disdetta con lettera raccomandata almeno _____ mesi prima della scadenza. In ogni caso Lei potrà recedere liberamente dal presente contratto trascorso il primo triennio, con _____ mesi di preavviso.

Lei avrà diritto ad un periodo di ferie di _____ giorni lavorativi. Al termine del rapporto Le verrà corrisposto un premio di fine lavoro nella misura di una mensilità di retribuzione per ogni anno intero di durata del rapporto. Una frazione di anno superiore a sei mesi viene a tal fine equiparata all'anno. Tale indennità non Le sarà dovuta nel caso che il rapporto si estingua per Sua colpa o per Suo recesso. La invitiamo a volerci rimettere l'unita copia della presente da Lei sottoscritta per accettazione.

(data, firma)

Dear Mr./Ms. _____:

In reference to the verbal agreements made, we communicate that starting from the date _____ you will be hired by us with the duties of _____ for the period of _____ and with the monthly salary of _____ lire for thirteen months. You will observe the following work schedule: _____. This contract will be assumed renewed under the same conditions for _____ more months and thus after unless it is canceled with a certified letter at least _____ months before its expiration. You are free to withdraw from this contract after the first three years, giving _____ months of advance warning.

You will have the right to a vacation period of _____ workdays. At the end of this agreement you will receive a termination of employment bonus equivalent to one month's pay for every year of this employment. Any fraction of a year exceeding six months will be treated as one year for this purpose. This indemnity will not be owed to you if the employment ends due to your fault or your withdrawal. We request that you sign and date the attached copy of this letter to indicate your acceptance of the position.

(date, signature)

APPRENTICESHIP CONTRACTS   If you are under the age of thirty, there is a special contract called the *contratto di apprendistato* or *tirocinio* that is limited to less than five years and was established to assist young people trying to penetrate the workforce. It's a training-period contract and carries reduced benefits and a slightly lower pay, which makes it attractive to employers who would otherwise not give young people a chance. When the contract expires, the employer has the option to renew it as an unlimited-duration contract.

TERMS OF EMPLOYMENT

The employer must pay all social security payments, or *contributi,* on behalf of employees in addition to annual bonuses and other benefits. Altogether these usually represent 40 to 45 percent on top of the worker's actual salary. Fringe benefits are rare, but when they do exist can include transportation, sports facilities, summer programs for children, and discounts on certain goods. These expenses, coupled with reduced work hours and other factors, make Italian labor one of the most expensive in Europe. Taxes due from employees are automatically deducted from their monthly paychecks by the employer. When employees receive their paycheck, they also get a *busta paga,* which is a document that keeps track of salary, the social security payments made on their behalf, the amount taken out for taxes, and the number of vacation days left. Here are the main terms of employment and benefits an employee can regularly expect.

WAGES, SALARIES, AND RAISES   All salaries (*le retribuzioni* or *lo stipendio*) are based on the category the worker falls into and are established by the state in published rate books called *tabelle professionali.* Most salaries are paid once a month. The three main categories are *operai* (manual workers), *impiegati* (office employees), and *dirigenti* (managers), each with varying salary scales based on hierarchy. Usually, first-time employees earn the minimum wage of their category, and all workers can expect a wage increase every two years called the *scatti di anzianità*. If workers fall into a category protected by a national union, their labor contracts are renewed every few years. Collective bargaining contracts regulate employees' conditions and establish new minimum wages each time the contracts are renewed.

WORKING HOURS AND OVERTIME   Many contracts call for forty hours of work per week, although it seems this will soon diminish to thirty-eight. Working overtime will earn you 115 to 130 percent of your basic pay for work completed during the day, and 120 to 175 percent for work completed on holidays or during the night. Some companies limit the number of overtime hours permitted each year to two hundred.

VACATION AND HOLIDAYS   Employees generally get twelve national holidays throughout the year, in addition to the saint's day of the town in which they live. If a holiday occurs on a Thursday or Tuesday, employees sometimes get the day in between off; this is known as *il ponte* (literally, "the bridge"). Otherwise, paid vacation ranges from four to six weeks per year, which often must be taken during the winter or summer seasons (most people take vacation during the entire month of August and two weeks around Christmas). If employees don't use the time allotted for vacation, they receive indemnity pay. To avoid this, some companies will suddenly require that employees take vacation days they've saved up, sometimes resulting in employees taking unexpected leaves of three months or more.

BONUSES   One of the greatest things about working for an Italian company is that, oddly enough, the work calendar has up to fourteen months per year in which employees receive a paycheck. The *tredicesima,* or "thirteenth month's pay," comes before Christmas, and the *quattordicesima,* "fourteenth month's pay," during the summer. A lucky few even get a "fifteenth month."

HEALTH INSURANCE   All hospitalization and medical assistance is free of charge to Italian residents and foreigners who pay medical contributions. (For more information on health care, see Chapter 7.)

MATERNITY LEAVE   A woman is entitled to five months of paid maternity leave—two months before giving birth and three months after. A mother gets 80 percent of her normal salary during this time and can take an additional six months off and still receive 30 percent of her salary. She is guaranteed her job back when she returns.

SICKNESS LEAVE AND DISABILITY PAY   Employees unable to work due to sickness receive 75 to 100 percent of their pay unless they are absent for more than 180 days. In that case they are considered disabled. If an injury occurs in the workplace, injured employees receive full salary during the recovery period. If they are permanently injured, they receive a pension.

PENSIONS   Following fifteen years of paying contributions, employees qualify for a partial pension. To collect the full pension, they must pay contributions for thirty-five years and must reach 61 years of age if they are male and 56 if they are female. By the year 2002 this will change to 65 for men and 60 for women. In the event of death, the pension is transferred to the remaining family. The maximum pension is 80 percent of the worker's average salary for his or her last six years of employment. In 2002 it will be ten years. Because the pension laws are currently being reformed, check with your company about its pension policies.

FIRING POLICIES   An employee can be fired only if the employer can prove "just cause" or "justified motive." Just cause means the employee is found guilty of a major offense, such as stealing or repeatedly not showing up for work. A justified motive includes downsizing. Justified-motive firings must include advance notice and must be negotiated with trade unions, making them nearly impossible to carry out. In both cases, if employees are fired they have two months to contest the dismissal, and if they have been fired unlawfully, they can claim back their job at the same salary with compensation for back salary lost. All dismissals must be made in writing; otherwise they are not valid.

TERMINATION INDEMNITY AND UNEMPLOYMENT BENEFITS   Whether or not an employee is fired or resigns, he or she gets a termination payment called the *trattamento di fine rapporto,* or *liquidazione,* which can be calculated by dividing the average one-month salary by 13.5. Employees can leave their jobs at any time without justification as long as they notify the employer in writing. Those who have lost a contracted position are paid unemployment benefits by the state.

CHAPTER SEVENTEEN

Business Etiquette

Italians put much emphasis on nonverbal communication and first impressions. A firm handshake, direct eye contact, and body gestures are often considered more revealing than words. Strange remnants of ancient superstition lurk in the shadows of contemporary corporate Italy: for example, someone who shies away from another person's eye contact is perceived as hiding something. In fact, Italians are probably the most proficient nonverbal communicators in the world. Their body language can quickly convey a complicated thought in just a few hand waves and shrugs of the shoulder. The concept of personal space does not exist as in the United States, and getting too close to someone is not considered an invasion; it communicates affection and camaraderie.

When doing business in Italy, it's important to know how to present yourself, your company, and your ideas in a proper way. The protocol you must follow when making professional contacts or giving business presentations is not unlike what you're used to in the United States. But subtle differences in business etiquette—such as limiting shop talk to the conference room and making a clear distinction between work and play—do exist. If you follow Italian business etiquette, you'll spend less time getting sidetracked by cultural differences and more time getting things accomplished. You'll also enjoy yourself more in the process.

Introductions

When setting up business meetings, remember that no matter how many telephone calls you make, faxes you send, and letters you mail, nothing can replace that first one-on-one encounter. When it occurs, there are two things you should be aware of: the *bella presenza* and the now-clichéd *bella figura*. Italians are very conscious of how people dress, and notice things such as unpolished shoes and dirty fingernails. They always look well groomed and fashionable, and so should you. That's what *bella presenza* communicates. In the United States, we dress formally for work and then let loose on "casual Fridays," changing into jeans and tennis shoes. Italians, on the other hand, are elegant seven days a week, and you rarely see an Italian man wearing shorts in the city or sandals to the workplace. Women usually wear heels and light makeup. Another accessory to the *bella presenza* is the *biglietto da visita* (business card). Italians always have elegant cards ready in their breast pocket or purse.

The *bella figura*, or good image, is like the *bella presenza*, but it's more about attitude, about expressing yourself in a way that projects confidence and self-importance. The *telefonino* (cellular phone) is the ultimate symbol of the *bella figura* because it conveys your professional importance to others nearby. It takes the *bella figura* a step higher: there's a bit of showmanship involved, a bit of playing the court jester and particularly a bit of displaying Italian charm. As an American you can make a *bella figura* by flaunting your international background, by showing that you feel confident of yourself in a foreign land, by showing off your knowledge of Italy, and by demonstrating your willingness to share your international experiences and languages. Know who the president of the Republic is and what the events of the day are, but keep your complaints about Italy to yourself and don't comment on Italian politics unless you are one of the few who actually understands it. Otherwise, the result will be a *brutta figura*, or bad image.

Italians are formal in a way that goes beyond physical appearance. They use titles when addressing superiors and people they haven't been introduced to before, and employees in a company will simply refer to their boss as *"Il Direttore"* or *"Il Presidente."* A handful of key business figures have been permanently branded by their titles: Gianni Agnelli, the former head of the Fiat Auto group, is simply known as *l'Avvocato*

Double date? The cellular phone is the ultimate way to make a bella figura.

(the lawyer); Carlo De Benedetti, the former CEO of Olivetti, is *l'Ingegnere* (the engineer); and media tycoon Silvio Berlusconi is *il Cavaliere* (the knight). You, too, will be introduced as *professore, professoressa, dottore,* or *dottoressa,* depending on your university degree. If you speak Italian, any introductions you make should be done in the formal *Lei* tense. If you don't know when to use the *Lei* or the informal *tu* form, it's always better to err by being too formal. (Don't use the *voi* form like the French "vous," because that form became outdated with the defeat of fascism.) Many Italians don't mind if you use the informal form with them on the first encounter, but every once in a while you'll meet someone who makes an issue of it. I applied for a job with an Italian company and almost lost my shot at the position because I said "*Ciao*" instead of "*Arrivederci*" to my interviewer at the end. He responded to my too-friendly good-bye salute with an annoyed look and said I would be excused for my impudence because "Americans don't know any better."

Professional Meetings

Setting up a business meeting usually entails an initial contact followed by a lengthy courtship of faxes: faxes to set a time for the meeting, faxes to establish who will attend, and faxes to express how pleased everyone is to do business together (after the meeting, thank-you faxes are standard, too). When you send your faxes, make an effort to write them in Italian unless you determine that your Italian colleagues know English well. If they don't, you risk miscommunication and wasted time as they try to understand what you want. After the faxing stage, the courtship between business partners continues up until the actual meeting. In fact, it's quite acceptable to get together for a quick "get-to-know-each-other" coffee a few days before the official date.

A common stereotype about Italians is that they're always late and that the farther south you go, the greater the problem becomes. Some say that the reason Italians often carry a folded newspaper under their arm is because they know they will have to spend a good portion of their day waiting for others. Others suspect that being late is part of the *bella figura* culture because tardiness shows that a person is very busy and hence very important—so important that you are expected to wait for him or her. But this is a stereotype. Our experience shows not only that Italians are punctual—especially where business is concerned—but that they make an extra effort to be on time. In turn, they do not expect others to be late either.

When it comes to scheduling business meetings, never plan them for the month of August since the country goes on vacation during that month, though summer lethargy really starts in mid-July and lasts well into mid-September. Scheduling business meetings around the Christmas holidays isn't such a good idea either, and you should avoid the smaller holidays sprinkled throughout the year (for a list of them, see the Appendix).

Mixing Business with Lunch

Italian business lunches are designed more for eating than for business. I went to a business lunch in Trieste and put my notepad and pen on the table next to my plate, planning to take notes during the conversation. When my colleagues saw I intended to pay little attention to the meal, they refused to order until I had put my work tools back into my bag. Don't mistake a restaurant or buffet for a conference room. In fact, don't be surprised if the food itself is the only substantial topic of conversation. People say that food is one of the closest things to an Italian's heart, so if you enjoy your meal make sure to say so. But Italians also appreciate honesty, and if you falsely praise a dish that you can't stomach, they will see right through you. Contrary to myth, Italians do not eat a lot, and they don't drink more than one or two glasses of wine with lunch at most. Lunch and dinner are also sometimes followed by an *amaro* (bitter) or other liquor *digestivo,* but a strong *espresso* is more common. If it's not clear who will pay, do some insisting, but remember that your Italian host will probably want to treat you. In my experience, suggesting to divide a bill is generally looked on unfavorably. If you are paying, remember not to overtip. The *servizio* (tip) is usually included in the bill, but if it isn't you should never leave more than 10 percent as tip.

MAKING AN IMPRESSIVE PRESENTATION

The most important thing to remember when preparing a business presentation is the language barrier. Many Italians speak English well but would prefer to receive pamphlets, brochures, and product material in Italian. If an important presentation will be conducted in English, make sure you provide your Italian guests with translations and simultaneous interpreters. By doing so, you will ensure that the Italians will be able to participate in the presentation by asking questions. Often Italian managers pride themselves on being able to make their own presentations in English, at times spending hundreds of hours preparing with tutors. If you suspect this has occurred, offer praise where it is due since they will be happy to know you appreciate their efforts. When Americans dazzle them with presentation gadgets such as slides, light pointers, and multimedia shows, they love it. In general, traditional Italian presentations can be long-winded and lack American-style conference room joke telling and computer wizardry though this, too, is changing.

THE ART OF NEGOTIATING

"Getting down to business" in the efficient-minded, hard-nosed American way is often considered a bit abrupt in Italy. Therefore, you should let your hosts determine the pace of the negotiations and follow their lead. Don't worry, Italians get down to business, too—they just do it with a softer touch. Following an interlude of friendly conversation, you can expect a good dose of haggling. Negotiation is a highly appreciated and practiced craft in Italy, and participants like to make the process last, whether it be wrangling over price, terms, or delivery dates. Since most Italian companies are family-owned, don't be surprised if you find sisters, mothers, sons, and daughters joining you at the bargaining table. Remember that if there are two qualities Italians appreciate overall in business partners, they are honesty and trust. Never promise something you can't deliver, and if you have concerns during the negotiations, point them out immediately. For example, if you foresee delays in your shipping schedule or if your supply is on back order, say so up front.

There is a certain sense of ceremony to Italian business, and this is best demonstrated by the custom of exchanging small gifts when you close a deal, such as umbrellas or watches with a company's logo printed on them, coffee-table photography books, calendars at the end of the year, bottles of wines, or desserts. Gift giving is also common in professions such as politics and journalism, where it is strictly prohibited in the United States.

Entertaining for Work

Business and pleasure are two separate universes in Italy, and the concept of "business entertainment" is fundamentally oxymoronic to Italians. I attended an international economic conference on the island of Sardinia and noticed that during the extensive debate on economic theory only the Italians seemed to be focused and attentive. The Americans stared longingly out of the window, distracted by the blue water and sun-drenched beaches only a few yards away. When the conference closed, the Italians economists stripped down to their swimming trunks and headed straight to the beach, while the Americans stood apart and watched, awkward and restrained. In this case, the best advice is to shed your reservations and follow suit if you want to fit in.

CHAPTER EIGHTEEN

Working in the Public or Private Sector

Italian companies, American companies, international organizations, and the American government—these all make up the public and private sectors where Americans can find employment in Italy. Without a doubt, the best way to get work in any of these fields is to get hired from the United States and then be transferred to an Italian branch. This is usually what occurs when people work for the American government offices and military bases in Italy. However, some Americans have succeeded in soliciting—and obtaining—jobs in the public and private sectors once they have arrived. The advantage of doing it this way is that you are already present for interviews, and by interviewing you have a better chance of convincing potential employers you're worth the bureaucratic hassle involved in hiring you. Yet finding full-time, contracted work in either of these sectors is not easy, even for Italians. The fact that you are American makes it even more difficult because of legal issues regarding work permits, paperwork, and local labor laws. On top of it, you are competing not only with unemployed Italians but with non-Italian members of the European Union, who have legal advantages you do not.

If you are willing to renounce full-time, contracted work, you might consider pursuing freelance or part-time opportunities with the more than one hundred American, international, and Italian companies and organizations listed at the end of this chapter (note that these addresses do not include Italian public sector organizations since the opportunities with them often require citizenship, fluency in Italian, and excellent connections). Many companies prefer to test candidates' skills by hiring them first on a freelance basis, then later consider them for regular positions. In addition, freelancers cost companies less overall because they aren't paid the costly employee benefits required by Italian law, and the paperwork required for hiring them is much simpler. Eventually, once you get your foot in the door, you may hear of full-time openings that become available, or you may even be able to create them for yourself.

Italian Companies

The only reason for an Italian company to hire a foreigner over the many unemployed Italians knocking on their doors is if the foreigner brings a new skill to Italy, whether it be a technical or managerial skill. Being able to speak and write Italian is, of course, fundamental. One of the biggest advantages is that when an Italian company hires you it is generally for life. Italian employees enjoy near-indestructible job security with up to fourteen months of salary per year, extended paid sick days, free health care, and protection by labor laws that makes firing them impossible unless they really deserve it. In fact, Italy ranks below only Switzerland in terms of job security in Europe. So if you land a job with an Italian company, you may have found your golden egg. Be aware, though, that differences, including the language barrier, procedures for dealing with bureaucratic details, and a lack of technology can make it frustrating. The fact that you're not Italian might also mean that you cannot rise above a certain level in the company's hierarchy, especially if it's a family-run business. Nevertheless, it can be an exciting experience because you will be able to perform your routine professional duties in a new cultural dimension.

Many Italian companies are smaller family-owned and -run operations, making it difficult for an outsider to break in. But there are also many large corporations which operate on a national or international level. Some of the better-known names abroad include the chic fashion houses of Armani and Versace, the computer company Olivetti, and auto manufacturers such as Fiat and Alfa Romeo. Italian companies that have made a splash on the American market in more recent years include Barilla, known for its pasta, and Parmalat, the milk products manufacturer.

American Companies

If you are coming back to Italy after a few years of absence, you'll be shocked to find how American it has become. In fact, you may be startled even if you've never been there before. The once glamorous Via Veneto in Rome is where the newest Hard Rock Café will be located, and a Planet Hollywood restaurant has opened nearby. There is a Foot Locker store sandwiched between Italian fashion giants such as Gucci and Fendi on the super posh Via dei Condotti. The *autostrade* are lined with the golden arches of McDonald's and Midas muffler repair shops. Blockbuster Video, the American movie rental chain, currently averages a new store in Italy every ten days. In addition to renting movies, Blockbuster sells Haägen-Dazs ice cream and frozen pizzas in boxes. Toys 'R' Us stores have already started dotting the peninsula. Just about the only thing missing is the Starbucks coffee giant, but rumors are that it's on its way, too.

If you understand where foreign money is being invested, you'll have a better chance of finding work in the corporate offices of an American company in Italy. The overwhelming majority of U.S. companies make their base in the Italian north, especially around Milan. This is because they can easily find the services and infrastructure they need to operate, such as fast trains with connections to the rest of Europe. (The Italian north is also where much of the Italian money is because it has a denser population and therefore a larger tax base.) The country's most significant industries are based in Turin, Milan, and the Veneto region, and you'll have a better chance of finding a job there. But there are Americans in unexpected places. For example, the University of Pittsburgh just formed a joint venture with two local hospitals to open Europe's largest organ transplant center in the Sicilian city of Palermo. The transplant center will use both American and Italian doctors.

The bad news is that it is difficult to be hired by a U.S. company in Italy because Italian labor law prohibits foreign companies from hiring Americans for jobs unemployed Italians could fill. Most American employees are hired back home and then transferred abroad. If you're interested in working for an American company in Italy, you should first inquire with its U.S. headquarters. Americans already abroad are either hired for low-paying positions, such as salesclerks, or high-paying positions given only to specialists with outstanding qualifications in their sector; there are few opportunities in between. But you do have a good chance of getting hired if you have special technical or managerial skills no one else does. For example, I know of an American movie director who was hired to work on an Italian television program because the program was to be broadcast in the United States and the director was deemed an "expert" in American television. Apparently, no Italian director could claim the same.

The good news is that there are new growth sectors emerging in Italy, making for a positive investment climate. This will translate into new job opportunities for those who are qualified and know what to look for. A big emerging sector is technology and telecommunications. You should target U.S. companies that develop new technologies for use in Italy, from Internet providers to software designers. For example, Microsoft has an Italian branch in Milan. As the Italian telecom system is becoming privatized, phone companies such as Motorola and AT&T have their eyes on what will be a very profitable market. UPS has recently invested more than $1 billion in Europe, including Italy, to expand overnight delivery services. Other American couriers, such as Federal Express and DHL, are doing the same. Mail Boxes Etc. now has more than one hundred stores in Italy. This expansion of services also applies to financial services. As the Milan stock exchange grows, more American banks will be on hand to trade on it. Citibank is already there, and so are large American investment brokers, as well as some big American law, accounting, and insurance firms, which are opening offices in Italy for the increasing number of U.S. companies requiring their skills. The "big three" American carmakers—Chrysler, Ford, and General Motors—already have a presence in Italy. Most Italians still drive Fiats, but the Americans are making inroads into the Italian auto market as consumers want different sets of wheels. Finally, the retail market is booming. American and European chain stores such as the Gap, Toys 'R' Us, Guess, Ikea, the Body Shop, and other big chain stores with specialized merchandise, are creating a strong presence in the market.

The U.S. Government

In 1861, the poet and novelist William Dean Howells was made consul to Venice, the painter William J. Stillman consul to Rome. Back then it was normal for consulships to be given to artists or writers. Their "training" for the positions was far from political: Stillman had spent the summer in the Swiss Alps sketching pictures, and Howells had written a campaign biography of Abraham Lincoln. In Italy, two of their prime duties were to help women traveling alone and to keep diaries on local commerce and trade. In their free time, they made excursions around the peninsula that became the basis of their art and writing. It was quite the life for a government employee.

Today, too, there are a few things that make working for the U.S. government stand out from other employment options in Italy. One is job security: you usually have an employment contract that lasts one or two years, and many of your living expenses are paid for. Another is that your salary is paid in dollars, which means that when you return to the United States, any savings you have won't immediately depreciate because of the lire-dollar exchange rate. Plus, by working for Uncle Sam, you are surrounded by Americans and American things at all times, such as traditional holiday celebrations and movies in English. If you're on a military base, you can buy American food and products at the base grocery stores, or commissaries. Your children can attend American schools and easily make the transition back to schools in the States when you return.

While you may be attracted to this employment possibility, you should be aware that there aren't many positions available each year. For example, the base in Aviano near Venice covers 1,500 acres of land and has 3,800 active personnel, but most of the employees are either spouses of Air Force officers or Italians (for whom there are quotas). However, there are sometimes positions open with the embassy, consulates, military bases, and cultural exchange programs. The most realistic possibilities are the civilian and academic positions at the military base schools, and Foreign Service careers. To find out about other positions that do open up occasionally, contact the Employment Information Office in Washington, D.C., for the latest updates.

THE FOREIGN SERVICE

It takes years of special education and training before you can make it to an Italian assignment with the Foreign Service. Once there, there's no saying you won't be shipped off to some other destination across the sea. In fact, one of the application requirements for the Foreign Service is that you are willing from the start to go anywhere it sends you. There are two categories of Foreign Service employees: Foreign Service officers and Foreign Service specialists. For both you must be a U.S. citizen and at least twenty years old. Both are governed by the Department of State, but working in the service doesn't necessarily mean working for that department: overseas careers with the service include jobs with the Agency for International Development, the Department of Agriculture, the Foreign Agriculture Service, the U.S. and Foreign Commercial Service, and the United States Information Agency (which is described separately). Each of these agencies has its own application requirements and procedures. The Department of State also sponsors the Woodrow Wilson National Fellowship Program to prepare students for Foreign Service careers by earning a master's degree and completing special professional preparation.

There are different kinds of Foreign Service officers, who are skilled in the following disciplines: administration, commerce, consular affairs, economics, information and cultural affairs, and politics. In order to be eligible for any of these positions, you must pass multiple screenings, an oral assessment, and a written examination. Foreign Service specialists have top security clearance and occupy more technical or administrative support positions. These positions include information management specialists, physicians, nurse practitioners, diplomatic security officers, financial management officers, personnel officers, psychiatrists, and administrative assistants, among others. You can't be more than fifty-nine years old when you begin your job or more than thirty-five years old if you want to be a diplomatic security officer. Generally, the application process also requires completing writing exercises, interviews about current events and the U.S. government, and technical questions regarding your specialization. In addition, you will have to obtain some degree of security clearance.

THE U.S. EMBASSY AND CONSULATES

The embassy in Rome is supported by three consulates in Naples, Florence, and Milan, as well as consular agents in Genoa, Palermo, and Trieste. Due to general downsizing, in 1995 the State Department proposed to close its consulate in Florence. Italian Americans and overseas residents, for whom the consulates represent one of the few familiar reference points they have, complained so loudly that it was allowed to stay open, for now. Some of the more routine embassy tasks include renewing passports, helping nationals in trouble, and issuing visas to foreign citizens. Many of the employees are Italian, and the Americans are generally part of the Foreign Service who have been sent from the United States. There are, however, occasionally lower-level positions posted at the consulates for which local American residents can apply. To increase your qualifications for getting a job with a consulate or embassy, focus on improving your fluency in Italian and your knowledge of international politics, economics, and culture. The more specialized you are in a given field, the greater chance you have of being hired.

THE UNITED STATES INFORMATION AGENCY

The United States Information Agency, or USIA (called the United States Information Service or USIS overseas), is a state-run organization that handles the government's overseas exchange of information, education, and culture. Its programs include the Fulbright Scholarship, which funds American students and researchers overseas, and the U.S. Speakers Program, which sends Americans to speak about specialized topics in other countries. It has offices in Milan, Rome, Naples, and Palermo. Their primary function is to organize student exchanges and provide information about the United States to Italians. They regularly sponsor conferences with American speakers to talk about American culture, ideas, and politics to an Italian audience. Most of the USIA overseas jobs are filled by people in the Foreign Service, but you can apply locally through the American Embassy or Consulate to work in one of the USIS offices.

THE ARMED FORCES: MILITARY BASES AND DoDD SCHOOLS

There are seven U.S. Air Force, Army, and Navy bases in Italy, located in Aviano, Livorno (Camp Darby), Naples, San Vito (Brindisi), Sigonella (Sicily), Vicenza, and La Madalena (Sardinia). Many of the bases opened during World War II to keep an eye on the Communists and the Middle Eastern oil fields. In 1993, the base in Aviano became a key figure in the Bosnia peacekeeping mission, housing the F-117 Stealth bomber planes. The North Atlantic Treaty Organization (NATO) used it and other Italian bases extensively to help maintain the "no-fly" zones over the ex-Yugoslavia. Since 1946, the Department of Defense has operated elementary and secondary schools on its overseas military bases, called "Department of Defense Dependents Schools" or simply "DoDDS." In general, only children of U.S. military and civilian personnel can attend these schools. However, American citizens, employees of other U.S. government agencies, and employees of international organizations such as NATO may also enroll their children, space permitting. Italy falls into the Mediterranean Region of the schools and has DoDDS in the following locations: Aviano (K–12), La Madalena (K–8), Livorno (K–12, as well as some college-level courses), Naples (K–12), Sigonella (K–12), and Vicenza (K–12). There is also a DoDD school in Verona (K–8) although there isn't a base there.

Each of these schools hires both teachers and other academic staff members (e.g., counselors), as well as general administrative personnel. Most positions are full-time, although part-time ones are occasionally available. Available positions include ones for teachers, training instructors in hands-on topics such as welding, student services (e.g., dorm counselors and guidance counselors), and support positions (e.g., nurses and reading improvement tutors). Each one usually requires a commitment of one or two school years. The salary is based on your educational degree and professional training. In 1997, the annual salary for a starting position was almost $25,000. In general, you also receive housing, medical insurance, and sometimes moving expenses. The hiring of teachers is done both through the DoDDS headquarters in Washington, D.C., and locally in Italy; the hiring of civilian personnel takes place only in Italy. The U.S. office says that your chances of getting a position are much higher if you apply directly to a school when you are already living in the vicinity (it sends only approximately ten teachers from the United States per year). However, if you apply from the United States, you must be willing to accept placement anywhere in the world and therefore may end up far from the Italian shores. Formal recruiting begins more than one school year in advance, and interviews generally take place in March and April. If you are accepted, you start your assignment in August.

Working at a DoDD school requires years of careful preparation. Aside from the basic requirement of U.S. citizenship, a bachelor's degree is necessary. Some positions require a master's degree or other graduate work as well. Specialized positions, such as nursing, require past experience in your field. If you want to teach, you must have teaching experience with an approved teacher education program at an accredited U.S. institution and course work in the field of professional teacher education. If you don't satisfy all of these requirements, concessions are sometimes made. For example, there are some positions (e.g., teachers of music, art, and physical education) for which state-approved certification programs can replace other academic requirements. All applicants must take the National Teacher Examination (NTE).

International Governmental Organizations

The United Nations has several organizations in Italy, almost all of them based in Rome. These include the Food and Agriculture Organization (FAO), the World Food Programme (WFP), the International Fund for Agricultural Development (IFAD), the International Plant Genetic Resources Institute (IPGRI), and the International Center for the Study of the Preservation and the Restoration of Cultural Property (ICCROM).

By far the largest of these is the FAO, with about 3,000 international employees in its Rome office. Although the FAO froze hiring of support staff about two years ago because of general cutbacks and the United Nations' decision to decentralize personnel by moving employees from its Rome headquarters to smaller offices worldwide, the FAO recruitment office does post about 100 job openings each year for what they call "high professional positions." That means positions for people specialized in certain areas of interest to the FAO, such as agriculture, forestry, fishery, and nutrition. All of these positions are listed on their Web site at www.fao.org. In fact, if you are interested in working for the FAO and qualify for a "high professional position," you should specifically apply for one of the job posts listed on the Web site rather than send in a general application. The FAO's recruitment staff receives so many applications each year it cannot process them all and responds only to those aimed at particular posts. Recent job opportunities have included positions for a fishery officer, an expert in agricultural policy, and a manager in plant protection services. Most positions also require that you speak at least two languages which must include English, French, Spanish, or Italian. Expect the application process to last several months.

Other international organizations accept general applications for posts in their Rome headquarters when openings become available. Because they are smaller than the FAO, they also sometimes advertise positions locally in the English-language *Wanted in Rome* magazine. For example, IPGRI, an organization that studies plant genetics and used to be part of the FAO, regularly advertises job openings for computer programmers. WFP deals with agricultural issues and food distribution and hires both for supporting staff positions and specialized professionals (WFP has about 700 employees and IFAD, which deals with similar issues, has about 400 in their Rome offices). ICCROM, which is dedicated to the conservation of historical sights, has about 35 full-time employees but rarely has job openings. It does, however, hire professionals specialized in a few specific areas for special projects. These include architecture, art restoration, paper restoration, painting, and sciences.

Useful Addresses

CORPORATE HEADQUARTERS OF THE
LARGEST ITALIAN COMPANIES

(*Note:* Some of these have offices throughout Italy.)

BELLUNO:

Luxottica Group
Ioc. Valcozzena, 10
32021 Agordo (Belluno)
tel (0437) 62641
fax (0437) 63223
(eyewear)

MILAN:

AGIP
Via Emilia, 1
20097 S. Donato Milanese (MI)
tel (02) 5201
fax (02) 52061819
(petrol/energy)

Alfa Romeo
Centro Direzionale
20020 Arese (MI)
tel (02) 93928111
fax (02) 9315746
(cars)

Banca Commerciale Italiana
Piazza della Scala, 6
20121 Milano
tel (02) 88501
fax (02) 88503026
(bank)

Ciga Hotels
Piazza della Repubblica, 32
20124 Milano

tel (02) 6266001
fax (02) 6266210
(hotel chain)

Feltrinelli Editore
Via Andegari, 6
20121 Milano
tel (02) 86463485
fax (02) 72001064
(publishing)

Ferruzzi-Montedison
Piazzetta Bossi, 3
20121 Milano
tel (02) 62705812
fax (02) 62705268
(finance)

Fininvest
Via Paleocapa, 3
20121 Milano
tel (02) 85411
fax (02) 85414283
(media and communications)

Fiorucci
Galleria Passarella, 2
20122 Milano
tel (02) 76021811
fax (02) 76005415
(clothing and accessories)

Gemina
Via Turati, 16/18
20121 Milano
tel (02) 63791
fax (02) 6379414
(finance)

Giorgio Armani
Via Borgo Nuovo, 11
20121 Milano
tel (02) 72318
fax (02) 72318453
(clothing and accessories)
Mediaset
Via Paleocapa, 3
20121 Milano
tel (02) 85411
fax (02) 85414283
(media and television)
Mondadori
Gruppo Mondadori
Via Anauldo, 1
20090 Segrate (Milano)
tel (02) 75421
fax (02) 75423020
(publishing)
Pirelli
Viale Sarca, 222
20126 Milano
tel (02) 64421
fax (02) 64423300
(tires)
RAS Gruppo
Corso Italia, 23
20122 Milano
tel (02) 72161
fax (02) 72162174
(insurance)
RCS Gruppo
Rizzoli Corriere della Sera
Via Angelo Rizzoli, 2
20132 Milano
tel (02) 2588
fax (02) 27201485
(publishing)
Versace
Via Manzoni, 38
20121 Milano
tel (02) 760931
fax (02) 76004122
(clothing and accessories)
NOVARA:
De Agostini
Via Giovanni da Verrazano, 15
28100 Novara

tel (0321) 4241
fax (0321) 471286
(publishing)
PARMA:
Barilla G. e R. Fratelli
Via Mantova, 166
43100 Parma
tel (0521) 2621
fax (0521) 270621
(pasta and pasta sauces)
PISA:
Piaggio Veicoli Europei
Viale Rinaldo Piaggio, 23
56025 Pontedera (Pisa)
tel (0587) 2725489
fax (0587) 290906
(mopeds and scooters)
ROME:
Alitalia
Via A. Marchetti, 111
00148 Roma
tel (06) 65621
fax (06) 65624707
(airline)
Banca d'Italia
Via Nazionale, 91
00184 Roma
tel (06) 47921
fax (06) 47922253
(bank)
Banca Nazionale del Lavoro
Via Vittorio Veneto, 119
00187 Roma
tel (06) 47021
fax (06) 47026469
(bank)
Cecchi Gori Group
Via Valadier, 42
00193 Roma
tel (06) 324721
fax (06) 32472300
(cinema and TV)
Confindustria
Viale dell'Astronomia, 30
00144 Roma
tel (06) 59031
fax (06) 5919615
(association for industry)

ENI
Piazzale E. Mattei, 1
00144 Roma
tel (06) 59821
fax (06) 59822141
(petrol/energy)
Esso Italiana
Viale Castello della Magliana, 25
00148 Roma
tel (06) 59951
fax (06) 59952956
(petrol/energy)
Fendi
Via Cornelia, 498
00166 Roma
tel (06) 614101
fax (06) 6246838
(clothing and accessories)
Ferrovie dello Stato
Piazza della Croce Rossa, 1
00161 Roma
tel (06) 84901
fax (06) 44241539
(trains)
Gruppo L'Espresso
Via Po, 12
00198 Roma
tel (06) 84781
fax (06) 8845603
(publishing)
INA-Assitalia
Istituto Nazionale delle Assicurazioni
Via Sallustiana, 51
00187 Roma
tel (06) 47221
fax (06) 47224465
(insurance)
Istituto per la Ricostruzione Industriale (IRI)
Via Vittorio Veneto, 89
00187 Roma
tel (06) 47271
fax (06) 47272308
(finance)
Radiotelevisione Italiana (RAI)
Viale Mazzini, 14
00195 Roma

tel (06) 3878
fax (06) 3725680
(radio and television)
Telecom Italia
Via Flaminia, 189
00196 Roma
tel (06) 36881
fax (06) 36882965
(telecommunications)
TREVISO:
Benetton Group
Via Villa Minelli, 1
31050 Ponzano Veneto (TV)
tel (0422) 4491
fax (0422) 969501
(clothing and accessories)
TURIN:
Fiat Auto
Corso Agnelli, 200
10135 Torino
tel (011) 6831111
fax (011) 6837591
(cars)
Iveco
Via Puglia, 35
10156 Torino
tel (011) 6872111
fax (011) 6874555
(cars)
Lavazza
Corso Novara, 59
10154 Torino
tel (011) 23981
fax (011) 2398324
(coffee)
Olivetti
Via Jervis, 77
10015 Ivrea (Torino)
tel (0125) 522639
fax (0125) 526220
(computers)
Pininfarina
Via Lesna, 78/80
10095 Grugliasco (Torino)
tel (011) 70911
fax (011) 700819
(automobile design)

(*Note:* A few of the companies listed below are not American, but all the companies and distributors have a large presence in both Italy and the United States. Many have offices in various Italian cities.)

AQUILA:

Texas Instruments Italia
Via Pacinotti, 5/7
67051 Avezzano (AQ)
tel (0863) 4231
fax (0863) 412763

BERGAMO:

Philco Italia
Via Marconi, 14/22
24030 Brembate di Sopra
(Bergamo)
tel (035) 608111
fax (035) 610594

CATANIA:

Cyanamid Italia
Via Franco Gorgone Zona
Industriale
95121 Catania
tel (095) 598111
fax (095) 7180134

COMO:

Avon Cosmetics
Via Venticinque Aprile, 15
22077 Olgiate Comasco (CO)
tel (031) 998111
fax (031) 998312

FLORENCE:

Pentax
Via A. Righi, 63
50010 Osmannoro (Firenze)
tel (055) 32851
fax (055) 308187

Ricoh
Via A. Righi, 63
50010 Osmannoro (Firenze)
tel (055) 32851
fax (055) 308187

LATINA:

Abbott
S. S. Pontina, 148 Km 52
Campoverde

04011 Aprilia (LT)
tel (06) 928921
fax (06) 9253193

MILAN:

A. C. Nielsen Italia
Via G. di Vittorio, 10
20094 Corsico (MI)
tel (02) 451971
fax (02) 45866235

Agfa
Via Grosio, 10/4
20151 Milano
tel (02) 30741
fax (02) 38000229

Apple Computer
Via Milano, 150
20093 Cologno Monzese (MI)
tel (02) 273261
fax (02) 27326555

AT&T Global Information Solutions Italia
Viale Cassala, 22
20143 Milano
tel (02) 581601
fax (02) 58160291

Bankers Trust Finanziaria
Via Turati, 16/18
20121 Milano
tel (02) 63691
fax (02) 6369334

Bayer
Viale Certosa, 126
20156 Milano
tel (02) 39781
fax (02) 39782896

Black & Decker Italia
Viale Elvezia, 2
20052 Monza (MI)
tel (039) 23871
fax (039) 2301447

Blockbuster Video Italia
Via Cola Montano, 33
20159 Milano
tel (02) 696131
fax (02) 69613500

The Boston Consulting Group
Via della Moscova, 18
20123 Milano

tel (02) 655991
fax (02) 65599655
Braun Italia
Via G. di Vittorio, 10
20094 Corsico (MI)
tel (02) 451701
fax (02) 45101480
Bridgestone-Firestone Italia
Centro Direzionale Colleoni
Pal. Taurus A3, Scala 2
Viale Colleoni, 3
20041 Agrate Brianza (MI)
tel (039) 656011
fax (039) 6899637
Buena Vista Home Entertainment
Via S. Sandri, 1
20121 Milano
tel (02) 290851
fax (02) 29085650
Business Software Alliance
Via Brera, 6
20121 Milano
tel (02) 8690419
fax (02) 86463892
Calvin Klein Europe
Via Montenapoleone, 29
20121 Milano
tel (02) 762091
fax (02) 76209201
Canon Italia
Via Mecenate, 90
20138 Milano
tel (02) 50921
fax (02) 58013296
Chrysler
Viale Certosa, 211
20151 Milano
tel (02) 380941
fax (02) 3085425
Citibank
Foro Buonaparte, 16
20121 Milano
tel (02) 864741
fax (02) 86474407
Coca-Cola Italia
Galleria Passarella, 1
20122 Milano
tel (02) 760971
fax (02) 76014428

Compaq Computer
Milanofiori Strada 7, Palazzo R
20089 Rozzano (MI)
tel (02) 575901
fax (02) 57500686
Condé Nast Edizioni
Piazza Castello, 27
20121 Milano
tel (02) 85611
fax (02) 8055716
Del Monte Foods Sud Europa
Via Grandi, 5
20060 Liscate (MI)
tel (02) 951281
fax (02) 9587961
DHL International
Viale Milanofiori, Strada 5
Palazzo U/3
20089 Rozzano (MI)
tel (02) 575721
fax (02) 89208099
Dow Italia (Dow Corning)
Via Patroclo, 21
20151 Milano
tel (02) 48221
fax (02) 48224366
Du Pont de Nemours Italiana
Via Volta, 16
20093 Cologno Monzese (MI)
tel (02) 253021
fax (02) 2547765
Elizabeth Arden
Via Aurelio Saffi, 28
20123 Milano
tel (02) 480621
fax (02) 48011735
Exxon Chemicals Mediterranea
Via Paleocapa, 7
20121 Milano
tel (02) 88031
fax (02) 8803231
Federal Express Italia
Palazzo Tintoretto
Via Cassanese, 224
20090 Segrate (MI)
tel (02) 21881
fax (02) 2188230
General Electric Plastics Italia
Via Brianza, 181

20092 Cinisello Balsamo (MI)
tel (02) 618341
fax (02) 61834211
Grace Italiana
Via Trento, 7
Passirana
20017 Rho (MI)
tel (02) 93321
fax (02) 9332555
Harley-Davidson
Viale delle Industrie, 10/17
20020 Arese (MI)
tel (02) 93582000
fax (02) 93581922
Hewlett-Packard Italiana
Via Giuseppe di Vittorio, 9
20063 Cernusco
sul Naviglio (Milano)
tel (02) 92121
fax (02) 92104473
Honeywell
Via P. Gobetti, 2/B
20063 Cernusco sul Naviglio (MI)
tel (02) 921461
fax (02) 92146888
IBM
IBM Semea
Circovalazione Idroscalo
20090 Segrate (Milano)
tel (02) 59621
fax (02) 59625937
Ingersoll-Rand Italiana
Strada Provinciale Cassanese
20060 Vignate (MI)
tel (02) 95056220
fax (02) 95056315
Intel Corporation Italia
Milanofiori Palazzo E/4
20094 Assago (MI)
tel (02) 575441
fax (02) 57501221
Johnson Wax
Piazza M. Burke, 3
20020 Arese (MI)
tel (02) 93371
fax (02) 9337399
JVC Professional Products Italia
Via Pannunzio, 4
20156 Milano

tel (02) 380501
fax (02) 33402391
Kellogg Italia
Centro Direzionale Colleoni
Palazzo Perseo, 2
20041 Agrate Brianza (MI)
tel (039) 66571
fax (039) 6657600
Kodak
Viale Matteotti, 62
20092 Cinisello Balsamo (MI)
tel (02) 660281
fax (02) 66010168
Kraft
Via Pola, 11
20124 Milano
tel (02) 69541
fax (02) 6888548
Levi Strauss Italia
Corso Como, 15
20154 Milano
tel (02) 290231
fax (02) 29003681
Mail Boxes Etc.
Piazza IV Novembre, 1
20124 Milano
tel (02) 6692661
fax (02) 6692928
McDonald's
Via Batistotti Sassi, 11/A
20133 Milano
tel (02) 748181
fax (02) 74818404
Microsoft
Centro Direzionale San Felice
Via Rivoltana, 13
Palazzo A
20090 Segrate (MI)
tel (02) 703921
fax (02) 70392020
Motorola
Centro Milanofiori, Strada 2
Palazzo OC/2
20090 Assago (MI)
tel (02) 82204
fax (02) 8220240
MTV Networks
Corso Europa, 7
20122 Milano

tel (02) 7621171
fax (02) 762117227
Nestlé Italiana
Viale Giulio Richard, 5
20143 Milano
tel (02) 81811
fax (02) 89123400
Panasonic Italia
Via Lucini, 19
20125 Milano
tel (02) 67881
fax (02) 6704895
PepsiCo Foods and Beverages International
Via Dante, 7
20123 Milano
tel (02) 724211
fax (02) 72421200
Philips
Piazza Quattro Novembre, 3
20124 Milano
tel (02) 67521
fax (02) 67522165
Pioneer Electronics Italia
Via G. Fantoli, 17
20138 Milano
tel (02) 50741
fax (02) 58012181
Polygram Italia
Via Carlo Tenca, 2
20124 Milano
tel (02) 67961
fax (02) 6796201
Purina Italia
Via dei Tulipani, 1
Palazzo A
20090 Pieve Emanuele (Milano)
tel (02) 904601
fax (02) 90782747
Rank Xerox
Direzione Generale
Strada Padana Superiore, 28
20063 Cernusco sul Naviglio (MI)
tel (02) 921881
fax (02) 92188209
Ray Ban (Bausch & Lomb)
Via Pasubio, 34
20050 Macherio (MI)

tel (039) 20731
fax (039) 2010081
Samsonite Italia
Via Enrico de Nicola, 18
20090 Cesano
Boscone (MI)
tel (02) 45860000
fax (02) 45869865
Seagram Italia
Centro Direzionale Milano 2
Palazzo Donatello
20090 Segrate (Milano)
Segrate (MI)
tel (02) 21261
fax (02) 26411903
Shell Italia
Viale Francesco Restelli, 1/A
20124 Milano
tel (02) 69861
fax (02) 6986411
Sony Music Entertainment Italy
Via Amedei, 9
20123 Milano
tel (02) 8536
fax (02) 860175
Sperling et Kupfer Editori
Via Borgonuovo, 24
20121 Milano
tel (02) 290341
fax (02) 6590290
Texaco Italiana
Via C. Farini, 81
20123 Milano
tel (02) 97255498
fax (02) 97255497
3M Italia
Via S. Bovio 1/3
San Felice
20090 Segrate (MI)
tel (02) 70351
fax (02) 70353090
Timberland Italia
Via Colleoni, 17
Palazzo Orione p. 8
20041 Agrate Brianza (MI)
tel (039) 68431
fax (039) 6899470

Time-Life International
Corso Vittorio Emanuele, II
20123 Milano
tel/fax (02) 76001222

Twentieth Century Fox Home Entertainment
Piazza Fontana, 6
20122 Milano
tel (02) 723251
fax (02) 8051371

Unisys Italia
Via Benigno Crespi, 57
20159 Milano
tel (02) 69851
fax (02) 6985588

United Airlines
Via Orefici, 2
20123 Milano
tel (02) 864831
fax (02) 72004030

Universal Music (formally MCA Music)
Corso G. Matteotti, 3
20121 Milano
tel (02) 760321
fax (02) 76032502

Upjohn
Via Robert Koch 1.2
20152 Milano
tel (02) 48381
fax (02) 48382734

UPS—United Parcel Service
Via Fantoli, 15/2
20138 Milano
tel (02) 50791
fax (02) 55400180

Virgin Music Italy
Via Porpora, 26
20131 Milano
tel (02) 29518305
fax (02) 29517891

Walt Disney Company Italia
Via Sandro Sandri, 1
20121 Milano
tel (02) 290851
fax (02) 6571423

Warner Entertainment Italia
Via U. Foscolo, 1
20121 Milano

tel (02) 721281
fax (02) 72128200

NAPLES:

Delta
Via Fratelli Cervi, 21
81030 Parete (CE)
tel (081) 5030251
fax (081) 5036028

NOVARA:

Mattel Toys
Via Vittorio Veneto, 119
28040 Oleggio Castello (NO)
tel (0322) 231311
fax (0322) 45842

REGGIO EMILIA:

Nike Italy
Via dell'Eronautica, 22
42100 Reggio Emilia
tel (0522) 929911
fax (0522) 921377

ROME:

American Express Company
Largo Caduti di El Alamein, 9
00173 Roma
tel (06) 722801
fax (06) 7222303

The Body Shop
Via del Corso, 168
00187 Roma
tel (06) 9069864
fax (06) 9069897

Bristol Myers–Squibb
Via Paolo di Dono, 73
00143 Roma
tel (06) 503961
fax (06) 50396523

Chiquita Italia
Via Tempio del Cielo, 3
00144 Roma
tel (06) 520831
fax (06) 5295499

Colgate-Palmolive
Via Giorgione, 59/63
00147 Roma
tel (06) 549061
fax (06) 54906351

Columbia TriStar Films Italia
Via Palestro, 24

00185 Roma
tel (06) 4941196
fax (06) 4469936
Ford Italia
Via Andrea Argoli, 54
00143 Roma
tel (06) 518551
fax (06) 51962349
GE Information Services
Via A. Vivaldi, 9
00199 Roma
tel (06) 86218661
fax (06) 86217909
General Motors Italia
Piazzale dell'Industria, 40
00144 Roma
tel (06) 5919750
fax (06) 5919751
Goodyear Italiana
Piazza Marconi, 25
00144 Roma
tel (06) 543901
fax (06) 54390231
Johnson & Johnson
Via Ardeatina, km. 23,500
00040 Santa Palomba, Pomezia (Roma)
tel (06) 910961
fax (06) 9194229
Litton Italia
Via Pontina, km. 27,800
00040 Pomezia (Roma)
tel (06) 911921
fax (06) 9122517
Mobil Oil Italiana
Via Vitaliano Brancati, 60
00144 Roma
tel (06) 502801
fax (06) 50280290
Pfizer Italiana
Via Valbiondone, 113
00188 Roma
tel (06) 331821
fax (06) 33626019
Philip Morris Corporate
Via del Pozzetto, 122
00187 Roma
tel (06) 69940673
fax (06) 6792129

Procter & Gamble Italia
Viale Cesare Pavese, 385
00144 Roma
tel (06) 500901
fax (06) 5011881
Revlon
Via Appia Nuova, 43/45
00043 Ciampino (Roma)
tel (06) 794931
fax (06) 79340458
TWA—Trans World Airlines
Via Barberini, 67
00187 Roma
tel (06) 47241
fax (06) 4746125
Twentieth Century Fox Italy
Largo Amilcare Ponchielli, 6
00198 Roma
tel (06) 85301030
fax (06) 85300971
United International Pictures
Via Bissolati, 20
00187 Roma
tel (06) 4820626
fax (06) 4820628
TREVISO:
Quaker Chiari & Forti
Via Cendon, 20
31057 Silea (TV)
tel (0422) 4631
fax (0422) 460420
TURIN:
Beloit Italia
Via Martiri del XXI, 76
10064 Pinerolo (TO)
tel (0121) 2311
fax (0121) 397637
Foot Locker
Via San Quintino, 28
10121 Torino
tel (011) 5625522
fax (011) 5628612
Nikon
Via Tabacchi, 33
10132 Torino
tel (011) 3102151
fax (011) 899622

Scott
Via della Rocca, 49
10123 Torino
tel (011) 88141
fax (011) 889120
VARESE:
Gillette Group Italy (Division Oral B)
Via Beato Angelico, 1
21047 Saronno (VA)
tel (02) 96702903
fax (02) 9620943
Ilford Anitec
C.P. 77
21047 Saronno (Varese)
tel (02) 967631
fax (02) 96701158
Polaroid Italia
Via Piave, 11
21051 Arcisate (Varese)
tel (0332) 470031
fax (0332) 478249
Whirlpool Europe
Viale Guido Borghi, 27
21025 Comerio (Varese)
tel (0332) 759111
fax (0332) 759347

THE U.S. GOVERNMENT

GENERAL INFORMATION AND
APPLICATIONS FOR JOBS WITH THE
FEDERAL GOVERNMENT

Employment Information Office
Office of Personnel Management
1900 E Street, N.W., Room 1416
Washington, DC 20415
tel (202) 606-2700
fax (202) 606-5049

FOREIGN SERVICE JOBS

U.S. Department of State
Employment Information Service
Recruitment Division
P.O. Box 9317
Arlington, VA 22219
tel (703) 875-7490
www.state.gov, then pick "careers"

Brochures and application forms:
Foreign Service Written Examination
P.O. Box 9317
Arlington, VA 22219
tel (703) 875-7490
Fellowships:
**The Woodrow Wilson National
Fellowship Foundation**
Foreign Affairs Fellowship Program
P.O. Box 2437
Princeton, NJ 08543-2437
tel (609) 452-7007
fax (609) 452-0066

UNITED STATES INFORMATION
AGENCY (USIA)

Office of Public Liaison
301 Fourth Street, S.W.
Washington, DC 20547
tel (202) 619-4355
(general information and applications)
fax (202) 619-6988
www.usis.it

DEPARTMENT OF DEFENSE
DEPENDENTS SCHOOLS

(*Note:* For information about teaching
at a DoDDS write to "Teacher Recruitment Section.")
**Department of Defense Dependent
Schools**
4040 North Fairfax Drive
Arlington, VA 22203-1634
tel (703) 696-3269
DODD SCHOOLS IN ITALY:
Aviano American Dependent Schools
Aviano Base
(ages 5–18)
tel (0434) 667233/667266
(elementary school)
tel (0434) 667283/667364
(middle school)
tel (0434) 667256/667287
(high school)
Livorno Unit School
Camp Darby
56018 Tirrenia (Pisa)

tel (050) 547111 (main switchboard)
tel (050) 547058 (elementary school)
tel (050) 547573 (high school)
The Naples High School
Via Scarfoglio, Palazzo AMM 21
80125 Agnano (Napoli)
tel (081) 7241110 (main switchboard)
tel (081) 7244350/7244380 (school)
The Naples Elementary School
Viale delle Acacie, Villaggio Coppola,
Pinetamare
81030 Castelvolturno (Napoli)
tel (081) 5093422
(ages 4–12)
U.S. Navy Base
Contrada Sigonella (CT)
95100 Catania, Sicilia
tel (095) 861112 (main switchboard)
tel (095) 564211 (schools)
Scuola Americana
Lunga Adige Altiraglio, 48
37025 Parona (Verona)
tel (045) 942203
fax (045) 941867
Vicenza Military Base
Via della Pace
Caserma Ederly
36100 Vicenza
tel (0444) 517111 (switchboard)
tel (0444) 517710 (school)
American Elementary School
PSC 816 Box 1755
FPOAE 09612
La Madalena (Sardinia)
tel (0789) 738294 (main switchboard)
tel (0789) 798209 (school)

INTERNATIONAL ORGANIZATIONS IN ITALY

**Food and Agriculture Organization of
the United Nations (FAO)**
Viale delle Terme di Caracalla
00100 Roma
tel (06) 52251
fax (06) 52253152
www.fao.org

World Food Programme (WFP)
Via Cristoforo Colombo, 426
00145 Roma
tel (06) 522821
fax (06) 59602111
www.wfp.org

**The International Plant Genetic Re-
sources Institute (IPGRI)**
Via delle Sette Chiese, 142
00145 Roma
tel (06) 518921
fax (06) 5750309
www.cgiar.org/ipgri

**International Center for the Study of
the Preservation and the Restoration of
Cultural Property (ICCROM)**
Via di San Michele, 13
00153 Roma
tel (06) 585531
fax (06) 58553349

**International Fund for Agricultural
Development (IFAD)**
Via del Serafico, 107
00142 Roma
tel (06) 54591
fax (06) 5043463
www.unicc.org/IFAD

CHAPTER NINETEEN

Teaching

Of all the jobs available to Americans in Italy, teaching is by far one of the most popular and accessible. However, in most cases you can arrange a position only once you've arrived. Teaching does not have to be limited to teaching English but can include other subjects taught in English, such as physical education at an American elementary school or marketing at a local college. A word of advice: teaching is a good way to earn a living—pay for rent, food, movies, and short weekend trips—but it is *not* a good way to get rich. This is true for both contracted positions (e.g., in the American overseas schools) and positions without contracts (e.g., in most private language institutes).

Teaching English

There are two kinds of English taught in Italy: English and ESL/EFL. When you teach "English," your students are other native English speakers (such as Americans at the American overseas schools) or foreigners fluent in the language (such as English literature students at an Italian university). When you teach ESL (English as a Second Language) or EFL (English as a Foreign Language), your students are Italians who are not fluent and often are encountering the English language for the first time. They study English the way we study French or Spanish in high school. There are many more ESL/EFL teaching opportunities available than "English" positions. Although English is taught in public and private Italian schools—students must pass rigorous exams that test their knowledge not only of grammar and vocabulary but of British/American history and culture—the emphasis is almost exclusively on grammar and not conversation.

There are six basic elements of teaching ESL/EFL: conversation, grammar, reading, listening comprehension, vocabulary, and writing. Each must be developed simultaneously and to varying degrees, depending on the level of the course. When you're in Italy, you'll want to go to one of the bookstores listed in Chapter 15. Some of the larger ones, especially Feltrinelli International, have entire ESL sections. They carry textbooks, grammars, picture dictionaries, and storybooks designed specifically for Italian students. In the United States, most college bookstores don't display ESL textbooks but do carry them; you can find them by searching for texts for specific ESL courses being taught. You may also want to contact publishers directly to request their catalogs.

When it comes to what kind of English you speak (British or American), some Italian students want an American teacher and won't settle for less; others say British English is the official language and American is a dialect. British English should be taught differently because it is different, including vocabulary ("lift" instead of "elevator"), grammar ("Have you got . . . ?" instead of "Do you have . . . ?") spelling ("colour" instead of "color"), idioms, and pronunciation. Because you may find yourself teaching with British texts, it's important to master these differences.

GETTING CERTIFIED

Many of the more prominent schools in Italy do require some kind of teacher certification, especially if you have only a high school diploma or a bachelor's degree. However, if you have a master's degree in English or some related subject, or if you already have solid teaching experience, they will often waive this requirement. If you are interested in obtaining a teaching certificate or degree in the United States, the most generic are the TEFL/TESL (teaching English as a foreign/second language) certificates, and the Royal Society of Arts/ University of Cambridge Certificate in Teaching English as a Foreign Language to Adults (also called the RSA/Cambridge CTEFLA). Do not confuse these with the "TOEFL" exam, which tests the English-language competency of foreign students. Most of the certificate programs take the form of intensive courses that last one to two months. Many require that you already have a B.A. or B.S. degree, and some also require foreign-language experience. In recent years, most of the four-week courses cost about $2,000 to $2,500. You can find a good list of the larger ones in the January–February issue of *Transitions Abroad*, available in the United States at some larger bookstores and by mail (see end of chapter for order information).

Some of the more advanced degrees include: the MATESOL, or Master's in Teaching English to Speakers of Other Languages; the Master of Arts in Teaching ESL; the Master of Arts or Science in Education with a concentration in ESL; and the Master of Arts in English with a concentration in ESL. These programs have stricter admission requirements and take one to two years to complete. The *Directory of Professional Preparation Programs in TESOL in the United States and Canada*, published by Teachers of English to Speakers of Other Languages, Inc. (TESOL), gives an in-depth description of more than four hundred programs from certificate courses to doctoral degrees. If you become a member of TESOL, you can consult the *TESOL Placement Bulletin*, which TESOL itself will supply (see end of chapter).

Where to Look for Teaching Work

PRIVATE AMERICAN AND BRITISH OVERSEAS SCHOOLS

In Italy, there are approximately twenty-five private American and British schools for children (K–12) where classes are conducted in English (see addresses at the end of this chapter). The campuses are similar to private school campuses back home, complete with baseball teams and Girl/Boy Scouts. The school year normally begins in September and ends in June. The tuition is high, and in general the students are children of diplomats, wealthy Italians, expatriates, and businesspeople who have been transferred overseas. At the American schools, teachers are normally paid less than their colleagues in the United States. Salaries are based on the academic degrees the teachers hold, the subjects they teach, and their years of prior professional experience. However, there is a U.S.-Italy tax treaty specifically for Americans who are not residents of Italy and are brought over with a contract to teach. They get a tax break for the first two years of work—a break so large that in the end it makes their salary comparable to an American one.

Outdoor markets such as the Mercato di San Lorenzo in Florence are popular job-hunting grounds with Americans.

Although these schools occasionally have unexpected openings, hiring is normally done in the spring for the following school year. You can contact the schools directly or through one of the agencies that sponsors international job fairs in the U.S. in February or March (see end of chapter for addresses). International Schools Services (ISS) and Search Associates sponsor fairs on both the East and West Coasts, whereas the others hold their fairs in the states in which they are located (Iowa, Ohio, and Massachusetts). Costs can include application fees, fair attendance fees, and placement fees. Make sure to contact the agencies around October in order to get your application filed early.

LANGUAGE SCHOOLS

These schools make up the bulk of the teaching opportunities. They are often small and run by foreigners. Most of the courses taught are ESL/EFL, though they often include specialized topics such as "Business English." Some schools have their own teaching method that you must follow if you want to work there; others are much more lenient and will only advise you as to which textbooks to use. Some pay weekly, others every two months. The standard hourly rate for English teachers in Italy in recent years has been 15,000 lire ($10) per hour. One of the most important things to look for in a school is a sense of trust, since the last thing you need is to worry that you won't be paid for the hours you've worked. Don't expect to get any paid vacation or sick days, training, a contract, housing, or meals; there are schools that offer one or more of these benefits, but they are few and far between.

In addition to the teacher certification requirements discussed earlier, the requirements to teach at these schools vary. The fact that you speak English well and are well educated, personable, reliable, and committed are the basics. You often don't need to prove that you know English grammar or how to teach in order to get the job, but it is necessary to learn before you begin classes. While many schools prefer to hire teachers who speak Italian well, some will hire you even if you don't. With intermediate- and advanced-level classes, it can be an advantage not to speak Italian because it forces students to ask you questions in English. I have taught absolute beginners without using any Italian during the lessons (as one does in a multicultural classroom), but it's more demanding and requires a better knowledge of ESL teaching techniques. Many of the teachers you will meet never taught before they were hired and taught themselves grammar on their own. In fact, if you are interested in teaching ESL as a career, the easiest way to start is overseas. When you return to the United States, you will find that potential employers are more receptive to your foreign experience.

ITALIAN UNIVERSITIES

At the universities there are positions open each year for English-speaking *lettori* (lecturers) whose job is to hold class discussion groups, help professors correct exams, and sometimes teach sections of big courses. They are often hired by the departments where English texts are used, such as science, medicine, and literature. The positions are hard to get, and it is almost a requirement that you know an Italian professor who will put in a good word for you. Because there are no longer annual searches for *lettori*, positions can open up at any time. The only way to find out about openings is through the Ufficio Lettori of the local university. You should call the office at least once a month and ask if they are accepting applications. A bachelor's degree and often a master's degree are needed, and sometimes a Ph.D. as well. In order to apply you must first have your degrees and transcripts translated and authenticated by an Italian consulate in the United States. When you apply, you will also have to present your résumé and any proof of previous teaching experience. Your application will be evaluated, and if you are judged eligible you will be given an interview. Nonresidents and residents alike can apply. Contracts for *lettori* commonly last eight months, one year, or three years. Italian universities tend to pay their English language/literature lecturers about 29 million lire (approximately $19,300 per year). For more details about the university system, refer to Chapter 13.

PRIVATE STUDENTS

Private students are a great source of income for the English teacher in Italy. They usually pay double what the schools pay and allow for a more flexible schedule. Unfortunately, this flexibility can often lead to lessons that are rescheduled or even skipped, especially around holidays. Private lessons are most often conducted one on one as *lezioni individuali*. In some cases they have to be catered to a specific topic and in others anything goes. For example, doctors and scientists often want to learn English for international conferences. They need help correcting presentations and speeches they have to present, but their biggest fear is that they won't be able to understand simple questions about nontechnical topics during lunches. You will have to determine what you think your services are worth, how often you wish to be paid, and how you want the lessons to function. Teachers tend to vary in their rates for private lessons. The more experienced ones (or sometimes simply the more confident) ask for 25,000 to 35,000 lire ($17–25) per hour for individual lessons.

If you speak Italian well and feel more daring, there are other private teaching opportunities. For example, some Italian companies hire teachers to provide English lessons in the conference rooms of their buildings. Also, the local governments of most major towns and cities sponsor inexpensive language classes for residents. You could try to get one of these positions or propose your own program if one doesn't already exist.

If you're looking for private students, you can advertise in the *bacheche* (kiosks) at the universities or the bulletin boards in the English-language bookstores. Typical teaching ads read something like this: *"Insegnante di madrelingua inglese impartisce lezioni a domicilio"* (Native-speaking English teacher offers lessons at home). Newspapers are not too helpful, and placing an ad yourself is expensive and not worth the trouble. Be particularly careful about ads in the secondhand goods papers. Because they usually can be placed free of charge, some-times people use the opportunity as a way of luring foreign women to their homes.

There are some general guidelines for making private lessons as productive and lucrative as possible. For example, if your students live far away, charge more per hour; try to do one two-hour lesson instead of two one-hour lessons each week. Work out a rate schedule for indi-vidual and group lessons; with groups, the amount each student pays per hour should decrease and the overall amount you earn should in-crease. To avoid losing money on canceled lessons, ask students to pay for a month's lessons in advance. If they cancel a lesson less than twenty-four hours in advance, you keep the money. Most important, spread the word through friends and acquaintances that you're looking for work.

DoDDS

The American government has many Department of Defense De-pendent Schools (DoDDS) in Italy. The requirements for teachers are strict (roughly the same as at public schools in the States) and are de-scribed in detail in Chapter 18.

Planning Your Job Search

There is little point in trying to contact schools while in the United States, except for the U.S. overseas schools and the DoDDS. If you write to most schools from the States, you won't usually get a response, so the best way to find a teaching job is to go there and look for one. Employers want to know you're actually serious about living overseas, and the best proof is that you've already made the move. The last thing they want is to hire someone from abroad who gets cold feet a week be-fore classes start and never shows up. In fact, many schools don't even advertise openings locally because they don't have to—they already know dozens of teachers looking for work. This means that you have to go out and solicit the jobs.

You can begin planning for your teaching jobs before you even leave home. First, go to a library or bookstore and look at ESL books; get to know the methodology and titles so that during an interview in Italy you can refer to them (one of the most popular American ESL texts is the Azar series published by Prentice Hall Regents); buy and study a good ESL grammar book, such as *The Advanced Grammar Book* by Steer and Carlisi (Heinle & Heinle Publishers). Next, start a folder of interesting English reading material that can be used for conversation lessons, especially newspaper and magazine articles that address topics of general debate such as newsworthy subjects, religion, famous people, travel, and cultural differences; underline any idioms, slang, or difficult vocabulary, and write a list of definitions that you can distribute to students. Most important, if you're unable to get paid teaching experience for your résumé before you leave, do some volunteer tutoring (try local universities and schools for potential students).

Once you arrive in Italy, the *pagine gialle*, or yellow pages, are the easiest way to identify schools in the area where you live. If you're interested in language schools, look under *"Scuole di Lingua"* and start making calls. Most of the time you'll find an English-speaking person on the other line who will tell you that they have no openings but that you can send your résumé and it will be kept in a file. Ask for the name of the school director and try to get an interview so that you will be remembered if someone decides to quit unexpectedly.

Teaching English in Italy is seasonal work for the most part, and you should plan to arrive at a time when hiring is being done. In general, this means during the first two weeks of September for work that will begin in mid-October to November, and in May for summer work. Since many Italians take a whole month of vacation during August and a couple of weeks around Christmas, those Italians who do have to stay in the cities for work are often interested in using the time to improve their English. Many summer students are children who failed public school year-end exams and have to pass in the fall in order to be promoted to the next year. Big corporations also regularly sponsor intensive summer business English courses for their employees.

Useful Addresses

TESOL
1600 Cameron Street, Suite 300
Alexandria, VA 22314
tel (703) 836-0774
tel (800) 329-4469 (fax on demand)
(push 999 for index)
fax (703) 518-2535
publ@tesol.edu
www.tesol.edu

Transitions Abroad
Dept. TRA
Box 3000
Denville, NJ 07834
tel (800) 293-0373
tel (413) 256-3414
fax (413) 256-0373
trabroad@aol.com
www.transabroad.com

Agencies That Sponsor International Job Fairs

International Educators Cooperative
212 Alcott Road
East Falmouth, MA 02536
tel/fax (508) 540-8173

International Schools Services (ISS)
15 Roszel Road
P.O. Box 5910
Princeton, NJ 08543
tel (609) 452-0990
fax (609) 452-2690

Ohio State University
Educational Careers Center
110 Arps Hall
1945 North High Street
Columbus, OH 43210-1172
tel (614) 292-2741
fax (614) 292-4547

Overseas Placement Service for Educators
University of Northern Iowa
SSC #19
Cedar Falls, IA 50614-0390
tel (319) 273-2083
fax (319) 273-6998

Search Associates
P.O. Box 636
Dallas, TX 18612
tel (717) 696-5400
fax (717) 696-9500

Private American and British Overseas Schools in Italy

FLORENCE:
American International School of Florence
Villa Le Tavernule
Via del Carota, 23–25
50012 Firenze
tel (055) 640033
fax (055) 644226
(ages 3–18)

GENOA:
American International School of Genoa
Via Quarto, 13/c
16148 Genova
tel (010) 386528
fax (010) 398700
staff@tn.village.it
(ages 3–14)

MILAN:
American School of Milan
Via C. Marx, 14
20090 Noverasco di Opera (Milano)
tel (02) 5300001
fax (02) 57606274
directorasm@planet.it
(ages 3–18)

International School of Milan
Via Caccialepori, 22
20148 Milano
tel (02) 48706030
fax (02) 48703644
ismmiddle@telemacus.it
(ages 2–18)

Sir James Henderson British School
Via Pisani Dossi, 16
20134 Milano
tel (02) 26413310
fax (02) 26413515
(ages 3–18)

NAPLES:
International School of Naples
AFSOUTH NATO
Building D
Viale della Liberazione
80125 Bagnoli (Napoli)
tel (081) 7212037
fax (081) 7628429
(ages 3–18)

ROME:
Ambrit International School
Via Filippo Tajani, 50
00149 Roma
tel (06) 5595305
fax (06) 5595309
ambrit@email.telpress.it
(ages 3–13)

American Overseas School of Rome
Via Cassia, 811
00189 Roma
tel (06) 33264841
fax (06) 33262608
aosr@mail.nexus.it
www.nexus.it/aosr
(ages 4–18)

Castelli International School
Via degli Scozzesi, 13
00046 Grottaferrata (Roma)
tel/fax (06) 94315779
www.pcq.it/cis
(ages 6–14)
Castelli Kindergarten
Via dei Laghi, Km. 8,600
00047 Marino (Roma)
tel (06) 93661311
(Ages 2–6)
Core: The Co-Operative School
Via Orvinio, 20
00199 Roma
tel/fax (06) 86211614
(ages 3–11)
Greenwood Garden School
Via Vito Sinisi, 5
00189 Roma
tel/fax (06) 33266703
(ages 2–6)
Kendale Primary International School
Via Gradoli, 86
(Via Cassia Km. 10,300)
00189 Tomba di Nerone (Roma)
tel/fax (06) 33267608
(ages 3–11)
Marymount International School
Via di Villa Lauchli, 180
(Via Cassia Antica, Km. 7)
00191 Roma
tel (06) 36301742
fax (06) 36301738
marymount@pronet.it
(ages 3–18)
The New School
Via della Camilluccia, 669
00135 Roma
tel (06) 3294269
fax (06) 3297546
newschool.rome@mclink.it
(ages 3–18)
Rome International School
Via Morgagni, 25
00161 Roma
tel (06) 44243328

fax (06) 44243090
(ages 2–10)
St. George's English School
Via Cassia, Km. 16
00123 Roma
tel (06) 30890141
fax (06) 30892490
(ages 3–18)
Saints Francis and Clare International School
Via Massimi, 164
00136 Roma
tel (06) 35341328
fax (06) 35348719
(ages 3–14)
St. Stephen's School
Via Aventina, 3
00153 Roma
tel (06) 5750605
fax (06) 5741941
mc0667@mclink.it
(ages 13–19)
Southlands English School in Rome
Via Teleclide, 20
(Via Epaminonda)
Casal Palocco
00124 Roma
tel (06) 5053932
fax (06) 50917192
(ages 2–14)
TRIESTE:
International School of Trieste
Via Conconello, 16
34016 Opicina (Trieste)
tel (040) 211452
fax (040) 213122
metzger@interbusiness.it
http://cef/mfa.org
(ages 2–14)
TURIN:
International School of Turin
Vicolo Tiziano, 10
10024 Moncalieri (Torino)
tel (011) 6407810
fax (011) 643298
(ages 2–17)

CHAPTER TWENTY

Freelancing and
Part-Time Work

Chances are you haven't lined up a job before moving to Italy, which means you will probably go through a phase of *lavoro indipendente* (freelance work) and do *lavoro part-time* (part-time work) once you get there. Being a *libero professionista* (freelancer) is the ideal starting point if you eventually plan to open your own business or work for a company, since you can become familiar with the Italian work world before committing to any particular full-time position. As a freelancer you will enjoy the freedom of working for different employers at the same time and taking vacation when you want, as well as the fact that many companies favor hiring freelancers over full-time employees to avoid burdening labor laws. Before you begin looking for work, you will have to identify the services and skills you have to sell, which means analyzing your training, experience, and expertise. One thing is certain: translating and interpreting skills are always hot commodities on the Italian market. The better you know Italian, the better your chances are of getting work.

Americans in Italy are hitting the freelance job market from all angles. They are doing computer programming, interior decorating, journalism, desktop publishing, and public relations. Some are tapping into the fashion world as makeup artists, hairdressers, and photographers. Others are selling their skills as designers and illustrators. Those who have superior linguistic abilities are providing simultaneous interpreting for conventions and business meetings or writing, translating, and editing reports and brochures in English for Italian companies with an international clientele. Because these companies often look to the United States for new ideas and techniques, Americans with special training or degrees are sometimes hired as *consulenti,* or consultants.

The Art of Freelancing

MARKETING YOURSELF TO CLIENTS

Generally speaking, it is a waste of money to advertise your services in Italian newspapers or to do direct mailings unless you are already well established. Sometimes advertising in the English-language papers works, as do flyers placed on bulletin boards. Networking like crazy is, without doubt, the best form of advertising. In order to do it well, have a business card made, including a good title for yourself. The title gives clients the sense that you are more professional and specialized. For example, "Anne Smith," "Anne Smith, U.S.-Italy Trade Expert," and "Anne Smith, Computer Consultant" have different rings to them. Another useful thing to do is to print a brochure in Italian and English describing your skills and past projects; it can make the difference between a professional presentation and an amateur one. Ask your current and past clients if they would be willing to serve as references and if you may list their names on your brochure.

GETTING PAID

As an American you are supposed to get a freelance visa and work permit to do freelance work. However, the "freelance visa" requires a letter from an Italian employer stating it will hire you as a consultant (see Chapter 2), which is nearly impossible to get before leaving the United States. In addition, you must prove that your skills are highly specialized. However, you can apply for the *codice fiscale* (personal taxpayer number) without any permit at all, and this *codice* is all employers need to withhold for you the *ritenuta d'acconto,* the 19 percent tax contribution required of all workers. In fact, most employers don't seem to care whether your paperwork is in order as long as you have that number. If you do have your paperwork in order, you can get a *partita IVA,* or VAT tax number, and include the 19 percent IVA tax on your invoice. If you do so, it is unnecessary for the employer to withhold the *ritenuta d'acconto.*

As a freelancer, ideally you should earn more on an hourly basis than you would at a full-time job, since you have to pay for your own

Enterprising freelancers will do just about anything to get work—including posing as Roman gladiators for tourists.

benefits, such as vacation and sick days. Because you set your own rate, it's important not to price your services above or below the market standard. It's also important not to ask for a "per project" rate if your colleagues are being paid per hour. It is inevitable that you will discover at some point that you were paid too little for a job you did, which is frustrating and makes you feel cheated. This happens to the best of freelancers when they first start, so don't get discouraged. One way around this problem is by asking employers what they think is fair pay for the job. Usually they will quote a lower price than what they are willing to pay, and you can simply say that you were hoping for more. There are also published professional rate books available through professional organizations that can be consulted to get a better idea of the going rates. Remember that Italians value quality over price and would rather pay more for better service. However, giving discounts is appreciated and will help you establish long-lasting work relationships.

SUBMITTING AN INVOICE

When you finish a job you submit a *fattura,* or invoice. If it's a big job, you could submit half of the total amount due midway through it. Sometimes people ask to be paid a certain amount up front, before the work even starts. On the invoice you should indicate the date (*data*), your name, address, phone number, *codice fiscale* or *partita IVA,* a description of the services you rendered (*servizi*), how many hours you worked (*ore lavorate*), the amount due (*somma da pagare*), and the *imposta da pagare* (the tax amount due, if you are using a *partita IVA*). Most invoices are paid after three months, and don't be surprised if you spend as much time soliciting payment as you did doing the work itself. I know a woman who gets regular freelance work from a large international organization that is constantly behind in payments. Her method is not to hand in completed projects until she gets paid for the previous ones. A less extreme method is to send a reminder letter to the client after six weeks, then start calling once a week.

Working in the
Expatriate Community

Many Americans get their first jobs in Italy through the expatriate network, and you can, too, if you know where to look and how to use your skills creatively. For example, you could provide services specifically designed for other expatriates, such as tax planning and preparation, psychotherapy, financial planning, accounting, and bookkeeping. You could work for an American high school as a substitute teacher or part-time art instructor, or you could get administrative work such as word processing with one of the American law offices, accounting firms, or newspaper bureaus. Even some of the expatriate publications, such as *Wanted in Rome,* might hire you to design covers, while others might pay you to write articles and take photographs. Finally, American expatriates who have been living in Italy for years may want to catch up on the latest trends from home. For example, if you know how to use a popular new computer program, perhaps you could give computer courses to employees at an American study abroad program. Being an expatriate yourself, the longer you stay in Italy the more you will understand their needs. Chapter 3 should give you more ideas, as should the *English Yellow Pages.*

Another possibility is to represent American or foreign companies doing business with Italy. These sometimes need a local contact person they can rely on when need be but don't want to hire anyone on a permanent basis. For example, if they import cloth, they may want a buyer to handle their Italian purchases; if they rent apartments in Italy, they'll need somebody to make sure the houses are ready for guests when they arrive. (There is a list of American companies that do business in Italy in Chapter 18.) Additionally, American universities abroad sometimes need people to take care of helping students get settled in when they first arrive (see Chapter 12).

Sometimes freelance work is available through the American Embassies or Consulates, or through international organizations such as the United Nations, the Food and Agriculture Organization (FAO), or the World Food Program (WFP). Their Italian branches regularly sponsor local conventions, events, and publications in English, but since many of their projects are funded for only several months at a time, it is impossible for them to hire anyone on a permanent basis. Since most are based in Rome, if you live there chances are you can get quite a bit of work with them doing graphic design or desktop publishing, editing of manuscripts and reports, and translating.

Jobs Requiring Italian Proficiency or Fluency

TRANSLATING AND INTERPRETING

Translating and interpreting are two of the most lucrative and steady forms of freelance work foreigners can get. In order to do them well, you must be fluent in Italian. The main difference between the two is that translating involves written Italian, while interpreting involves spoken Italian. Of these, the most difficult forms include simultaneous interpreting (much needed by important organizations such as the United Nations for international conferences) and legal translating. The more technical the vocabulary, the more difficult the projects are. Generally, translators earn less than interpreters on a per project basis but have more opportunities for work, including everything from museum brochures to advertisements to textbooks.

Most translators and interpreters begin their careers taking any work they can get, which results in a hodgepodge of experience. However, they eventually learn which kinds of projects they enjoy more and then begin to specialize. For example, some interpreters specialize in business Italian, while others focus more on politics, medicine, or science. If you already have specialized knowledge of some topic (e.g., banking or art history), make it known to potential clients. However, beware of making your specialization seem a limitation on your general abilities. If you're planning to be in Italy for a long time, you may want to pursue a local two-year university diploma (the so-called *diploma universitario* or *laurea breve*) in your field. For example, there are diplomas for interpreters and translators at the Universities of Bari, Bologna, Florence, Milan, Naples, Rome, and Turin, about which you can get information through the Italian Cultural Institutes (see Chapter 13 for addresses).

Leading Tours

If you are interested in leading tour groups in Italy, there is one important thing you should know before starting: the difference between a "tour guide" and a "tour director." Tour guides must obtain a permit issued by the Italian state that verifies that they are experts in the history and sights of a city. They can practice their trade only in a single Italian city, the one the permit has been issued for. To become a state-certified tour guide, you must have the proper work credentials, pass a lengthy exam, and be able to speak Italian well. Becoming a "tour director" is a different story—one that is much more accessible to foreigners. A tour director is responsible for accompanying a tour and for overseeing accommodation and transportation arrangements. However, a tour director is prohibited from giving historical information about sights and monuments because that's the tour guide's job. Theoretically, a tour director should also pass a state exam before working, but the exam is rarely administered and most operate without having taken it.

Tour directors should be amiable and tolerant and should know some Italian (though fluency is not necessary), as well as at least one other foreign language, such as French or Spanish. Many tour directors lead groups of American high school students on their first trip to Europe, and the trick of the trade is to be extremely patient when it comes to explaining differences between the United States and Italy, especially where food and public toilets are concerned. Most tours last about ten days and take place during the spring and summer months. However, the pay is good enough to permit a tour director to work only eight to ten tours per year. Pay includes a per day salary, tips collected from members of the group, and commissions made by bringing members to certain shops and restaurants. I spoke with one tour director who, on a single ten-day trip, made as much as $800 in tips and $500 in commissions on top of his salary.

To become a tour director, you should contact one of the large tour group operators in the United States listed at the end of this chapter, such as Education First (EF), the Council for International Educational Exchange (CIEE), Youth for Understanding, Backroads, or the American Institute for Foreign Study (AIFS). You could also contact the European Travel Commission in New York (see end of chapter) for other related job ideas. If you are already in Italy, look through the tourism yellow pages published by the local phone company, which lists all local hotels and travel agencies (this can often be found at the hotels and agencies themselves). Keep in mind that many tour group operators have a strict application procedure, and some require you apply in the United States six months in advance of your expected departure.

Working for Club Méditerranée

Club Méditerranée has six vacation resorts, or "villages," in Italy where you can be what the company calls a *"gentil organizateur,"* or "congenial host." The Italian resorts are located in Caprera (on the island of Sardinia), Donoratico (on the coast of Tuscany), Metaponto (in southeastern Italy, near Taranto), Otranto (in the southernmost part of the peninsula's "heel"), Santa Teresa (on the island of Sardinia), and Sestriere (in Piedmont, where Italian ski champ Alberto Tomba trains). Positions range from resort administrators to child care personnel to tour guides to medical practitioners. They include jobs in entertainment, too, from technical positions such as sound engineers to performance-based positions such as nightclub DJs, circus performers, and comedians. You can work in the Club Med restaurants, bars, or shops. You can teach silk painting or instruct land, water, or snow sports, depending on the location. If you are based in Sestriere, you will surely be involved in snow activities and winter sports; if you are in Caprera your activities will involve the sea and sand.

Club Med positions last a minimum of six months and require a seven-day-per-week commitment. The minimum age requirement is twenty years, but most Club Med "hosts" are in their late twenties. In addition, "hosts" must be willing to be transferred to any Club Med resort in the world. In fact, if you apply from the United States you will have to spend your first months in Florida, Colorado, the Bahamas, the Caribbean, or Mexico for training. Club Med jobs include transportation to the resort, room, board, and access to the village facilities where you work. The average starting salary is about $500–600 per month, though this figure can vary according to your degree of specialization and previous work experience.

Requirements for each position also vary. For example, to be an aerobics instructor you must have the proper certification and at least two years of teaching experience. To be a bartender, you must be over twenty-one years of age and have at least one year of bartending experience. A bartending diploma is not required but is preferred, as is fluency in foreign languages. If you want to work as a tour guide, you must have a college degree, be fluent in at least two languages, have tour-leading experience, know a lot about history and geography, and have traveled extensively.

To apply for a position, you should send the following to the U.S. office if you are a resident there or to the Milan office if you have Italian residency: a résumé and cover letter stating which positions you are interested in and why you are qualified to fill them; copies of diplomas, certificates, or letters of recommendation that prove your qualifications; and a photocopy of your passport. Eventually, you will also have to attend an interview.

Jobs Requiring Little Italian

Non capisci italiano? If this is the case, you're up against an obstacle if you want to work in Italy. Generally, the Italian workplace is for Italian speakers only. But there are a few key industries, such as tourism, that offer employment opportunities to foreigners who speak little Italian. If you take advantage of them, you can support yourself as you study the language. Once you become comfortable with Italian, you can choose from a wider selection of jobs. This section will provide you with some basic ideas on how to begin earning a living in Italy as you perfect your fluency skills. Although you are required by law to have the proper work permit to earn money, many of the jobs listed below are paid *al nero*, or "under the table" (which is, of course, illegal). If you plan to work part-time or for short intervals, many employers look the other way if your paperwork is not in order. If you are caught, however, the penalties are high.

BEING AN AU PAIR

If you are eighteen to twenty-seven years old, female, and good with children, becoming an au pair, or *alla pari*, live-in baby-sitter is one of the best ways to learn Italian (male au pairs do exist but are rare). In general, au pairs take care of children for about twenty-five to thirty-five hours per week. In exchange, they receive housing with an Italian family and are paid a small stipend of about 100,000 lire (or $65) each week. An au pair is not expected to be a maid or full-time nanny but is asked to speak English to the children, care for them, help with their homework, and do some light housework or occasional cooking. One of the more common perks of being an au pair is accompanying the host family on vacation. Some au pair positions can last years, although the majority last only a couple of months during the summer. Au pair candidates should be patient and open-minded, and they should expect to follow the "house rules" of the family they live with, including curfews and proper behavior.

If you are interested, you should contact one of the au pair agencies in Europe or the United States (some are listed at the end of this chapter). The agencies screen au pair candidates and match them with Italian families according to compatibility and location. Many also arrange the paperwork required and assist the au pair to enroll in local Italian-language schools. Generally, an au pair should obtain a study visa instead of a work visa if she plans on staying in Italy for more than three months. Because the stipend is not considered a salary, agencies say that technically there is no need for a work visa. If the au pair is also a university student, some foreign language departments of U.S. schools will accept au pair work for academic credit.

WAITERING AND SEASONAL HOTEL WORK

In Italy waitering is a career, and the *camerieri* and *cameriere* who choose it are impeccably trained and committed to their profession. In fact, many agree that Italy has the best waiters in the world. It is a salaried job with benefits, and by norm waiters do not receive tips—their incentive to provide excellent service often comes simply from a willingness to preserve the traditions of the craft. In addition, there is not a high turnover rate, making it difficult for Americans to break in, especially if they intend to work for a short period of time. Recently, however, trendy new restaurants, discotheques, and franchised theme bars have mushroomed all over the peninsula, and tend to hire young people looking for part-time or temporary work. It would be impossible to provide a list of these places, but the kinds you should target include Irish pubs, American-style sports bars, foreign-food restaurants, local *trattorie* or *osterie* (inns), nightclubs and discotheques, fast-food restaurants, and outdoor food stands. Other than learning the daily menu, no extensive conversational skills are required.

If you'd like to work for a hotel, the scenario is similar. You will have a hard time finding year-round work because these positions are usually dominated by professionals and require special work/health permits. However, many hotels desperately need extra part-time English-speaking employees during the summer, especially ones located by the sea. You can find employment cleaning rooms, guarding the hotel's private beach, or helping out with organized activities. The best months to try are from April to September, and you should focus on big hotels or resorts located in coastal towns such as Rimini, on the Ligurian coast, the south, or islands such as Sardinia and Elba. During winter months you might try ski resorts in the Italian Alps.

WORKING IN AN OUTDOOR MARKET OR STORE

If you walk through the San Lorenzo outdoor market in Florence, you will be astonished by how many Americans work there. As you go from stand to stand admiring the polished leather bags, intricate lace, and colorful suede gloves, you will hear nothing but conversations in English between salespeople about the latest American football scores or the hottest updates on who's dating whom on daytime soaps back home. There are outdoor markets like this one in all of the popular tourist destinations such as Venice, Rome, and the Amalfi coast, as well as an abundance of small stores selling souvenirs which have the same need for English-speaking salespeople. As a job hunter, the key is to target markets and stores that cater to English-speaking clients so that you can be a valuable employee despite your limited knowledge of Italian.

FITNESS AND HOLISTIC MEDICINE

If you are an experienced aerobics, step, or yoga instructor or a personal fitness trainer, you may find work at the *palestre* (gyms) nearest you. The language requirements are minimal, and most important, you should be able to demonstrate your professional experience and qualifications with any certificates you have earned. Some Americans with larger apartments also organize aerobics classes in their homes, often charging 10,000 lire per person per class. Others trained in massage, reflexology, and acupressure also have private clients come to their homes, asking going rates upward of 50,000 to 60,000 lire ($33–$40) per hour.

MESSENGER WORK

Foreigners with a *motorino* (moped) or bicycle can inquire about becoming messengers with a courier service such as Speedy Boys or Motopost or look in the Italian yellow pages under "*Corrieri*" for more companies. In Italian, a messenger is called *il pony,* and local newspapers report that the need for messengers is rapidly increasing. To be good at this job, you should master the art of Italian body language to fight your way through traffic. Speaking skills are less important.

MODELING

Even if you've never considered modeling in the United States, you might do so in Italy. Models often start at 600,000 lire ($400) per day at larger agencies in Milan and Rome. But jobs are not limited to these larger cities, as there are smaller agencies throughout the country. There are many opportunities for both males and females to pose for ads, catalogs, and brochures. In addition, small boutiques and design houses seek models to wear clothing and accessories when they host "showrooms," or mini–fashion shows, for their wealthiest clients. If you are a perfect size, you could also try becoming a model for fittings. That's when designers in the designing phase of clothing production use your body as a template for adjustments and cuts. If you're interested, you should have your photo taken by a professional photographer and create a composite card with your height, measurements, and eye and hair color listed (make sure to put information in centimeters, not inches). Then you can start calling modeling agencies to inquire about work possibilities.

As an American you have the advantage that the Italian fashion industry is always on the prowl for foreign beauty, especially what they call the "classic American look" (i.e., blond hair and blue eyes). I attended an American high school in Italy and remember that television producers were often making the rounds of our classrooms looking for Americans to sell Italian products such as Mulino Bianco cookies. One of Italy's most recognizable television personalities, Wendy, started her very successful career inadvertently. The Californian was standing in front of the Trevi Fountain when an Italian television producer noticed her golden hair and cheerleader's body. Now she's too famous to go by the fountain unnoticed—stand back, Anita Ekberg. In recent years, Italian notions of beauty have been changing and more ethnic looks have also become hot commodities.

Nude modeling for art schools and workshops is another type of modeling some Americans pursue. Nude modeling can pay anywhere from 20,000 to 30,000 lire per hour ($15–20) and models usually pose in one position in ten-minute intervals. If it is your first time, you should ask to observe a class with a working nude model first. You should also heed one important piece of advice shared by experienced nude models: go to the schools or workshops yourself and ask if you can model; never respond to a published ad. By going in person, you choose whom you will model for after you have seen the facilities and met with the instructors and students. In Italy, as everywhere else in the world, there is an evil underworld in the shadows of the modeling industry. It was recently disclosed that many young girls on some of Italy's most popular prime-time television shows had been asked to trade sexual favors for a few seconds in the spotlight. Don't be naïve, and be extremely careful about finding legitimate art schools.

Freelance Survival Tips

The golden ingredients of freelancing in Italy are creativity, persistence, optimism, organization, and expertise. You need creativity to think of services you can market and ways to do so, persistence and optimism to keep pursuing new clients and jobs, and organization to keep track of all your possible job leads and invoices. Expertise, of course, is what you are selling. Above all, remember that anyone you meet in any situation is a possible job lead and that it is fundamental to keep an eye on the competition. In order to keep yourself marketable, improve your skills regularly to keep your brochure and/or résumé updated.

There are negative aspects to freelancing that you must consider as well. The first is that when you're not working, you're not earning. This means no paid vacations or sick days. It also means that some months you earn more than others, according to the number of jobs you get. If you want to have a pension plan or health insurance, you have to create it yourself and pay for it out of your own pocket. Between searching for new clients and maintaining old ones, many freelancers end up working more hours per week than if they had a salaried job. They don't separate their free time from work time and often work at night or on weekends. Many use their apartments as their offices but don't distinguish between "office space" and "living space," which can become stressful.

There are some things you can do to alleviate these problems. The first is to set regular hours of operation and to stick to them (make sure that your hours match local office hours). The second is to create a clear "office" area in your home, for example, by investing in a file cabinet to eliminate clutter. Finally, make yourself as technologically savvy as possible to make it easy for clients to contact you and less expensive for you to contact them. Buy an answering machine, fax machine, computer, and modem, and get an e-mail account. If your work requires much commuting, consider renting or buying a cellular phone.

Useful Addresses

Au Pair Agencies in the
United States

AIPT
Association for International Practical Training
10400 Little Patuxent Parkway, Suite 250
Columbia, MD 21044
tel (410) 997-2200
fax (410) 992-3924

Alliances Abroad
18 Buena Vista Terrace
San Francisco, CA 94117
tel (415) 487-0691
fax (415) 487-1164

Council on International Educational Exchange (CIEE)
205 East 42nd Street
New York, NY 10017
tel (212) 822-2600
fax (212) 822-2699
info@ciee.org
www.ciee.org

InterExchange
161 Avenue of the Americas
New York, NY 10013

tel (212) 924-0446
fax (212) 924-0575

Au Pair Agencies in Italy

Agenzia Intermediate
Via Bramante, 13
00153 Roma
tel (06) 5747444
fax (06) 57300574

Euro Au Pair
Corso dei Tintori, 8 (Tintari)
50122 Firenze
tel (055) 242181
fax (055) 241722

La Lampada da Aladino
Via Sebenico, 9
20124 Milano
tel (02) 6884325
fax (02) 66804071

Mix Culture
Via Baccina, 16
00184 Roma
tel (06) 6783887
fax (06) 6783607

TOUR DIRECTOR AGENCIES

Abercrombie and Kent
1520 Kensington Road
Oak Brook, IL 60521
tel (630) 954-2944
fax (630) 954-3324
akintl@xnet.com
**American Institute for Foreign Study
(AIFS)**
102 Greenwich Avenue
Greenwich, CT 06830
tel (800) 727-2437
tel (203) 869-9090
fax (203) 869-9615
info@aifs.org
www.aifs.org
Backroads
1516 5th Street, Suite Q333
Berkeley, CA 94710
tel (800) 245-3874
fax (510) 527-1444
CIEE
Council for International Educational
Exchange
(See "au pair" listing above.)
Education First (EF)
Institute for Cultural Exchange
1 Memorial Drive
Cambridge, MA 02142
tel (617) 252-6060
fax (617) 621-1930
jobs@ef.com
www.edtours.com
European Travel Commission
630 Fifth Avenue, Suite 565
New York, NY 10111
tel (212) 307-1200
fax (212) 307-1205
www.visiteurope.com
Experience Plus
1925 Wallenberg Drive
Fort Collins, CO 80526
tel/fax (800) 685-4565
tel (970) 484-8489
tours@xplus.com

Progressive Travels
224 West Galer Street
Seattle, WA 98119
tel (800) 245-2229
tel (206) 285-1988
fax (206) 285-1987
Youth for Understanding
3501 Newark Street, N.W.
Washington, DC 20016
tel (202) 966-6800
fax (202) 895-1104

CLUB MÉDITERRANÉE

GENERAL CLUB MED INFORMATION
tel (800) 258-2633 (for resort information)
tel (407) 337-6660 (for employment
opportunities)
www.clubmed.com (for Club Med
locations)
www.cooljobs.com/clubmed (for Club
Med jobs)
CLUB MED—ADMINISTRATIVE
HEADQUARTERS
Club Med Human Resources
4500 S.E. Pine Valley Street
Port Saint Lucie, FL 34952
tel (561) 335-4400
fax (561) 337-6677
Club Méditerranée
Largo Corsia dei Servi, 11
20122 Milano
tel (02) 77861
fax (02) 7786261

MESSENGERS

Motopost
Via Parini, 9
20121 Milano
tel (02) 6224
fax (02) 6572803
Speedy Boys
Via Buccari, 8
00195 Roma Prati
tel/fax (06) 39888
(Metro Ottaviano)

CHAPTER TWENTY-ONE

Starting Your Own Business

In 1981, a housewife from Los Angeles moved to Rome with her two small children to follow her husband and his job. She didn't speak Italian and had been to Italy only a handful of times before on brief holiday trips. But as a foreigner she had something many Italians did not: a keen sense of American-style businesses that was missing in her adopted country. She realized this when she took four rolls of family snapshots to the nearest photo laboratory. She waited weeks before the pictures were developed, and when they finally were, not a single picture came out. The lab couldn't even confirm if the blank negatives were hers because so much time had passed. Despite this, she was asked to pay an exaggerated 80,000 lire ($50). That's when she knew Italy needed faster, less expensive labs. By February 1984, she had opened Foto Quick, Italy's first one-hour photo store.

The road to success was not an easy one. Before the store opened, she spent three years learning Italian, taking courses in the United States on one-hour photo processing, and battling Italian bureaucracy. She estimates that 90 percent of her time and energy was spent on bureaucratic matters. The first obstacle was finding financing, and she eventually took a second mortgage on her home in California. The second obstacle was finding a suitable location for the business. Besides needing a store with a good water supply, ample space for the photo machinery, and an above-average electrical supply, she hoped to find a position in the center of Rome that would be visible to pedestrian traffic and easily discovered by tourists. Following months of scanning classified ads and observing the foot traffic in front of stores for rent, she finally found the perfect place: a roomy ground-floor store. It had huge windows through which people could watch the one-hour process and enough space in the rear to set up a studio for portraits and still-life photography. But the best thing was that it was located adjacent to the Trevi Fountain, one of Rome's most visited monuments.

She soon ran into three other bureaucratic problems so difficult to resolve that she actually considered abandoning the Foto Quick idea altogether. First, she had to apply for a store license. Because Italian bureaucrats had never seen her type of business, they didn't know how to categorize it. In their books, it was neither a laboratory nor a retail store. The confusion caused a year-long delay. Second, Italian labor laws required that she hire Italian personnel, but she couldn't find any Italians experienced in one-hour photo technology. She was fortunate to find two young, enthusiastic wedding photographers who were willing to train themselves by tediously deciphering badly translated Japanese instruction manuals. Third, she had to get a sanitation permit from the Sanitation Department for approval of her store and its necessary use of photo chemicals, as the Department feared they would contaminate the waters of the Trevi Fountain. In the end, she actually tore down a store wall to demonstrate to the officials that she had invested in the proper filters and discharge tubing. Finally, all of the bureaucratic obstacles had been overcome.

From its first day, Foto Quick was a success. It developed an average of 100 rolls of film per day, while similar stores in the United States were lucky to get 25. The housewife kept the momentum going by using American-style advertising techniques Italians hadn't seen before. For example, on weekends she put colorful Foto Quick flyers onto car windshields. By her second year in operation, profits had doubled, and following summer holidays she always saw record-breaking returns. Her main expenses included the lease on the photo machinery, the monthly rent, worker's salaries and social security benefits, and her operational expenses, including chemicals and paper. Nevertheless, her profits were sufficient to allow her to cover those expenses, pay off her debts, and pay for her entire family's life abroad. And she had enough left over to buy an apartment in Rome.

A few years later, the one-hour photo craze hit Europe. The number of stores in Italy rapidly increased as others saw the market potential. But Foto Quick had an edge over the competition because it had been there first and had already developed a steady clientele with contracts to service the needs of big companies such as Fendi, Valentino, and Bulgari. Her success was due to good timing, a good idea, and persistence. She believes it was also due to the fact that she is American. Foto Quick gained the reputation of being "American owned," and for Italians this translated into speedy service, competitive prices, quality, and friendly customer service.

Types of Businesses

When starting your own business, there are different types of business structures you can choose from, depending on your professional activity and desired tax liability. For all of them you'll need a *codice fiscale* (individual taxpayer number) and *partita IVA* (VAT tax number), and you'll need to register with the nearest *camera di commercio* (chamber of commerce). The main types include representative offices, branch offices, sole proprietorships, partnerships, and corporations.

REPRESENTATIVE OFFICES
An *ufficio di rappresentanza,* or representative office, is for those who do not actually want to set up business operations in Italy but want to come and research available markets, distribute information, or promote the image of a foreign company locally. Sometimes they exist for no other reason than to establish an address in Italy. For example, a newspaper's foreign bureau or a university's research center could be representative offices. Because a representative office does not make money and all its expenses are covered by its foreign headquarters, it is usually not subject to Italian taxes.

BRANCH OFFICES
A *sede secondaria* is the branch office of a nonresident company that wants to do business in Italy. The branch office is subject to Italian corporate law, income taxes, and IVA (VAT tax). For example, an American software company or record distributor might open an Italian branch. The procedures required to open one are complicated, and

The tourism industry is one of the largest sectors to consider when starting your own business.

you will need the help of a *notaio* (notary public) to register the branch office with the local tax authorities.

SOLE PROPRIETORSHIPS

A *ditta individuale,* or sole proprietorship, is the simplest business structure because there is no capital requirement. The owner must have a *partita IVA* tax number and must be registered with the *camera di commercio* within one month of starting operations. You should be careful with a sole proprietorship because you will have to bear all the tax consequences and liability of the company. This means that if the business goes bankrupt, your assets, both personal and company-related, are liable for all business debts.

PARTNERSHIPS

There are two types of *società di persone,* or partnerships: a general partnership and a limited partnership. As in the case of the sole proprietorship, there is no capital requirement for partnerships, and profits and losses are passed on to the partners, who are also responsible for debts incurred. In a general partnership, or *società in nome collettivo* (S.n.c.), all partners are liable without limit for the debts of their business. In a limited partnership, or *società in accomandita semplice* (S.a.s.), the liability of each partner is determined by his or her original investment. There is no limit to the number of partners permitted with the S.n.c. and S.a.s., as long as there are at least two. Partnerships are subject to local income tax and IVA, in addition to the personal income tax of each partner. You will need the help of a *notaio* to set one up, and you will need court approval.

CORPORATIONS

By forming a *società di capitali,* or corporation, you are protected against liabilities incurred by the enterprise, except where the original investment is concerned. If the corporation goes bankrupt, shareholders' personal effects cannot be taken to pay off debts. There are two types of corporations, and each has its own set of capital requirements. Both can be managed by a single director or a board of directors, and both can be fully foreign-owned. Both are subject to local income tax, IVA, and corporate tax (IRPEG).

The first is a limited-liability company, or *Società a responsabilità limitata)* (S.r.l.). It requires a minimum quota capital of 20 million lire ($13,300). It cannot be listed on the stock exchange and has quotas, rather than shares. The capital is divided into quotas of no less than 1,000 lire ($0.67) that represent the interests of the quotaholders. Generally, each quotaholder has one quota, but these vary in size according to investment. The size of the quota determines the liability and the voting right of the quotaholder. If the S.r.l. is incorporated by one person, he or she will have limited liability. An S.r.l. usually does not require an outside auditor. Foto Quick, for example, was an S.r.l.

The second type of corporation, and the more complex, is the *Società per Azioni* (S.p.A.). This is a joint-stock corporation. It must have a minimum capital of 200 million lire ($133,000) and is usually set up for large businesses that want to be traded on the stock exchange, or *borsa*. It is a limited liability vehicle with the liability of shareholders limited to their investment. Before the S.p.A. is registered, its capital must be underwritten by at least two shareholders and a bit less than one-third of the capital must be deposited with a bank (this is refunded following registration). If the S.p.A. is to be listed on the stock market, it is required to submit its accounts to outside auditors.

Setting up a corporation, be it an S.r.l. or S.p.A., is costly. First, there is a tax due upon registration that is equal to 1 percent of the capital, and there is a state concessions tax of about 500,000 lire ($300). The fees of the *notaio* alone can run from 4 million to 5 million lire ($3,000 to $4,000).

Setting Up Shop

To set up a business, you will most likely need the help of a *notaio*. Each business structure has its own requirements, but in general the *notaio* will help you do the following:

- Ask for approval for the business from the local court.
- Register with the Ufficio Registro (tax registrar's office).
- Register with the Registro delle Imprese (registrar of enterprises).
- Register with the Registro delle Ditte (registrar of companies) at the nearest *camera di commercio*.
- Register with the Ufficio delle Imposte (local tax authority).
- Publicize the formation of the company in the official bulletin of companies called *BUSARL*.

Italian tax laws are so complicated that you should also depend on the services of a trustworthy *commercialista*, or accountant, to prepare your income tax returns and keep your books in order. All books and receipts should be kept for ten years. Make sure you also seek the services of a financial and legal advisor. If you have a large business, you might want to get advice from the Italian offices of Arthur Anderson,

Ernst & Young, or Price Waterhouse (see Chapter 5), or the American Chamber of Commerce (see end of this chapter). You can also contact one of the trade specialists at the U.S. Embassy in Rome or the American consulates. They have counselors for economic affairs, commercial affairs, and agricultural affairs. The commercial section of the Italian Embassy in Washington, D.C., is also staffed with people who can help you obtain information for opening a business in Italy.

PERMITS, LICENSES, AND "KEY MONEY"

Permits and licenses must be acquired for the type of commercial activity you wish to pursue. Permits are issued for things such as sanitation and labor, and allow the state to be sure your business is in accordance with the law. Police will routinely visit your store to verify that your permits are in order. If they're not, you will have to pay a fine that can cost more than the permit itself. A license provides a definition of your business (e.g., grocery store versus shoe repair shop). Licenses help the state control the density of businesses per area, which is why there are limited numbers of *alimentari* stores per zoning area and why only certain stores are allowed to sell newspapers or cigarettes. You should definitely look into obtaining a license before you invest large sums into your new business at the *circoscrizione,* or local office of your comune.

"Key money," called a *buon uscita* or *buon entrata* in Italian, is a fee you are sometimes asked to pay to buy off the previous tenant of the property you want to rent (this also often applies to renting residential property). Even though key money is illegal, don't be surprised if you are confronted with a tenant who refuses to leave the property you want to rent unless it is paid. There are stories of tenants asking for as much as $100,000 in "key money." Although you can report this to the police as extortion, the practice is so common that some renters actually believe it's a legitimate expense, led into thinking that the money covers the former tenant's moving expenses. If you do decide that you want to rent a property badly enough to pay a *buon uscita,* remember that it is not a tax-deductible expense.

FINANCING, AID, AND LOANS

American banks usually don't give loans to businesses abroad, and Italian banks shy away from giving loans to small businesses in general. (Italian banks' interest rates are so high that you'd probably want to avoid them anyway.) Sometimes, if you have big expenses (e.g., the photo-developing machinery for Foto Quick), you can arrange leasing agreements whereby you pay in installments and can eventually buy the equipment outright.

The Italian government gives much freedom to foreign investors, so that there are hardly any limitations that apply to Americans opening businesses in Italy. The only exceptions are where state monopolies such as telecommunications, railways, and electricity are concerned; Americans may not enter these sectors. A nonresident who wants to invest in Italy does not need authorization, and profits made in Italy can be transferred back to the United States after taxes have been paid in Italy. A foreigner can either open a business following Italian laws or set up a branch office in Italy under the rules of a foreign company by entering into a joint venture with an Italian company. The Italian government offers tax breaks to both resident and nonresident entrepreneurs to encourage them to open businesses in depressed areas such as the Mezzogiorno (south) or to create export companies, small enterprises, or research and development companies. Tax credits can be applied in these cases, and additional tax breaks are given if you hire first-time employees, the unemployed, or people with disabilities. Or you might qualify for a low-interest government loan or grant. In some cases these grants can cover as much as half of your total investment.

HIRING EMPLOYEES

As a small-business owner, you will be responsible for paying your employees' salaries, social security benefits, and annual bonuses. Workers' salaries are determined by preset standards according to profession. There are *tabelle professionali* that classify each kind of worker and how much he or she should earn. (See Chapter 16 for more detailed information.) If you want to hire American employees, you will have to do so according to Italian labor laws.

AMERICAN CHAMBERS OF COMMERCE

There are two chambers of commerce geared toward American businesses, and they can help provide you with ideas and advice. The first is the American Chamber of Commerce in Milan, sponsored by the American government. The second is the private, bilateral, nonprofit Italy-America Chamber of Commerce (IACC) in the United States. It is affiliated with the U.S. Chamber of Commerce and has branches in Atlanta, New York, Los Angeles, Boston, Chicago, Houston, Miami, Pittsburgh, and Philadelphia, in addition to thirty-eight foreign countries. The Italy-America Chamber of Commerce also offers a plethora of online business-related information, such as economic data, information for investors, a trade directory, and a newsletter. You can access the Italy-America Chamber of Commerce West in Los Angeles on line at www.italchambers.net/losangeles/, which includes pages for most IACC branches and links to affiliate chambers all over the world. The IACC in New York has its own Web site at www.italian-chamber.com.

Both of these chambers provide members with information regarding import and export between Italy and the United States, and facilitate trade by matching manufacturers and distributors. The membership fee ranges from $500 to $2,500 per year. In addition, they each publish an extensive annual directory of all the U.S. companies that do business in Italy and Italian companies that do business in the United States. They are considered the "bibles" of U.S.-Italy trade and can be purchased by contacting them at the addresses at the end of this chapter.

ITALIAN CHAMBERS OF COMMERCE

The Italian government operates branches of its own *camere di commercio* (chambers of commerce) throughout the country, and anyone opening a business in Italy must register with the local branch. The primary task of the *camera* is to keep track of the businesses in any given area through its master list called the Registro delle Ditte (Register of Companies). These chambers are also on the Internet. There is one main site (www.camcom.it/) that provides links to Web sites of more than twenty-five local branches and six Unioncamere Regionali (Regional Chamber Unions), such as the Unioncamere Lombardia of the Lombardy region. The individual sites offer information about the chambers' locations, services, and events. For example, the Milan Chamber of Commerce has a *Milan Business Mall—Doing Business in Italy* page where you can find databases of Italian and ECU company profiles.

CONFCOMMERCIO AND THE ISTITUTO DI COMMERCIO ESTERO (ICE)

There are two other organizations that address the needs of local businesses: Confcommercio and the Istituto di Commercio Estero (ICE, or Italian Trade Commission). The function of Confcommercio is to stimulate business in key sectors (such as cosmetics, fashion, construction, computers, software, retail, import, and export) through promotional ac-

Theme bars like this Irish Lion's Fountain Pub in Florence are profitable businesses for American entrepreneurs.

tivities as well as free legal and financial advice for members. It publishes a monthly magazine called *Impresa Italia* and organizes the country's biggest trade fairs. ICE is a public organization based in Rome with more than thirty-four offices in Italy and seventy-seven offices abroad, including in New York, Atlanta, Chicago, and Los Angeles, all of which promote trade between Italy and the United States. Each ICE branch has its own specialty. For example, Los Angeles oversees trade in eyewear and bicycles, Chicago is in charge of motor vehicles and machine tools, Atlanta follows arts and crafts, and New York supervises textiles and food. ICE also organizes international trade fairs, provides members with valuable business contacts, and matches suppliers with products. You'll find the U.S. and Italian addresses of these organizations at the end of this chapter or by looking at ICE's Web site (www.ice.it).

Small-Business Ideas to Consider

There is a wide range of business possibilities for foreigners with an outsider's perspective on what's missing in the Italian market. From American-style restaurants and stores to schools and medical practices, for those of you who have entrepreneurial spirit, determination, and the dream of opening a business in Italy, it can be done. No one can give you the character traits necessary, but there are guidelines for surviving the bureaucratic challenges. As the owner of Foto Quick says, "It's not for the weak." So if you're ready, here are some ideas to get your mind working:

Computer Technology   This one of the fastest-growing sectors, and Italy needs computer experts versed in the latest programs, as well as Internet Web masters.

Tourism   Tourism in Italy is valued at about $20 billion per year, and Americans have been able to capitalize on the market by organizing walking tours, wine-tasting trips, and bike tours. Some open small hotels or bed and breakfasts with accompanying courses on the city or surrounding area.

Import-export   It could prove successful to introduce inexpensive but good-quality home items similar to what Pottery Barn, Crate and Barrel, and Pier One sell, as well as office supplies. Italians go crazy for things like placemats, wicker baskets, Rolodexes, and modern desk accessories.

Real estate agents/realtors   Anyone with experience renting or buying a home in Italy can tell you there is a shortage of professional realtors knowledgeable of American and Italian real estate concerns.

Accountants   Few Italians accountants are experienced with American taxes, and residents who owe an annual payment to Uncle Sam need someone to turn to at least once a year.

Attorneys   There are few lawyers specialized in American and Italian law. I was able to find only one attorney who knew about U.S. trust law.

Theaters and art galleries   Americans with a passion for the arts should consider opening a business that bridges the diverse art worlds of the United States and Italy, including art galleries and English-language cinemas and playhouses.

Restaurants, bars, and discotheques   Franchised theme bars such as Irish pubs and Mexican restaurants are popping up all over the country, and many of them have been opened by Americans. Others open restaurants or catering businesses from home. I know of a woman whose specialty is preparing Asian food. She cooks dishes in front of her guests in an informal cooking school setting and then serves them for 65,000 lire a head. Ethnic dance clubs with live bands are becoming popular with Italians as well.

Health foods   There is a demand for businesses that specialize in health food, such as frozen-yogurt shops, protein drink stands, vegetarian restaurants, organic groceries, and vitamin stores.

Medicine   Italy lacks English-speaking chiropractors, acupuncturists, and doctors specialized in holistic and homeopathic medicine. One American chiropractor opened a very successful practice in Rome, and an American woman opened a practice specializing in the Alexander technique for back and joint trouble.

Schools and student services   Italian students need help preparing for exams, writing résumés in English, learning interview techniques, and applying for scholarships and internships in the United States. You could start a business that provides these services. Many Americans open in-house schools that teach things such as fitness, stress release, birthing, and pottery. Others open English-language nurseries.

Business services   Foreign clients doing business in Italy often need someone to organize conventions, arrange office space, transportation, and accommodations, or provide translating and interpreting. Many companies need the language services of an English speaker for help in preparing annual reports or newsletters.

Elderly care   Because homes for senior citizens are not as common as in the United States, Italian families are always searching for companionship and care for grandparents. You could organize a staff of caretakers and farm out the work.

Wedding services   One American opened a travel agency that specialized in setting up romantic honeymoons in Venice for American newlyweds. Since many Americans dream of getting married in Italy, too, it might be profitable to start a company that helps them do it.

Useful Addresses

ITALY-AMERICA CHAMBERS OF COMMERCE
IN THE UNITED STATES

ATLANTA:

Italy-America Chamber of Commerce
South Regional Chapter
1050 Crown Pointe Parkway, Suite 310
Atlanta, GA 30338
tel (404) 913-9999
fax (404) 671-8513

BOSTON:

**Italy–New England Chamber of
Commerce**
100 Boylston Street
Boston, MA 02116
tel (617) 482-5949
fax (617) 482-6434

CHICAGO:

**Italian-American Chamber of
Commerce of Chicago**
30 South Michigan Avenue, Suite 502
Chicago, IL 60603
tel (312) 553-9137
fax (312) 553-9142

HOUSTON:

**Italy-America Chamber of Commerce
of Texas**
4605 Post Oak Place, Suite 226
Houston, TX 77002
tel (713) 626-9303
fax (713) 626-9309

LOS ANGELES:

**Italy-America Chamber of Commerce,
West**
10350 Santa Monica Boulevard
Los Angeles, CA 90025
tel (310) 557-3017
fax (310) 557-1217
www.italchambers.net/losangeles/

MIAMI:

**Italy-America Chamber of
Commerce—Miami**
1 S.E. 15th Road, Suite 150
Miami, FL 33129
tel (305) 577-9868
fax (305) 577-3956

NEW YORK:

**Italy-America Chamber of
Commerce—New York**
730 Fifth Avenue, Suite 600
New York, NY 10019
tel (212) 459-0044
fax (212) 459-0090
www.italian-chamber.com

PHILADELPHIA:

The Mid-Atlantic Chapter of the IACC
2400 Eleven Penn Center
Philadelphia, PA 19103
tel (215) 963-0998
fax (215) 963-8821

PITTSBURGH:

The Pittsburgh Chapter of the IACC
200 First Avenue, 4th Floor
Pittsburgh, PA 15222
tel (412) 261-2580
fax (412) 261-2678

THE ITALIAN TRADE COMMISSION
(L'ISTITUTO NAZIONALE
PER IL COMMERCIO ESTERO)

**Istituto Nazionale per il Commercio
Estero (ICE)**
Via Liszt, 21
00144 Roma
tel (06) 59921
fax (06) 59926899
www.ice.it

NEW YORK:

Italian Trade Commission
499 Park Avenue, 6th Floor
New York, NY 10022
tel (212) 980-1500
fax (212) 758-1050

ATLANTA:

Italian Trade Commission
233 Peachtree Street, N.E.
Peachtree Center—Harris Tower, Suite
2301
Atlanta, GA 30343

LOS ANGELES:
Italian Trade Commission
1801 Avenue of the Stars, Suite 700
Los Angeles, CA 90067
tel (213) 879-0950
fax (310) 203-8335
CHICAGO:
Italian Trade Commission
401 North Michigan Avenue, Suite 3030
Chicago, IL 60611
tel (312) 670-4360
fax (312) 670-5147

OTHER CHAMBERS AND AUTHORITIES

**American Chamber of Commerce
in Italy**
Via Cantù, 1
20123 Milano
tel (02) 8690661
fax (02) 8057737
Camera di Commercio—Florence
Piazza dei Giudici, 3
50100 Firenze
tel (055) 27951
fax (055) 2795259
Camera di Commercio—Milan
Via Meravigli, 9/b
20123 Milano
tel (02) 85151
fax (02) 85154232

Camera di Commercio—Naples
Via S. Aspreno, 2
80133 Napoli
tel (081) 7607111
fax (081) 5526940
Camera di Commercio—Rome
Via de' Burrò, 147
00186 Roma
tel (06) 520821
fax (06) 6786521
Confcommercio
Piazza Gioacchino Belli, 2
00153 Roma
tel (06) 58661
fax (06) 5809425
Dipartimento della Dogana
(Customs Department)
Viale delle Province, 103
00162 Roma
tel (06) 4452741
Ufficio Italiano dei Cambi
(Currency Exchange Office)
Via Quattro Fontane, 123
00184 Roma
tel (06) 46631
fax (06) 4825591

CHAPTER TWENTY-TWO

Internships and Volunteering

Both internships and volunteering provide a good way for foreigners to become active participants in the Italian work world while avoiding much of the legal and bureaucratic red tape that other employment opportunities entail. Both also provide a great way to improve your Italian without enrolling in a school. Though most of these opportunities are unpaid, some of the more structured programs offer room and board, insurance, and even airfare. Furthermore, you can expect the time and energy you invest to be rewarded with a letter of recommendation and a new overseas experience to add to your résumé. Occasionally, companies you intern with or larger volunteer associations even have openings for part-time or full-time paid positions. If you are already involved with an organization, you will be among the first to know about them. However, at that point legal factors involving visas and permits would apply to you as well since nonprofit organizations must adhere to the same Italian labor laws as for-profit enterprises.

Internships

In Italy, internships are not nearly as common as in the United States, but the concept of the internship is ancient. Old artisans who have perfected their skills over a lifetime pass them on to the next generation by taking young students under their wing as apprentices, exchanging free labor for professional training. The Florentine painter Domenico Ghirlandaio operated a little workshop in the fifteenth century with his brothers and had an apprentice named Michelangelo Buonarroti. By the time Michelangelo worked on the Sistine Chapel, he'd already passed his skills on to numerous apprentices of his own. A similar tradition continues with the modern-day Italian internship, which is quickly catching on. Companies are accepting it as a way of introducing young people into the job market who would otherwise have difficulty entering it.

The majority of organized internship programs in Italy are with American companies or international organizations. Most of these are limited to the biggest Italian cities, most notably Rome, and they are almost always unpaid. The Italian companies that do offer *stage*, as internships are often called in Italian, structure them like American internships: they are usually limited to a few months and are also unpaid. If there were a salary involved, internships would be protected by strict Italian labor laws, making access to them nearly impossible. With the internship, employers have no legal obligation to hire the intern on a permanent basis at the conclusion of it.

To apply for any internship, you generally need a résumé, a cover letter describing what kind of internship you want and how long you want it to last, a letter of recommendation from a professor, and a portfolio of work if relevant. Not all internships require Italian fluency, but most internship coordinators will tell you the better you speak the language, the more you will gain from the experience. When you apply, you should stress your language ability and any international experience on your résumé, as well as any relevant past academic or professional experience. In your cover letter, explain why doing an internship in Italy is more important to you than doing one back home. To do this, you might offer examples of things you can learn only in Italy. For example, if you want to do an internship related to the arts, you could say that being close to the museums in Florence is essential.

MEDIA INTERNSHIPS

Most media internships are in Rome, home of the Stampa Estera (Foreign Press Club), although there are few foreign newspaper bureaus there since many of them closed decades ago, when newspapers decided that the cost of keeping foreign bureaus was too high. Of those that have stayed, most have their offices in the Stampa Estera building.

You can post your résumé there on the main bulletin board, contact the Stampa Estera administrative office, or consult its annual membership directory of American bureaus in Italy.

The Associated Press, one of the two main news agencies, has as many as five interns at any given time in its Rome bureau, and it sometimes hires an intern for its Milan bureau. This is the biggest and most structured of all the print journalism internships in Italy. It is a great way to work alongside seasoned foreign correspondents in a smoke-filled, coffee-stained newsroom and observe them reporting the news under pressure-cooker-tight deadlines. You can watch as they handle foreign dignitaries and the fallen stars of the Italian political scene during one-on-one interviews. I interned there for six months and found the hands-on training invaluable. If breaking news happens, expect to be thrown into the high-stress, high-speed environment of the newsroom. Some interns thrive on the adrenaline; others swear off journalism for good. You must stay with the program for at least three months before you will be given a writing assignment, but if you're in the market for fine-tuning your reporting skills, it can be useful and a great résumé builder. If the staff recommends you, the internship can lead to paid freelance jobs. To apply, you should present any published clippings you may have from college papers or from previous internships.

Reuters, the British news agency, has a similar program but does not hire as many interns at once. It usually needs an intern during the summer months, when the staff journalists go on vacation. A Reuters intern I spoke with who also did the AP internship says she got more writing experience with Reuters. Since it does not have a structured program, the internship can last as little as three weeks or as long as you are needed.

If you want to be in Florence, *Vista* magazine (see Chapter 3 for address) takes about ten interns per year. Because *Vista* is a smaller operation than most, interns have the chance to participate in all areas of production, from ad copy and photos to editorial meetings with writers and graphic designers. In the past, some interns have written articles, worked on the photo archive, and helped with office work. The internship is unpaid and is even open to people who don't speak Italian well. The Managing Editor recommends that potential candidates contact the magazine in writing by sending a cover letter and résumé (no phone calls), emphasizing their particular areas of interest.

If you're interested in broadcast journalism, try CNN (Cable Network News), WTN (World TV News), Reuters TV, or APTV (Associated Press Television) in Rome. CNN says, "We're lucky to have one intern a year," but adds that whether or not it has an intern depends on what's going on in Italy. If you're interested, you might try to apply at election time or when big news is breaking. CNN interns help with research, accompany video crews on location, and learn how to synchronize stories and log tapes. It accepts only university students as interns, and you should send the Rome office a copy of your résumé, a letter of recommendation from a professor, and a college transcript. APTV and Reuters TV take more interns at once and offer similar work experience. WTN has a small, informal unpaid internship program, but it encourages people to apply and says that interns are given crucial work, including doing their own stories with a crew. The WTN program is the most hands-on of all the broadcast journalism internships.

INTERNSHIPS IN THE ARTS

Venice is home to one of the most prestigious art internship programs in the world: the Peggy Guggenheim Collection internship. The Peggy Guggenheim Collection, located on the Grand Canal, needs people in their early twenties with an interest in art and a knowledge of Italian to help with daily operations. Interns are responsible for preparing the galleries each morning before the museum opens and closing them at night. Interns also guard the rooms, answer questions from museum visitors, sell tickets and catalogs, and assist with other administrative details. Although interns aren't paid, the Guggenheim organizes lectures on modern art and arranges visits to sights and exhibitions in the Lagoon City for the interns as part of their training program.

LAW INTERNSHIPS

Two law organizations specializing in international law offer unpaid internships in Italy. The first is the International Juridical Organization for Economic and Social Development (IJO), many of whose activities deal with the environment. Interns clerk, collaborate on projects, and assist the legal team with research and procedures that often involve spending long hours in the legal library. The second is an international organization called the International Development Law Institute (IDLI). It offers six- to nine-month-long internships that focus on logistics and other international legal issues. Internships are limited to students interested in becoming lawyers and advisers to developing countries. The main task interns face is assisting in research, and in compensation they receive special law courses prepared by IDLI. To apply to either of these programs, you should have a law background or be currently enrolled in, or have recently graduated from, law school.

INTERNSHIPS WITH INTERNATIONAL ORGANIZATIONS

Italy is home to many international organizations, such as the United Nations, IFAD, IOM, OXFAM, UNICEF, and UNESCO. All offer internships for students with backgrounds in international relations, political science, social science, public relations, and economics. They also all share two basic requirements: that candidates be proficient in spoken Italian and that they send the organizations a cover letter and résumé before calling.

The United Nations has two offices in Italy with internship programs: the U.N. High Commissioner for Refugees (UNHCR) and the U.N. Information Center. Internships with the UNHCR involve researching issues vital to refugees, and occasionally interns are sent to help out in poor areas of Italy or even to Third World nations to collect data. Internships with the U.N. Information Center involve distributing information related to the United Nations' functions. Positions last for at least three months and include three half days per week, either in the library or in the press office. Library positions include research, filing, and keeping archives up to date. Press office positions include answering phones, doing legal research, and helping with public relations, but because the office is small, your duties can expand if you demonstrate commitment and enthusiasm.

The International Fund for Agricultural Development (IFAD) regularly has unpaid internships in its public relations, agricultural studies, and economics departments. There is also an in-house roster where you can post your résumé so that members of various departments can determine individually if they could use your services. If they do, you would probably be assigned to help with a short-term project such as an annual report or a special presentation.

The International Organization for Migration (IOM) has formal internship programs in both its Rome and Milan offices. These programs are organized by the headquarters in Geneva, and it is to the Geneva office that you should send your résumé and cover letter. Internships last two or three months on average but depend largely on the individual student and the availability of assignments. Officials at the Geneva headquarters say they'd like to see more interns in Italy, so this promises to be a great opportunity.

OXFAM describes its program more as "volunteer work" rather than an internship, but volunteers can ask for a letter of recommendation from the OXFAM program director if they need one for university credit. Activities that volunteers/interns participate in include organizing projects such as concerts and raffles and running the OXFAM thrift shop in Rome, which sells used goods to raise money for developing nations.

UNICEF, the international organization dedicated to helping children in Third World countries, sometimes takes interns as well. An intern's duties are limited to office work and include clerking, filing, and research. UNESCO also has similar internships in Italy, but you must send your résumé to the headquarters in France.

INTERNSHIP ORGANIZATIONS

The Association of International Students for Economics and Commerce (AISEC) is a nonprofit, student-run group affiliated with fifty-five American universities. It organizes what are called "traineeship programs" for university students interested in gaining professional experience with large Italian companies in economics, marketing, business, and computer science. The internships can last anywhere from six weeks to eighteen months, and you must apply from the United States to participate—AISEC says it will not help American students who are already in Italy. If you are interested, you should contact the New York office to find out which branch office is closest to you. To qualify, you must become a member by paying the $150 membership fee, and you must make an appointment with one of the local AISEC counselors to discuss your qualifications and professional goals. Once you've determined what kind of internship you'd like, you'll have to wait six months to a year before being placed. Another Italian organization that might help is the Mercurius Association in Turin, which publishes an annual directory (available for about 15,000 lire, or $10, plus shipping) of all the large Italian companies that accept interns. The Mercurius directory also offers practical tips on preparing your résumé, as well as a listing of graduate programs both in Italy and abroad.

In the United States, there are a number of other organizations like AISEC that arrange internships abroad for American students. Some of these organizations charge high fees for their services and limit their assistance to supplying you with a list of Italian company addresses. Others that definitely do more to help are listed at the end of this chapter; however, you should ask as many questions as possible concerning the internship possibilities, the type of professional experience you will gain, and the availability of housing. One way to judge the quality of the organization is to ask if it requires a lengthy interview to determine what kind of internship is best suited for you; if it does, you can probably assume it has your best interests at heart.

FINDING INTERNSHIPS THROUGH UNIVERSITIES AND CREATING YOUR OWN

Many American schools, including Brown University and Syracuse University, offer internship opportunities as part of their study abroad package for students enrolled in their Italy programs (see Chapter 12 for addresses of American universities). In addition, the Institute of European Studies (IES), based in Chicago, has a branch in Milan that offers college credit internships for its students, as well as students from affiliated universities. If your university does not offer internships as part of its study abroad program, ask if it is affiliated with IES. Currently, many Italian universities—most notably the Università di Parma—also have services to help their students find internships. In the next few years, it is anticipated that all Italian public universities will begin to offer this type of service.

There are countless other internship possibilities in Italy that are not listed in this chapter. Because internships are flexible and beneficial to all parties involved, many more Italian employers would surely accept interns if they knew how they could benefit from the situation. Of course, you'll have to convince them of these benefits on your own. You could make cold calls to personnel offices or post announcements with professional organizations in your field such as the Associazione Italiana degli Analisti Finanziari (AIAF, or Italian Association of Financial Analysts) or the Associazione Italiana Editori (AIE, or Italian Publishers' Association). To find such organizations, check in the Milan and Rome phone books since most are headquartered there. If that doesn't work, you might try sending your résumé and a cover letter to the addresses listed in Chapters 3 and 18.

Volunteering

There are more than 35,000 volunteer associations, cooperatives, and foundations in Italy, and about 10 million Italians actively contribute to a cause in one form or another. Volunteer opportunities involve everything from archaeological digs to animal protection, from teaching to medical assistance. Besides the obvious payoff of feeling you have contributed to helping society, volunteers form social and professional contacts important for future opportunities. For practical purposes, volunteer organizations in Italy can be divided into a few different categories. The first category is made up of foreign organizations headquartered in other countries that organize specific large-scale volunteer projects in Italy. These programs often require an application fee, a minimum age, and a length of commitment ranging from three weeks to two years. The second category is made up of Italian branches of international organizations with offices in the United States, such as Greenpeace and Amnesty International. Sometimes the American office can help you get into touch with its Italian affiliate. The third category is composed of Italian organizations that function exclusively in Italy, such as local architectural restoration associations. With these organizations, you will have to write directly to them from the United States or set up the position once you arrive. In addition, aside from the large-scale volunteer organizations listed at the end of this chapter, every Italian town has small local groups, which you can find under *"Associazioni"* (Associations) in the local Italian yellow pages.

ARCHAEOLOGY AND ARCHITECTURE

Volunteering on an archaeological dig usually means sleeping in a trailer or tent, getting up before dawn, and sweating in a field all day under the hot sun. Scuttling around on their hands and knees covered in dust, archeologists spend much of their time carefully scraping away layers of dirt and dividing pieces of pottery into bags. Those who are artistically inclined are often placed in the "small finds" office, where they make detailed drawings of the artifacts alongside people cleaning the pottery with brushes and water. Although the archaeological work can often be backbreaking and tedious, most people who have done it say they would do it again without giving it a second thought, just for the thrill of hands-on discovery.

Even the Roman Forum can be the site of an archaeological dig for enthusiastic volunteers.

One of the biggest Italian archaeological organizations, Gruppo Archeologici d'Italia (Archaeologists of Italy Group), has chapters in more than seventy towns from Piedmont to Sicily. It needs volunteers to help with excavations all over the peninsula, especially during summer months, and should be contacted directly for more information. There are also several specific digs taking place in Italy that you can help out with. If you want to work on an Etruscan farm, for instance, professors from the University of Rome are excavating one in San Mario, in the valley of the Cecina River. For more information, you should contact Earthwatch in Massachusetts. Hunter College (of the City University of New York) and the University of Bradford in the United Kingdom sponsor the Anglo-American Research Project in Pompeii. Their dig focuses on studying the urbanization of this ancient city and includes weekly field trips to other sites. College credit is available (for information, see the Hunter College entry at the end of this chapter). For an experience that is less demanding physically, the Centro Camuno di Studi Preistorici, an Italian research institute that studies the prehistoric period, looks for volunteers interested in archaeology, anthropology, and primitive art to help with all aspects of research from exploration to data entry.

There are a few associations operating in Italy that have "adopted" abandoned architectural sites in the countryside and are working to restore them to livable condition. Three examples are La Sabraneque (based in France), International Bouworde–IBO (based in the Netherlands), and Bouworde (based in Belgium). Another, Involvement Volunteers Association, based in Australia, also restores buildings in Italy and performs other projects related to archaeology, research, and teaching. Concordia (Youth Service Volunteers Ltd.), a British organization, restores local Italian monuments and palaces, does social work, heads archaeological digs, and places volunteers in work camps.

ENVIRONMENTAL AND ANIMAL CARE

Two of the most important and active volunteer associations in Italy are the World Wildlife Fund, or WWF (pronounced "vu-vu-effay" by Italians), and Greenpeace. The Italian headquarters of WWF was opened in 1966 and now has 260 local branch offices. A third, Amici della Terra (Friends of the Earth), was founded in the United States in 1969 and now has offices in thirty-eight countries, including Italy. One of the most important and active is the Legambiente, the Italian national equivalent of the WWF. Another, the Associazione Mare Vivo (Living Sea Association), located on the bank of the extremely polluted Tiber River in Rome, is dedicated to saving the oceans from pollution.

When it comes to animal protection, one of the largest national groups is the Ente Nazionale Protezione Animali (ENPA, or National Animal Protection Agency). It was founded in 1871 by Giuseppe Garibaldi, an avid animal lover, just ten years after he united Italy. Garibaldi also served as its honorary president, bringing animal rights to the attention of Italians and their new government. Today, ENPA has more than one hundred local branches and 50,000 members. Other important animal protection associations include the Associazione Nazionale Protezione Animali (ANPA, or National Animal Protection Association) and the Lega Nazionale per la Difesa del Cane (National Dog Defense League). The latter runs shelters to house abandoned and abused animals and promotes general animal protection awareness. Founded in

1950, it now has more than 30,000 members and saves upward of 13,000 cats and dogs each year.

SOCIAL SERVICES AND HUMAN RIGHTS

Most opportunities in the field of social services and human rights lie with big organizations such as the Croce Rossa Italiana (Italian Red Cross), whose volunteers include nurses, military corps members, and first aid assistants, and Amnesty International, which has more than 24,000 members and two hundred local branches. Another, Medici Senza Frontiere (Doctors Without Borders) is famous for sending volunteer medical help to war-torn areas (it has had a satellite office in Italy since 1994). Active American organizations in Italy include Global Volunteers, which promotes education by placing volunteer teachers in remote areas of the peninsula, and the Center for Interim Programs, which helps refugees in Rome by providing legal assistance, language classes, and job training.

Of the more prominent Italian national social service organizations, there is the Associazione per la Pace (Association for Peace); Associazione per la Gestione dei Servizi e la Solidarietà (AUSER, or Association for the Management of Services and Solidarity), which provides assistance to elderly people; and SEAC, which is active in prisons. Others include Mani Tese and Movi Mondo MOLISV. The Associazione Nazionale Lotta Contro l'AIDS (ANLAIDS, or National Association for the Fight Against AIDS), and the Lega Italiana Lotta AIDS (LILA, or Italian League Fighting AIDS) are two national associations helping in the fight against AIDS. The Associazione Volontari Ospedalieri (AVO, or Hospital Volunteers Association), with more than 15,000 members, provides assistance to hospital patients in the form of physical and moral support. In Florence, there is a section that provides interpreting for English-speaking patients.

On a regional level there are hundreds of such organizations. For example, in Turin the Associazione Italiana Zingari Oggi (Italian Gypsies Today Association) has about 1,000 active volunteers and about 6,000 members. Started in 1971, this association helps Gypsies with social services, legal matters, health problems, and education. In Rome, the Associazione Cultura Assistenza Popolare Comunità di Sant'Egidio (ACAP) provides free drug rehabilitation and counseling. SOS Razzismo Italia (SOS Racism Italy) is active in Lazio against racism. Gruppo Abele provides assistance and counseling to people in the Turin area with drug addiction problems.

Religious Organizations

There are several national and international religious organizations that are particularly active in the peninsula, but all are overshadowed by Caritas, the Catholic volunteer organization, which is operated by the Vatican and has branches throughout Italy. Another large one is Misericordia, a volunteer medical service that was started centuries ago and today offers nearly free health care and ambulance services to anyone who needs them. Members who are not trained doctors and nurses help out by driving ambulances and assisting the medical staff. The Società San Vincenzo de'Paoli was started in 1850 and now has approximately 30,000 volunteer members nationwide. It focuses on helping immigrants, the elderly, and the unemployed. Other such associations include the Associazione di Cooperazione Cristiana Internazionale (AACRI, or International Christian Cooperation Association) and the Papa Giovanni XXIII.

When it comes to international religious volunteer organizations operating in Italy, there are a few big ones. The YMCA Federazione Italiana Associazioni Cristiane dei Giovani (YMCA Italian Federation of Christian Youth Associations) organizes activities for young people and provides them with counseling. The Gioventù Operaia Cristiana, which was started in Belgium in 1925 and is now present in more than fifty countries including Italy, also provides assistance to youth. L'Arche, an interdenominational Christian organization, gives shelter to people with developmental disabilities and organizes volunteer positions in twenty-six countries. There are two L'Arche houses in Italy, commonly called "Il Chicco." Or, if you're looking for a summer position that's a little more academic, try the Agape Centro Ecumenico, a Christian conference center in the Italian Alps. It needs a small handful of volunteers each year to help the regular staff.

Work Camps and Summer Camps

Each year Volunteers for Peace (VFP) and Servizio Civile Internazionale (SCI, or Civil Service International) collaborate to create more than seventy-five "international work camps" all over Italy with positions for hundreds of volunteers. The camps are divided into general categories revolving around common themes, such as antiracism, solidarity, peace, and ecology, among others. Volunteer projects can include anything from organizing a multicultural festival in Tuscany to raising money for refugees in Rome, from farming in the Piedmont countryside and helping shepherds on the island of Sardinia to counseling people with drug-related problems in Florence. Camp workers build flood prevention structures, restore medieval towns, and set up forest fire protection. All of the available positions are listed in detail in VFP's annual directory, which can be purchased by mail at little cost. Because the registration deadline changes each year, make sure to inquire with VFP before March.

If you would like to move to Italy for a summer, there are many Italian volunteer summer camps you can become involved with. Some are for children; others are also for adults. Many of the positions fill up quickly, so you should make arrangements several months in advance. Most also require that you pay a registration fee, as well as your own room and board. For example, Gruppo Archeologici d'Italia sponsors nine summer camps for children, mostly in Lazio and Calabria, where volunteers even help in underwater excavations of sunken Roman ships. World Wildlife Fund Italia has summer camps for children of all ages in the regions of Puglia, Sicily, and Emilia-Romagna with lodgings in authentic medieval castles. Tasks involve studying and tending to local wildlife and fauna, leading trekking expeditions, and working on the first Italian marine reserve lying underwater off the coast of Sicily.

Legambiente has more than one hundred camps in Italy that, like the association itself, are oriented toward saving the environment. Volunteers help to clean coastlines, construct new facilities, take care of reserves, and help protect against brush fires. Nuova Acropoli Associazione Culturale (New Acropolis Cultural Association) also has a volunteer summer camp for people interested in helping to prevent forest fires. Europe Conservation Italia, an international environmental association, has camps for those interested in monitoring endangered birds and whales in the Mediterranean. The Lega Italiana Protezione Uccelli (Italian Bird Protection League) has a junior camp for children who want to study the birds on a reserve in Sardinia and protect them from poachers. Other summer camps include Lunaria, which focuses on human rights protection activities, assisting disabled children, and building playgrounds, as well as Mani Tesi, which organizes events to promote intercultural relations and recycling.

INTERNSHIPS

INTERNSHIPS WITH THE MEDIA

**Associazione della Stampa Estera in Italia
(Foreign Press Association)**
Via della Mercede, 55
00187 Rome
tel (06) 675911
fax (06) 67591262
Associated Press
Piazza Grazioli, 5
00186 Roma
tel (06) 6784201
fax (06) 6784591
Associated Press Television (APTV)
Piazza Grazioli, 5
00186 Roma
tel (06) 69942362
fax (06) 69942364
CNN
Via Col di Lana, 8
00195 Roma
tel (06) 3614266
fax (06) 3614238
Reuters
Via della Cordonata, 7
00187 Roma
tel (06) 6782501
fax (06) 6794248
Reuters Television
Via della Cordonata, 7
00187 Roma
tel (06) 69984381
fax (06) 6795103
Worldwide Television News (WTN)
Via Monte della Farina, 42
00186 Roma
tel (06) 6875002
fax (06) 68807209

INTERNSHIPS IN THE ARTS

Peggy Guggenheim Collection
Fondazione Solomon R. Guggenheim
Dorsoduro, S. Gregorio, 701
30123 Venezia
tel (041) 5206288
fax (041) 5206885

LAW INTERNSHIPS

**IDLI
(International Development Law
Institute)**
Via di S. Sebastianello, 16
00187 Roma
tel (06) 69922745
fax (06) 6781946
**International Juridical Organization for
Economic and Social Development (IJO)**
Via Barberini, 3
00187 Roma
tel/fax (06) 4742117

INTERNSHIPS WITH INTERNATIONAL ORGANIZATIONS

**International Fund for Agricultural
Development (IFAD)**
Via del Serafico, 107
00143 Roma
tel (06) 54591
fax (06) 5043463
**International Organization for
Migration (IOM)**
Chief Division Personnel
17 Route des Morillons
1211 Geneva 19 (Switzerland)
tel (4122) 7179111
fax (4122) 7986150
OXFAM
Vicolo Doria, 7
00186 Roma
tel (06) 6791129
fax (06) 6781125
UNESCO
J. Larrauri PER/TRA
1, rue Miollis
75732 Paris Cedex 15 (France)
tel (331) 45683758
fax (331) 45685666
UNICEF—Italian Committee
Via Vittorio Emanuele Orlando, 83
00185 Roma
tel (06) 478091
fax (06) 47809270

United Nations High Commissioner for
Refugees
Via Caroncini, 19
00197 Roma
tel (06) 8077119
fax (06) 8082338
United Nations Information Center
Piazza San Marco, 50
00186 Roma
tel (06) 6789907
fax (06) 6793337

INTERNSHIP ORGANIZATIONS

AISEC
(Association of International Students
for Economics and Commerce)
135 West 50th Street, 20th Floor
New York, NY 10020
tel (212) 757-3774
fax (212) 757-4062
www.aisec.org/us
aisec@us.aisec.org
Internships International, LLC
1116 Cowper Drive
Raleigh, NC 27608
tel/fax (919) 832-1575
intintl@aol.com
http://rtpnet.org/~intintl
Worldwide Internships and Service
Education (WISE)
303 South Craig Street
Pittsburgh, PA 15213
tel (412) 681-8120
fax (412) 681-8187
wise@unix.cis.pitt.edu
Institute of European Studies (IES)
223 West Ohio Street
Chicago, IL 60610
tel (800) 995-2300
fax (312) 944-1448
iesiascr@mcs.net
Associazione Mercurius
Via Bel Fiore, 82
10126 Torino
tel (011) 6693054
fax (011) 6692625

VOLUNTEERING
ITALIAN VOLUNTEER UMBRELLA
ORGANIZATIONS

ANPAS
(National Public Assistance Association)
Via Baracca, 209
50127 Firenze
tel (055) 374887
fax (055) 375002
CNCA
(National Coordination of Welcoming
Communities)
Via Vallescura, 47
63010 Fermo (AP)
tel (0734) 672504
fax (0734) 675539
Fondazione Italiana per il Volontariato
(Italian Foundation of Volunteering)
Via Nazionale, 39
00184 Roma
tel (06) 474811
fax (06) 4814617
Movimento Volontariato Italiano
Via San Nicolao, 6
20123 Milano
tel (02) 72004317
fax (02) 72002281

ITALIAN VOLUNTEERING INTERNET SITES

Associazioni
www.mi.cnr.it:80/IGST/Associazioni.htm
Nonprofit (*Città Invisibile*)
www.citinv.it
Solidarity
www.crs4.IT/HTML/Solidarity.html
ADDRESSES OF VOLUNTEER
ORGANIZATIONS IN ITALY

(*Note:* Only the main headquarters of
each organization are included; many
have branches all over the country.)
ACAP (Comunità di Sant'Egidio)
Piazza Sant'Egidio, 3/A
00153 Roma
tel (06) 5895945
ACLI
Via G. Marcora, 18/20
00153 Roma

tel (06) 58401
fax (06) 5840436
Agape Centro Ecumenico
Borgata Agape, 1
10060 Prali, Torino
tel (0121) 807514
fax (0121) 807690
Amici della Terra
(Friends of the Earth)
Via di Torre Argentina, 18
00186 Roma
tel (06) 6875308
fax (06) 68308610
Amnesty International
Viale Mazzini, 146
00195 Roma
tel (06) 37513860
fax (06) 37515406
ARCI
Via dei Mille, 23
00185 Roma
tel (06) 4453995
fax (06) 4465934
Associazione di Cooperazione Cristiana
Internazionale (ACCRI)
Via Cavana, 16/A
34124 Trieste
tel/fax (040) 307899
Associazione Italiana Zingari Oggi
Corso Monte Grappa, 118
10145 Torino
tel (011) 7496016
fax (011) 740171
Associazione Nazionale Lotta Contro
L'AIDS (ANLAIDS)
Via Barberini, 3
00187 Roma
tel (06) 4820999
fax (06) 4821077
Associazione Nazionale Protezione
Animali
Via Attilio Regolo, 27
00192 Roma
tel (06) 3242873
fax (06) 3221000
Associazione Mare Vivo
Lungotevere Arnaldo da Brescia
Scalo De Pinido
00196 Roma

tel (06) 3202949
fax (06) 3222564
Associazione per la Gestione dei Servizi
e la Solidarietà (AUSER)
Via dei Frentani, 4a
00185 Roma
tel (06) 44481298
fax (06) 44481247
Associazione per la Pace
Via G.B. Vico, 22
00196 Roma
tel (06) 3212242
fax (06) 3216705
Associazione Volontari
Ospedalieri (AVO)
Via San Marino, 30
10134 Torino
tel (011) 3198918
Caritas Italiana
Viale F. Baldelli, 41
00146 Roma
tel (06) 541921
fax (06) 5410300
Centro Camuno di Studi Preistorici
Via Marconi, 7
25044 Capo di Ponte (Brescia)
tel (0364) 42091
fax (0364) 42572
Il Chicco (L'Arche)
Via Ancona, 1
00043 Ciampino (Roma)
tel (06) 7963850
fax (06) 7962104
Croce Rossa Italiana
(Italian Red Cross)
Via Toscana, 12
00187 Roma
tel (06) 47591
fax (06) 44244534
www.crossnet.org (Red Cross
International site)
Ente Nazionale Protezione Animali
(ENPA)
Corso San Maurizio, 71
10124 Torino
tel (011) 8122894
fax (011) 8127482

Europe Conservation Italia
Via del Macao, 9
00185 Roma
tel (06) 4741241
fax (06) 4744671
Gioventù Operaia Cristiana
Via Vittorio Amedeo II, 16
10121 Torino
tel (011) 541806
fax (011) 5626253
Greenpeace
Via Gelsomini, 28
00153 Roma
tel (06) 5750053
fax (06) 5783531
Gruppo Abele
Via Giolitti, 21
10123 Torino
tel (011) 8395444
fax (011) 8395577
Gruppo Archeologici d'Italia
Via degli Scipioni, 30a
00192 Roma
tel (06) 39733786
fax (06) 39734449
Lega Nazionale per la Difesa del Cane
Via Germagnano, 9
10156 Torino
tel (011) 2620902
Lega Italiana Lotta AIDS (LILA)
Viale Tibaldi, 41
20136 Milano
tel (02) 58114980
fax (02) 89400941
Lega Italiana Protezione Uccelli (LIPU)
Via Trento, 49
43100 Parma
tel (0521) 273043
fax (0521) 273419
Legambiente
Via Salaria, 403
00199 Roma
tel (06) 86268324
fax (06) 86268319
Lunaria
Via Salaria, 89
00198 Roma
tel (06) 8841880

fax (06) 8841859
ics.apax.lun@agora.stm.it
Mani Tese (MATE)
Via Cavenaghi, 4
20149 Milano
tel (02) 48008617
fax (02) 4812296
manitese@planet.it
Medici Senza Frontiere
Via Ostiense, 6/e
00154 Roma
tel (06) 57300900
fax (06) 57300902
Misericordia
Piazza San Giovanni, 1
50129 Firenze
tel (055) 283756
fax (055) 288484
Movi Mondo MOLISV
Piazza Albania, 10
00153 Roma
tel (06) 57300330
fax (06) 5744869
Nuova Acropoli—Associazione Culturale
Piazza Colonna, 355
00187 Roma
tel (06) 6792405
Papa Giovanni XXIII
Via Tiberio, 6
47037 Rimini
tel (0541) 55025
fax (0541) 23040
SEAC
Via della Conciliazione, 1
00193 Roma
tel (06) 6868751
fax (06) 68802088
Servizio Civile Internazionale (SCI)
Via G. Cardano, 135
00142 Roma
tel (06) 5580661
fax (06) 5585268
Società San Vincenzo de'Paoli
Corso Matteotti, 11
10121 Torino
tel (011) 5621986
fax (011) 5627793

SOS Razzismo Italia
Via XX Settembre, 49
00186 Roma
tel (06) 4820965
World Wildlife Fund (WWF) Italia
Via Garigliano, 57
00198 Roma
tel (06) 844971
fax (06) 85300612
YMCA Federazione Italiana
Associazioni Cristiane dei Giovani
Via Varese, 5
00185 Roma
tel (06) 490539
fax (06) 491857

AMERICAN AND FOREIGN ASSOCIATIONS
OPERATING IN ITALY

Amnesty International
322 Eighth Avenue
New York, NY 10001
tel (212) 807-8400
fax (212) 627-1451
L'Arche
The Association of L'Arche North
America
7401 Sussex Avenue
Burnaby, BC V5J 3V6
Canada
tel (604) 438-6883
Bouworde
Tiensesteenweg 145
3010 Leuven, Belgium
tel (32) (16) 259144
fax (32) (16) 259160
Center for Interim Programs
P.O. Box 2347
Cambridge, MA 02238
tel (617) 547-0980
fax (617) 661-2864
interimcip@aol.com
Concordia Ltd.
(Youth Service Volunteers)
8 Brunswick Place, Hove
East Sussex BN3 1ET, England
tel (44) (273) 772086
Earthwatch
680 Mt. Auburn Street
P.O. Box 9104
Watertown, MA 02272-9104

tel (800) 776-0188
tel (617) 926-8200
fax (617) 926-8532
info@earthwatch.org
www.earthwatch.org
Global Volunteers
375 East Little Canada Road
St. Paul, MN 55117
tel (800) 487-1074
tel (612) 482-1074
fax (612) 482-0915
Greenpeace
1436 U Street, N.W.
Washington, DC 20009
tel (202) 462-1177
fax (202) 462-4507
www.greenpeace.org
Hunter College, CUNY
Department of Anthropology
Anglo-American Research Project in
Pompeii
Attn: Bernice Kurchin
695 Park Avenue
New York, NY 10021
tel (212) 772-5672
fax (212) 772-5423
bxkgc@cunyvm.cuny.edu
International Bouworde-IBO
St. Annastraat
172 6524 GT Nijmegen
The Netherlands
tel (31) (80) 226074
Involvement Volunteers Association
P.O. Box 218
Port Melbourne, Victoria 3207
Australia
tel/fax (61) (3) 646-5504
La Sabraneque
Centre Internationale
rue de la Tour de l'Oume
30290 Saint Victor la Coste, France
tel (033) (66) 500505
—or—
Jaqueline Simon
217 High Park Boulevard
Buffalo, NY 14226
tel (716) 836-8698

"Spoken words fly away and written ones remain"—the credo for the slogans splashed across the boardwalk of Rome's Tiberina Island.

Volunteers for Peace
43 Tiffany Road
Belmont, VT 05730
tel (802) 259-2759
fax (802) 259-2922
www.vermontel.com/~vfp/home.htm

World Wildlife Fund
1250 24th Street, N.W.
Washington, DC 20037
tel (202) 293-4800
fax (202) 293-5211
www.panda.org (WWF International)

For Further Study:
Books and Films

EXPATRIATE TRAVELOGUES AND LITERATURE SET IN ITALY

James Fenimore Cooper, *Excursions in Italy; The Letters and Journals of James Fenimore Cooper*

Charles Dickens, *Pictures from Italy*

George Eliot, *Romola*

E. M. Forster, *Twilight in Italy; A Room with a View; Where Angels Fear to Tread*

Margaret Fuller, *The Portable Margaret Fuller*

Johann W. von Goethe, *Italian Journeys*

Robert Graves, *I, Claudius*

Nathaniel Hawthorne, *The Marble Faun, Or the Romance of Monte Beni; Passages from the French and Italian Notebooks; Rapaccini's Daughter*

Ernest Hemingway, *A Farewell to Arms*

Oscar Hijuelos, *The Fourteen Sisters of Emilio Montez O'Brien*

Washington Irving, "The Inn at Terracina" (from *Tales of a Traveller by Geoffrey Crayon, Gent.*); *Notes and Journals of Travel in Europe, 1804–1805*

Henry James, *The Portrait of a Lady; Roderick Hudson; The Aspern Papers; Daisy Miller; Italian Hours; Portraits of Places; Henry James on Italy*

Thomas Jefferson, *Thomas Jefferson's European Travel Diaries* (James McGrath Morris and Persephone Weene, eds.)

D. H. Lawrence, *Aaron's Rod; Twilight in Italy; Sea and Sardinia; Etruscan Places*

Thomas Mann, *Death in Venice*

Mary McCarthy, *The Stones of Florence; Venice Observed*

Herman Melville, *The Writing of Herman Melville: Journals* (Howard C. Horsford with Lynn Horth, eds.)

Ann Radcliffe, *The Mysteries of Udolpho*

Harriet Beecher Stowe, *Agnes of Sorrento*

Mark Twain, *The Innocents Abroad; A Tramp Abroad; Tom Sawyer Abroad; The Autobiography of Mark Twain*

Horace Walpole, *The Castle of Otranto*

Edith Wharton, *Italian Backgrounds; Italian Villas and Their Gardens; Roman Fever; Souls Belated; Edith Wharton Abroad: Selected Travel Writings, 1888–1920* (Sarah Bird Wright, ed.)

NONFICTION BOOKS ABOUT ITALY

Nicoletta Alegi and Deirdre Ryan, *Rome for Children*

Arthur Andersen & Co., *Doing Business in Italy*

Phebe Archer (ed.), *Business Guide to Italy*

Paul Baker, *The Fortunate Pilgrims: Americans in Italy, 1800–1860*

Arturo Barone, *Italians First! An A to Z of Everything Achieved First by Italians*

Luigi Barzini, *The Italians*

Gloria Brolatti, *Come cavarsela con la burocrazia*

Van Wyck Brooks, *The Dream of Arcadia: American Writers and Artists in Italy, 1760–1915*

Jacob Burckhardt, *Civilization of the Renaissance in Italy*

Carlo M. Cipolla, *Storia facile dell'economia italiana dal medioevo a oggi*

Martin Clark, *Modern Italy, 1871–1982*

Toby Cole (ed.), *Florence: A Traveler's Anthology*

Mario Costantino and Lawrence Gambella, *The Italian Way: Aspects of Behavior, Attitudes, and Customs of the Italians*

Christopher Duggan, *A Concise History of Italy*

Raymond Flower and Alessandro Falassi, *Culture Shock! Italy*

Matt Frei, *Getting the Boot: Italy's Unfinished Revolution*

Paul Furlong, *Modern Italy*

Paul Fussell, *Abroad*

Paul Ginsborg, *A History of Contemporary Italy: Society and Politics, 1943–1988*

Barbara Grizzuti Harrison, *Italian Days*

Paul Hofmann, *That Fine Italian Hand*

Anne Holler, *Florencewalks*

William Dean Howells, *Tuscan Cities*

Peggy Kenna and Sondra Lacy, *Business Italy: A Practical Guide to Understanding Italian Business Etiquette*

David I. Kertzer, *Sacrificed for Honor*

Ronald L. Krannich and Caryl Rae Krannich, *The Complete Guide to International Jobs and Careers*

R. W. B. Lewis, *The City of Florence*

Valerio Lintner, *A Traveller's History of Italy*

William Murray, *Italy, the Fatal Gift*

Tim Parks, *Italian Neighbors, or a Lapsed Anglo-Saxon in Verona*

Walter Pater, *The Renaissance*

Martin Penner, *Teaching English: Italy*

John Ruskin, *The Stones of Venice*

Hugh Shankland, *Simple Etiquette in Italy*

Michael Sheridan, *Romans: Their Lives and Times*

Anya Shetterly, *RomeWalks*

Tobias Smollet, *Travels Through France and Italy*
Frederic Spotts and Theodor Wieser, *Italy: A Difficult Democracy*
Stendhal, *Rome, Naples and Florence*
Michael Stern, *An American in Rome*
Irving Stone, *The Agony and the Ecstasy*
Time Out, *Time Out Guide: Rome*
Virginia Valentini, *Destination Rome: A Guide to Roman Living*
William B. Whitman, *Literary Cities of Italy*

ITALIAN LITERATURE

Dante Alighieri, *La divina commedia (The Divine Comedy)*
Ludovico Ariosto, *Orlando Furioso*
Alberto Bevilacqua, *Questa specie d'amore; Una città in amore*
Giovanni Boccaccio, *Decameron*
Dino Buzzati, *I sette messageri; Un amore*
Italo Calvino, *Le città invisibile; Se una notte d'inverno un viaggiatore*
Carlo Cassola, *La ragazza di Bube; La visita*
Baldesar Castiglione, *Il libro del cortegiano (The Book of the Courtier)*
Gabriele D'Annunzio, *Il piacere; Il fuoco; L'innocente*
Umberto Eco, *Il nome della rosa (The Name of the Rose)*
Oriana Fallaci, *Un uomo*
Dario Fo, *Morte accidentale di un anarchico; Il papa e la strega*
Natalia Ginzburg, *È stato così; Caro Michele*
Carlo Goldoni, *Il bugiardo; La bottega del caffè*
Carlo Levi, *Cristo si è fermato a Eboli*
Primo Levi, *Se questo è un uomo*
Niccolò Machiavelli, *Il principe (The Prince)*
Eugenio Montale, *Ossia di seppia*
Elsa Morante, *Menzogna e sortilegio; La storia*
Alberto Moravia, *Racconti romani; La ciociara; L'uomo che guarda; La noia; Gli indifferenti; Agostino*
Cesare Pavese, *Paesi tuoi; La luna e i falò; La bella estate; La spiaggia*
Francesco Petrarca, *Il canzoniere; Trionfi*
Luigi Pirandello, *Il fu Mattia Pascal; Cosi è (se vi pare); Sei personaggi in cerca d'autore (Six Characters in Search of an Author)*
Leonaro Sciascia, *Il giorno della civetta; A ciascuno il suo*
Italo Svevo, *La coscienza di Zeno*
Giuseppe Tomasi di Lampedusa, *Il gattopardo (The Leopard)*
Federigo Tozzi, *Il podere*
Giorgio Vasari, *Vite de' più eccellenti architetti; pittori e scultori italiani*
Giovanni Verga, *Malavoglia; Il marito di Elena*
Paolo Volponi, *Memoriale; Macchina mondiale*

ITALIAN FILMS

Michelangelo Antonioni: *Il grido* (1957), *L'avventura* (1960), *La notte* (1961), *L'eclisse* (1962), *Blow-up* (1967), *Zabriskie Point* (1969), *Professione: Reporter (The Passenger,* 1975)

Cinecittà is where many famous Italian films were made, as well as some major American films such as Ben Hur, which left its props behind on the film studio grounds.

Bernardo Bertolucci: *Il Conformista* (*The Conformist*, 1971), *Ultimo tango a Parigi* (*Last Tango in Paris*, 1972), *Novecento* (*1900*, 1976), *L'ultimo imperatore* (*The Last Emperor*, 1987), *Il tè nel deserto* (*The Sheltering Sky*, 1990), *Io ballo da sola* (*Stealing Beauty*, 1996)

Giuseppe De Santis: *Riso amaro* (*Bitter Rice*, 1949)

Vittorio De Sica: *Sciuscià* (1946), *Ladri di biciclette* (*The Bicycle Thief*, 1948), *Umberto D* (1952), *La ciociara* (*Two Women*, 1960), *Il giardino dei Finzi-Contini* (*The Garden of the Finzi-Continis*, 1971)

Federico Fellini: *Lo sceicco bianco* (1952), *I vitelloni* (1953), *La strada* (1954), *Le notti di Cabiria* (*Nights of Cabiria*, 1957), *La dolce vita* (1960), *Otto e Mezzo* (8 ½, 1963), *Satyricon* (1969), *Roma* (1972), *Amarcord* (1973), *Casanova* (1976), *Ginger e Fred* (1985)

Sergio Leone: *Per un pugno di dollari* (*A Fistful of Dollars*, 1964), *C'era una volta il West* (1968)

Daniele Lucchetti: *Il Portaborse* (1991)

Mario Monicelli: *I soliti ignoti* (*Big Deal on Madonna Street*, 1958), *La grande guerra* (1959)

Nanni Moretti: *Ecce Bombo* (1978), *Bianca* (1983), *Palombella rossa* (1989), *Caro diario* (1994)

Pier Paolo Pasolini: *Accattone* (1961), *Mamma Roma* (1962), *Uccellacci e uccellini* (1966), *Edipo Re* (1967), *Il Decameron* (1971)

Dino Risi: *Poveri ma belli* (1957), *Una vita difficile* (1961), *Il Sorpasso* (1962), *I Mostri* (1963)

Francesco Rosi: *Cadaveri eccellenti* (*Excellent Cadavers*, 1976), *Cristo si è fermato a Eboli* (*Christ Stopped at Eboli*, 1979)

Roberto Rossellini: *Roma città aperta* (*Open City*, 1945), *Paisà* (*Paisan*, 1946), *Germania anno zero* (*Germany Year Zero*, 1947), *Stromboli—terra di Dio* (*Stromboli*, 1949)

Gabriele Salvatores: *Marrakech Express* (1989), *Mediterraneo* (1991), *Nirvam* (1997)

Ettore Scola: *Una giornata particolare* (1977), *La famiglia* (1987)

Giuseppe Tornatore: *Nuovo cinema paradiso* (*Cinema Paradiso*, 1988), *L'uomo delle stelle* (1995)

Carlo Verdone: *Un sacco bello* (1980), *Borotalco* (1982), *Compagni di scuola* (1988)

Luchino Visconti: *Ossessione* (*Obsession*, 1942), *La terra trema* (1948), *Bellissima* (1951), *Senso* (1954), *Rocco e i suoi fratelli* (1960), *Il gattopardo* (*The Leopard*, 1963), *Morte a Venezia* (*Death in Venice*, 1971)

Lina Wertmüller: *Mimì metallurgico ferito nell'onore* (*The Seduction of Mimi*, 1971), *Travolti da un insolito destino nell'azzurro mare d'Agosto* (*Swept Away*, 1974), *Pasqualino settebellezze* (*Seven Beauties*, 1975), *Ciao, Professore* (1994)

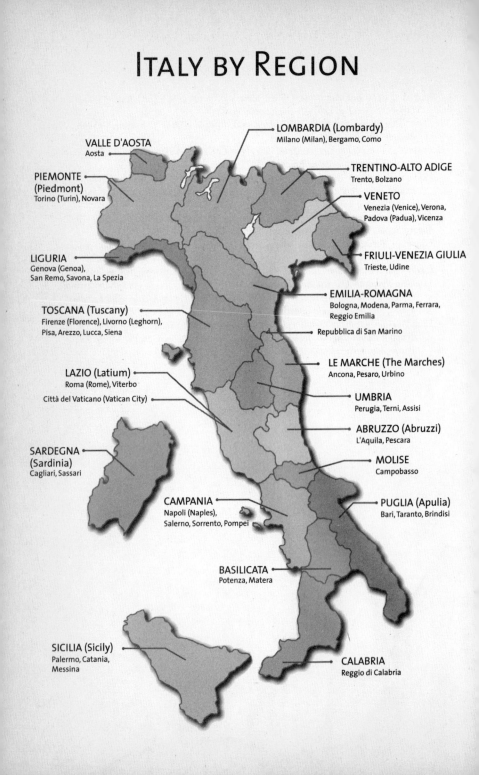

ITALY BY REGION

LOMBARDIA (Lombardy)
Milano (Milan), Bergamo, Como

VALLE D'AOSTA
Aosta

TRENTINO-ALTO ADIGE
Trento, Bolzano

PIEMONTE (Piedmont)
Torino (Turin), Novara

VENETO
Venezia (Venice), Verona,
Padova (Padua), Vicenza

FRIULI-VENEZIA GIULIA
Trieste, Udine

LIGURIA
Genova (Genoa),
San Remo, Savona, La Spezia

EMILIA-ROMAGNA
Bologna, Modena, Parma, Ferrara,
Reggio Emilia

TOSCANA (Tuscany)
Firenze (Florence), Livorno (Leghorn),
Pisa, Arezzo, Lucca, Siena

Repubblica di San Marino

LE MARCHE (The Marches)
Ancona, Pesaro, Urbino

LAZIO (Latium)
Roma (Rome), Viterbo

UMBRIA
Perugia, Terni, Assisi

Città del Vaticano (Vatican City)

ABRUZZO (Abruzzi)
L'Aquila, Pescara

SARDEGNA (Sardinia)
Cagliari, Sassari

MOLISE
Campobasso

CAMPANIA
Napoli (Naples),
Salerno, Sorrento, Pompei

PUGLIA (Apulia)
Bari, Taranto, Brindisi

BASILICATA
Potenza, Matera

SICILIA (Sicily)
Palermo, Catania,
Messina

CALABRIA
Reggio di Calabria

Appendix: Technical Information You Should Know

GENERAL INFORMATION

Capital city: Rome

Official name: Repubblica Italiana (Italian Republic)

Type of government: Parliamentary republic

Head of government: Prime Minister

Size: A bit larger than the state of Arizona

Area: 301,262 square kilometers (116,317 square miles)

Length: 660 miles

Maximum width: 150 miles

Geographic highlights: Alps, Apennine Mountains, volcanoes Etna and Vesuvius, islands of Sicily and Sardinia

Independent states within Italy: San Marino, Vatican City

Languages and dialects: Italian (official), French (Valle d'Aosta), Slovene (Friuli–Venezia Giulia), German and Ladin (Alto Adige), Sardo (Sardinia), Friulano (Friuli), Franco-provençal and Arpitano (Valle d'Aosta and some valleys of Piedmont), Occitanian and Provençal (Val Argentina), Catalan (Alghero), Greek (Salento and Aspromonte), Albanian (mainly in Siciliy and Calabria)

Bordering countries: France, Switzerland, Austria, Slovenia

Surrounding seas: Ionian (south), Tyrrhenian (west), Ligurian (west), Adriatic (east)

Population: 57.8 million

Religion: Mostly Roman Catholic

GDP: 1,785 trillion lire, $115.6 billion

GDP growth rate: In 1995, 2.9 percent

GDP per head: $18,400

Unemployment: 12 percent (average)

MAIN POLITICAL PARTIES OF THE 1990s

Alleanza Nazionale (AN): This right-wing party, currently headed by Gianfranco Fini, has its roots in the MSI (Movimento Sociale Italiano) of Fascist sentiment.

Forza Italia: Named after the soccer chant "Go, Italy," this party was created by media tycoon—and soccer team owner—Silvio Berlusconi, who served as prime minister just as the Clean Hands investigations died down in 1994.

Lega Nord: This is Umberto Bossi's party, which grew in popularity by preaching federalism, meaning that Italy should be divided into autonomous states. It lost popularity when it started advocating splitting Italy into two separate nations.

Partito Democratico della Sinistra (PDS): When the Berlin Wall fell in 1989, the Italian Communist Party (PCI) split over what its role should be in the post–Cold War period. The moderate side of the PCI became the PDS, and the hard-line Communists became the Rifondazione Comunista. Both are members of the current Ulivo coalition government.

Partito Popolare: This is the new name for the Christian Democratic Party, which held a monopoly on power for much of Italy's postwar period (Giulio Andreotti was a Christian Democratic prime minister seven times). When many of its leaders were put under investigation in the Operation Cleans Hands anticorruption probe, the party attempted to split from its past by changing its name to Partito Popolare.

Partito Socialista Italiano (PSI): This was the party of Bettino Craxi, who served as the nation's longest-lasting prime minister in the 1980s. But, when it was discovered that his tenure had created a climate for corruption, the party vanished and Craxi went into self-imposed exile in Tunisia to avoid corruption charges.

MAJOR MEDIA

Newspapers: Corriere della Sera (Italy's largest-circulation newspaper with a center-left stand, considered to have the best foreign coverage); *La Repubblica* (a little more to the left, this is Italy's second largest paper and is printed in a tabloid format, mixing serious news with more local gossip and a great culture page; good local news in special local inserts.); *La Stampa* (owned by the Agnelli clan, this centrist paper is based in Turin and has a good arts section); *L'Unità* (highly respected paper, founded by the Italian Communists, is now very mainstream).

Magazines: L'Espresso (weekly magazine, left-leaning with heavy coverage of national politics, as well as international business, arts, and culture); *Panorama* (like *L'Espresso* but more centrist; vies with it for the number one spot); *Oggi* and *Gente* (more gossip, less news).

TV channels: Government-run channels, called collectively Radiotelevisione Italiana (RAI-UNO, RAI-DUE, RAI-TRE); private TV channels (Canale 5, Italia Uno, Rete 4, founded by Silvio Berlusconi; TeleMonteCarlo, broadcast from over the border in Monte Carlo and owned by Mario Cecchi Gori); satellite dish channels (NBC Superchannel, with many American shows and news though the packaging is strictly British; MTV International; CNN International).

THE FOUR BRANCHES OF ITALIAN POLICE

Italy is protected by four separate police forces, each with their own specialty and jurisdiction. These forces were created to limit the possibility of a single police force growing too powerful, and each is controlled by a separate ministry. The differences between them are as varied as the designers responsible for their stylish uniforms (the *carabinieri*'s uniforms were designed by Giorgio Armani and the *vigili urbani*'s by Fendi).

Carabinieri work for the Ministry of Defense and in the past have been implicated in shady operations with the Italian secret police in attempted *colpi di stato*, such as the 1964 scandal, when the Italian military intelligence service, or *servizio informazioni forze armate*, had planned a coup d'état down to the most minute detail. The *carabinieri* are an all-male military police although this might soon change as women will be allowed to volunteer for the military, and very well trained (there are also horse-mounted *carabinieri*). There are currently about 86,000 active members of the *carabinieri*, and their headquarters are at the *caserma* or *commando*.

The *polizia* are regulated by the Ministry of the Interior, and their headquarters are at the *questura*. If they want to get your attention, they will wave a lollipop-like red-and-white paddle at you. There are about three thousand fewer *poliziotti* than *carabinieri*, but 5 percent of the force is female.

The *guardia di finanza* is responsible for combating tax evasion and smuggling. Its roots go back to the older police force that watched over borders between the many states of the Italian peninsula before unification. But in 1881 it became the tax police and is regulated by the Ministry of Finance.

Vigili urbani do not carry guns and therefore are not after major crimes. They leave that to the *carabinieri* and *polizia*. They are ever present at public *piazze* in search of traffic offenses, building permit infringements, and tourists without their shirts on. They are like a neighborhood police force.

HOLIDAYS AND CULTURAL EVENTS

National Holidays

There are national, regional, and local *feste* (holidays). Because Italy is primarily a Catholic country, the majority of these are related to events in the Bible. Many Italians, however, do not celebrate them in any religious way, and they are more regarded as time to spend with the family.

January 1	**Capodanno or San Silvestro (New Year's Day)** People traditionally celebrate with fireworks and champagne, as well as by throwing dishes and furniture from windows.
January 6	**Epifania (Epiphany)** Characterized by a Santa-like figure, *la Befana,* an old woman on a broomstick who scales roofs and gives gifts or coal to children depending on whether they've been bad or good.
March or April	**Pasqua (Easter Sunday); Pasquetta (Easter Monday)** *La colomba pasquale,* a dove-shaped cake, and *le uova di pasqua,* chocolate eggs, are given as gifts.
April 25	**Anniversario della Liberazione (Liberation Day)** Freedom from Germany, 1945.

May 1	**Primo maggio (Labor Day)**
June 2	**Festa della Repubblica (Celebration of the Republic)** Characterized by military parades and *bersaglieri* (army riflemen) running around town squares.
August 15	**Azzunzione (Assumption)** Commonly known as *ferragosto*, the day when many Italians go on summer vacation until the end of the month.
November 1	**Ognissanti or Tutti i Santi (All Saints' Day)**
November 2	**Tutti i Morti (All Souls' Day)** People go to cemeteries to visit graves of loved ones.
December 8	**L'Immacolata Concezione (Immaculate Conception)**
December 25	**Natale (Christmas)**
December 26	**Santo Stefano (Saint Stephen's Day)**

Festivals and Celebrations

In Italy it seems that there can never be enough festivals. Many are based on Renaissance traditions, and most of the celebrations include dinner, dance, and song. Aside from the ones listed here, there are dozens of regional antique markets and *sagre*, festivals celebrating a specific food such as cheese or mushrooms.

January–March	**Carnevale (Carnival) in Venice, Viareggio, and Ivrea** Celebrated the week before Lent, usually late February or early March but sometimes in January. It is characterized by costume balls, fireworks, masked parades, and joyful chaos.
February	**Festival della Canzone Italiana (Festival of the Italian Song) in San Remo** A televised song competition that is as popular in Italy as the Grammy Awards are in the United States.
March 8	**Festa delle Donne (Women's Day)** Italians give yellow mimosa flowers on this day to women they love/appreciate.
May 15	**Corsa dei Ceri in Gubbio (Umbria)** Shrines are carried by worshipers to a church on a mountaintop.
June	**Calcio in Costume (Historical Soccer in Costume) in Florence** Burly men dressed in sixteenth-century costumes fight a bloody battle over a soccer ball in Piazza Santa Croce. No protective padding or helmets are allowed, except for masking tape over the ears to protect them from being torn off.
	Biennale di Venezia During even-numbered years this international art exhibition is held from June to September.
	Verona Music Festival An opera and music festival held every year, June to August.
July–August	**Palio horse race in Siena** Horses representing various quarters of the city race around the

Carnival in Venice is a surreal experience with midnight parades and elaborate costumes, such as the one worn by this participant.

main *piazza* while spectators crowd about cheering. The racetrack is so narrow that sometimes horses are injured and die.

La Festa di Noantri (middle two weeks of July) in Trastevere
This celebration is held in honor of Madonna del Carmine on the other side of the Tiber River from the historic center of Rome. Fireworks, *porchetta* (a spicy pork delicacy), boxing, and Roman folk songs are among the usual attractions. See the end of Fellini's film *Roma* for an authentic taste of it.

Festivale dei Due Mondi in Spoleto (Umbria)
This "Festival of the Two Worlds" celebrates music and performing arts for two months.

Panatenee Pompeiane
A music festival in Pompeii during the last week of August.

September   **The historical Regatta boat race** in Venice
Boaters from all over Italy migrate north to gather in the Grand Canal in rowing sculls, kayaks, canoes, and antique crafts.

Mostra Internazionale d'Arte Cinematografica (Venice Film Festival)
During the first two weeks of the month, filmmakers from all over the world exhibit their works in this highly prestigious competition.

Saints' Days

Each Italian town has its own saint's day. Often businesses close on these days, though stores usually remain open. Within any given city there is a myriad of jokes about the saints of other cities, usually to illustrate the ignorance of the rival townspeople. Here the competition left over from past centuries really shows through. The religious importance given to the saint's day depends on the city, and generally speaking, the farther south you go the more religious celebrations take place. San Gennaro, the saint of Naples, is much loved and honored there, as he is in New York City's Little Italy. In many Italian cities there are nonreligious celebrations on these days. For example, in Florence there are fireworks for the *festa di San Giovanni*. Florentines flock to the banks of the Arno River, and members of the two local boat clubs crowd the water in all kinds of crafts to watch the display of lights. Here the greatest challenge is to avoid being hit by the people spitting from the bridges above. The saint's day is also known as the *onomastico*, or name day. People with the same name as the saint are often given cards or presents on these days. Each saint represents a different virtue. For example, Padua's Sant' Antonio represents health. Others represent happiness, love, and good fortune. Some of the more celebrated saint's days include:

Month	Saint	Place Celebrated
April 25	San Marco	Venice
May 1	Sant' Elisio	Cagliari, Sardinia
June 13	Sant' Antonio	Padua
June 24	San Giovanni	Turin, Genova, Florence
June 29	San Pietro	Rome
July 10–15	Santa Rosalia	Palermo
July 23–25	Caltagirone; San Giacomo	Sicily
July 26	Santa Anna	Island of Ischia
September 19	San Gennaro	Naples
October 4	San Petronio	Bologna
October 4	San Francesco	Assisi
December 7	Sant' Ambrogio	Milan

TIME

In Italy, the twenty-four-hour time system (what we commonly call "military time" in the United States) is used not only for train and movie schedules but also in common speech for setting up appointments. For example, someone might say to you, *"Vediamoci alle quindici,"* meaning literally "Let's meet at fifteen o'clock" (i.e., three in the afternoon). Unless it's eight o'clock and you're making an appointment for nine, it is always safer to use military time. For foreigners who don't normally use this system, it is especially difficult to get used to this, so we have supplied an easy table below to help you remember. Note that you put a comma (2,00) between the hours and minutes instead of a colon (2:00).

Late Night and Morning		Afternoon and Evening	
English	*Italian*	*English*	*Italian*
1:00 a.m.	1,00	1:00 P.M.	13,00
2	2,00	2	14,00
3	3,00	3	15,00
4	4,00	4	16,00
5	5,00	5	17,00
6	6,00	6	18,00
7	7,00	7	19,00
8	8,00	8	20,00
9	9,00	9	21,00
10	10,00	10	22,00
11	11,00	11	23,00
12 p.m. (noon)	12,00 (*mezzogiorno*)	12 A.M. (midnight)	24,00 (*mezzanotte*)

Time Differences Between Italy and the United States

Italy is in the Central European time zone. There is no time difference between Italian cities. Summer time (+1 hour) begins at the end of March and lasts until September. Because summer time begins and ends on different days than in the United States, for a week or more there is often a seven-hour (instead of six-hour) difference between New York and Italy, a ten-hour (instead of nine-hour) difference between California and Italy. Under normal circumstances Italy is six hours ahead of New York, seven hours ahead of Dallas, eight hours ahead of Denver, and nine hours ahead of Los Angeles.

1:00	2:00	3:00	4:00	10:00
Los Angeles	Denver	Dallas	New York	Italy

GENERAL MEASUREMENTS
Distance

General English-to-Metric Conversions

To Convert	*Multiply*	*By*
Inches to millimeters	No. of inches	25.4
Inches to centimeters	No. of inches	2.54
Inches to meters	No. of inches	0.0254
Centimeters to inches	No. of centimeters	0.39
Feet to centimeters	No. of feet	30.48
Feet to meters	No. of feet	0.3048
Meters to feet	No. of meters	3.28
Yards to meters	No. of yards	0.9144
Meters to yards	No. of meters	1.09
Miles to kilometers	No. of miles	1.61
Kilometers to miles	No. of kilometers	0.62

Specific English-to-Metric Conversions

United States	*Italy*
0.394 inch	1 centimeter
1 inch	2.54 centimeter
1 foot	30.48 centimeters = 0.3048 meter
1 yard (36 inches)	91.4 centimeters = 0.9144 meter
39.4 inches	1 meter
0.6214 miles	1 kilometer
1 mile = 5,280 feet	1.6093 kilometers
0.5 mile	0.8 kilometer
1 mile	1.6 kilometer
5 miles	8.0 kilometers
10 miles	16.0 kilometers
50 miles	80.4 kilometers
100 miles	160.9 kilometers
1,000 miles	1,609 kilometers

Square Measurements (Rooms, Houses, and Land)

Rooms are measured in square meters in Italy. Also, remember that:

144 square inches = 1 square foot

9 square feet   = 1 square yard

1 acre   = 4,840 square yards or 4,047 square meters

To Convert	*Multiply*	*By*
Square inches to square centimeters	No. of inches	6.452
Square inches to square meters	No. of inches	0.000645
Square centimeters to square inches	No. of centimeters	0.1550
Square feet to square meters	No. of square feet	0.0929
Square yards to square meters	No. of square yards	0.836
Square meters to square yards	No. of meters	1.196
Square miles to square kilometers	No. of square miles	2.59
Square kilometers to square miles	No. of kilometers	0.386
Acres to hectares	No. of acres	0.4047
Hectares to acres	No. of hectares	2.47

Weight

When dealing with weights and measures, there are a few key points to keep in mind. First of all, dry weights and liquid weights are different. Second, the United Kingdom and the United States use many of the same terms for measurements, but they represent different amounts. You will find that many English-language cookbooks you buy in Italy are published in England, which means you should consult the British conversion scales, not the American ones (see Liquid Measurements). Last, there are probably many conversions that you just never learned in English or learned in a fifth-grade home economics course. For people who need some refreshers, we have included the basic U.S. conversions as well.

In Italy there are two important units of measure that are used in daily life. The first is the *etto*, which is actually an abbreviation of *ettogrammo,* or 100 grams. The most important thing to remember about this unit is that one *etto* is the standard dry portion of pasta cooked per person, assuming you're making the usual multicourse Italian meal. The other unit is the *fetta,* or slice. When shopping for sandwich meats in an *alimentari,* or when requesting bread in a restaurant, you use this word.

General U.S.-to-Italian Conversions

To Convert	Multiply	By
ounces to grams	No. of ounces	28.35
grams to ounces	No. of grams	0.035
liters to quarts	No. of grams	1.06
quarts to liters	No. of quarts	0.95
pounds to kilos	No. of pounds	0.45
kilos to pounds	No. of kilograms	2.21

Specific U.S.-to-Italian Conversions

United States	Italy
1.00 ounces	28.50 grams
3.53 ounces	100 grams (*un etto*)
¼ pound	125 grams
½ pound	250 grams
1 pound (16 ounces)	453.60 grams
5 pounds	2.25 kilograms

Temperature and Weather
In Italy temperature is measured in Centigrade or Celsius. To you 40 degrees may sound cold, but that actually means it's *HOT.* The actual calculation for making the conversion is complicated to do without a calculator, so the second table below should come in handy.

To Convert	To	Step 1	Step 2	Step 3
Fahrenheit	Centigrade	Subtract 32	Multiply by 5	Divide by 9
Centigrade	Fahrenheit	Multiply by 9	Divide by 5	Add 32

Common Weather Temperatures

Fahrenheit	Centigrade
104	40.0
90	32.2
70	21.1
60	15.5
50	10.0
32	0
14	−10.0
0	−18.0

BODY MEASUREMENTS

Height

United States	Italy	United States	Italy	United States	Italy
4 ft	122 cm	5 ft	152.40 cm	6 ft	182.88 cm
4'1"	124.46	5'1"	155.94	6'1"	185.42
4'2"	127	5'2"	157.98	6'2"	187.96
4'3"	129.54	5'3"	160.02	6'3"	190.50
4'4"	132.08	5'4"	162.56	6'4"	193.04
4'5"	134.62	5'5"	165.10	6'5"	195.58
4'6"	137.16	5'6"	167.64	6'6"	198.12
4'7"	139.70	5'7"	170.18	6'7"	200.66
4'8"	142.24	5'8"	172.72	6'8"	203.20
4'9"	144.78	5'9"	175.26	6'9"	205.74
4'10"	147.32	5'10"	177.80	6'10"	208.28
4'11"	149.86	5'11"	180.34	6'11"	210.82

Body Temperature

Unless you bring your own thermometer that has measurements in Fahrenheit, you will have to get used to the Italian thermometer when you're sick. For some people it is more consoling to have the familiar sight of the thermometer from home. In addition, most Italian thermometers are designed to be held under your armpit or are rectal. Children have slightly different standards from adults.

Adults, Oral Temperature

Fahrenheit	Centigrade
96.8°	36.0°
97.5°	36.5°
98.6° (normal body temperature)	37.0°
99.5°	37.5°
100.4°	38.0°
101.3°	38.5°
102.2°	39.0°
103.1°	39.5°
104.0°	40.0°

Children

Placement	Normal Temperature	Fever
Oral	98.6°F (37°C)	100°F (37.7°C)
Rectal	99.6°F (37.6°C)	100.4°F (38.1°C)
Under the arm	97.6°F (36.5°C)	99°F (37.2°C)

Body Weight

The key calculations to remember are:

1 pound	= 450 grams
No. of pounds × 0.45	= No. of kilos
No. of kilos × 2.21	= No. of pounds

Pounds	Kilos	Pounds	Kilos	Pounds	Kilos	Pounds	Kilos
10	4.5	110	49.5	210	94.5	310	139.5
20	9.0	120	54.0	220	99.0	320	144.0
30	13.5	130	58.5	230	103.5	330	148.5
40	18.0	140	63.0	240	108.0	340	153.0
50	22.5	150	67.5	250	112.5	350	157.5
60	27.0	160	72.0	260	117.0	360	162.0
70	31.5	170	76.5	270	121.5	370	166.5
80	36.0	180	81.0	280	126.0	380	171.0
90	40.5	190	85.5	290	130.5	390	175.5
100	45.0	200	90.0	300	135.0	400	180.0

Clothing and Shoe Sizes

The biggest problem with clothing sizes is that they are not standardized and vary from brand name to brand name. Also, men's trousers generally include a waist size but not a length measurement because they have to be hemmed.

Women's Clothes—General

United States	2	4	6	8	10	12	14	16	18
Italy	36	38	40	42	44	46	48	50	52

Women's Stockings

United States	Petite	Small	Medium	Large
Italy	I	II	III	IV

Men's Shirts

United States	14	14.5	15	15.5	16	16.5	17	17.5
Italy	36	37	38	39	40	41	42	43

Men's Suits, Sweaters, and Overcoats

United States	36	38	40	42	44	46	48
Italy	46	48	50	52	54	56	58

Men's Trousers

United States	26	28	30	32	34	36	38	40
Italy	42	44	46	48	50	52	54	56

Children's Clothes

United States	1	2	3	4	5	6	7	8	9	10	11	12	13	14
Italy	35	40	45	50	55	60	65	70	75	80	85	90	95	100

Women's Shoes

United States	5.5	6.5	7	7.5	8	9	10
Italy	35	36	37	38	38.5	39–40	41

Men's Shoes

United States	7.5	8	8.5	9	9.5	10	11	12
Italy	41	41.5	42	42.5	43	43.5	44–44.5	44.5

Children's Shoes

United States	8	9	10	10.5	11	12	13	1	2
Italy	24	25	26	27	28	29	30	1	2

COOKING AND BAKING

Oven Temperature
When you are baking, be sure to remember that the dial on the Italian oven has the temperature in Centigrade.

Definition	*Fahrenheit*	*Centigrade*
Very slow	250°	121°
Slow	300°	149°
Moderately slow	325°	165°
Moderate	350°	177°
Moderately hot	375°	190°
Hot	400°	205°
Hot	425°	218°
Very hot	450°	232°
Very hot	475°	246°

Water Temperature

Water	*Fahrenheit*	*Centigrade*
Boiling	212°	100°
Simmering	185°	85°
Freezing	32°	0°

Solid Ingredients (United States Only)

Amount	Equals
1 pinch	A bit less than ¼ teaspoon
1 dash	a few drops
3 teaspoons	1 tablespoon
2 tablespoons	1 ounce
8 tablespoons	½ cup = 4 ounces = 1 dL
2 cups	1 pint = ½ quart
4 cups	2 pints = 1 quart
4 quarts	1 gallon = 128 fluid ounce

Butter

500 grams = ½ kilo

No. of Ounces	Equals	No. of Grams
0.5	1 tablespoon	15
1	2 Tbs. = ¼ stick	30
2	4 Tbs. = ¼ cup = ½ stick	60
4	8 Tbs. = ½ cup = 1 stick = ¼ pound	115
16	32 Tbs. = 2 cups = 4 sticks = 1 pound	450

Sugar

No. of Ounces	Of	Equals	No. of Grams
0.16	granulated sugar	1 teaspoon	5
0.5	granulated sugar	1 tablespoon	15
1.75	granulated sugar	¼ cup or 4 Tbs.	60
2.25	granulated sugar	⅓ cup or 5 Tbs.	75
6.75	granulated sugar	1 cup	200
16	brown sugar	1 pound or 2⅓ cups	450
16	confectioner's sugar	1 pound or 4 cups	450

Flour

No. of Ounces	Equals	No. of Grams
¼	1 tablespoon	8.75
1.25	¼ cup = 4 Tbs.	35
1.5	⅓ cup = 5 Tbs.	45
5	1 cup	140

*Note: measurements listed here are for unsifted flour; 1 cup unsifted flour minus 1.5 tablespoons = 1 cup sifted flour

Liquid Measurements

Again, make note of the fact that the British and American conversions are different in some cases. They have been listed separately in the table below. Remember, "tsp" is "teaspoon" (*cucchiaino da tè*) and "Tbs." is "tablespoon" (*cucchiaio da mines-*

tra). Small amounts can be written as portions of liters (l) or as centiliters (cl) and milliliters (ml). One liter equals 100 centiliters and 1,000 milliliters. For example, 0.35 liter is equal to 35 centiliters and 0.01 liter equals 10 centiliters. Or, 0.2366 liter equals 236 milliliters and 23.6 centiliters. Also, one U.S. gallon equals 0.833 British Imperial gallons, and 1.201 U.S. gallons equals one British Imperial gallon.

Liquids (United States Only)

Measurement	Equivalent
1 gallon	4 quarts or 128 ounces
1 tablespoon	0.5 fluid ounce
½ pint	1¼ cups
⅛ pint	¼ cup + 1 tablespoon
¼ pint	⅔ cup
1 quart	4 cups or ¼ gallon (U.S.)
1 quart	2 pints (U.K.)
1 pint	2.5 cups or 0.5 quart (U.K.)
1 pint	16 ounces or 2 cups (U.S.)

Specific U.S.-to-Italian Liquid Conversions

United States	Italy
⅕ teaspoon	1 milliliter
1 teaspoon	5 milliliters
1 tablespoon	15 milliliters
⅛ pint	75 milliliters
¼ pint	150 milliliters
½ pint	300 milliliters
8.5 fluid ounces	0.25 liter
1 pint	0.4732 liter
1 pint	0.5683 liter
33.5 fluid ounces	1 liter
1 quart	0.9463 liter
1 quart (U.K.)	1.137 liter
1 gallon (U.S.)	3.7853 liters
1 gallon (U.K.)	4.546 liters
3.3 fluid ounces	0.01 liter
1 fluid ounce	29.574 milliliters
1 teaspoon (tsp.)	4.9288 milliliters
1 tablespoon (Tbs.)	14.786 milliliters
1 cup	0.2366 liter

ELECTRICAL STANDARDS AND ELECTRONICS

Italy and Europe have a different standard of electrical current than the United States. For this reason, appliances brought from the United States cannot function without a transformer. For smaller machines, a converter is usually enough. For larger ones, a heavy-duty transformer is needed. Some of these converters and transformers have outlets for two-prong American plugs; buy some three-to-two-prong adapters in the United States just to be safe. In addition to the difference in current, the plugs themselves are different. In Italy, the average plug has two or three round metal tubes where the flat, rectangular metal prongs are on an American plug. In the United States, the standard is 110 volts, and in Italy it is 220 volts and 50-Hz AC cycles (in some areas of Italy it is 125 or 115 volts). When it comes to phone jacks, modern Italian homes have the RJ11 jack we use in the United States, but older ones still have three-pronged Italian jacks. You can easily find an adapter at a local hardware store.

When it comes to videocassette recorders (VCRs), the difference has to do with the speed at which the cassette turns. A videocassette designed for an American VCR will not function in Italy unless it is first converted using a special machine. There are many stores that specialize in converting such tapes, but the procedure is not cheap. The American VCR standard is "NTSC," while the Italian one is "PAL." There are video rental stores (including Blockbuster Video) all over the peninsula.

NUMBERS

One of the problems that plagues expatriates is the many zeroes in Italian numbers. What is a million or billion in English, and what is it in Italian? This is especially confusing when large amounts of money are written. For example, during the "Tangentopoli" bribe trials, every day newspapers reported how much money people had obtained illegally. The numbers were so large that it was hard to keep the equivalencies in dollars straight or imagine that any money was left. There is one basic concept you have to get straight: in Italian numbers the period goes where our comma goes, and the comma goes where our period does. In Italy, a decimal point is written using a comma and not a period; to separate thousands, Italians use the period.

English	Italian
8.5	8,5 (otto virgola cinque)
1,300	1.300 (milletrecento)
1,000,000	1.000.000 (un milione)
1,000,000,000	1.000.000.000 (un miliardo—USA)

TELEPHONE AND MAIL

Italian phone numbers come in all colors and sizes. Green numbers (*numeri verdi*) all start with "167" and are toll-free. Sky blue numbers (*numeri azzurri*) are to report child abuse. Pink numbers (*numeri rosa*) are to report abuse of women. Violet numbers (*numeri viola*) are to report any other kind of abuse. Red numbers (*numeri rossi*) are for prenatal medical advice. Orange numbers (*numeri arancioni*) are for general psychiatric counseling. One important thing to remember: when dialing an Italian number from within Italy, you add a zero to the city code; when dialing it from outside Italy, you do not. For example, the city code for Florence is "055" within Italy and "55" from other countries. But this may change. Here are some less colorful national numbers you should have:

Emergency Numbers

Police (Polizia)	113
Carabinieri	112
Fire (Vigili del Fuoco)	115

Appendix: Technical Information You Should Know

Highway emergency (Soccorso Stradale ACI)		116
Sanitary emergency (Emergenza Sanitaria)		118

Directory Assistance and Operators

AT&T operator	1721011
Sprint operator	1721877
MCI operator	1721011
Local Italian directory assistance and operator	12
Telephone communication problems, calls within Italy	182
European and international directory assistance	176
International operator	170
Telephone communication problems, international calls	1723535

Other National Numbers

Neighborhood information	110
Wake-up calls	114
Time	161
TIM, cellular information	119
OMNITEL, cellular information	190

Calling the USA

If you want to dial the United States directly, dial 001, the area code, and the phone number. To make a call using an American calling card or an operator in the United States, use one of the numbers listed in the previous section under "Directory Assistance and Operators." Because Italian phones do not include letters on the dialing pad, here is the U.S. pad: 1 (no letter); 2 (ABC); 3 (DEF); 4 (GHI); 5 (JKL); 6 (MNO); 7 (PRS); 8 (TUV); 9 (WXY).

Spelling over the Phone

Italians have a precise set of words they use to aid spelling over the phone. While in the United States we say "B as in boy," in Italy they simply say words starting with the letter needed (e.g., "Bologna"). When they need to spell a whole word, they say a series of words, often very quickly. For the most part, these words are the names of Italian cities. The American tendency to confuse "i" and "e" makes it only more confusing. For example, if Italians want to spell the word *"barca,"* they say "Bologna Ancona Roma Como Ancona." The word "egg" would be spelled "Empoli Genova Genova."

A	Ancona	G	Genova	M	Milan	S	Savona	Y	York
B	Bologna	H	Hotel	N	Napoli	T	Torino	Z	Zara/Zeta
C	Como	I	Imola	O	Otranto	U	Udine	
D	Domodossola	J	Ilunga/Jolly	P	Perugia	V	Venezia	
E	Empoli	K	Kappa/Kursaal	Q	Quarto	W	Washington	
F	Firenze	L	Livorno	R	Roma	X	Ics	

Postal Codes and Area Codes

Though the number of digits in an Italian area code can vary greatly, the postal code always has five digits. The area code is called *il prefisso,* and the postal code is *il codice avviamento postale* (CAP). Each city has one principal area code and many others specific to the neighborhood. If you don't know the specific one, use the principal one instead, as listed below.

City	Area Code	Postal Code
Agrigento	0922	92100
Alessandria	0131	15100
Ancona	071	60100
Aosta	0165	11100
Arezzo	0575	52100
Ascoli Piceno	0736	63100
Asti	0141	14100
Avellino	0825	83100
Bari	080	70100
Belluno	0437	32100
Benevento	0824	82100
Bergamo	035	24100
Bologna	051	40100
Bolzano	0471	39100
Brescia	030	25100
Brindisi	0831	72100
Cagliari	070	09100
Caltanisetta	0934	93100
Campobasso	0874	86100
Caserta	0823	81100
Catania	095	95100
Catanzaro	0961	88100
Chieti	0871	66100
Como	031	22100
Cosenza	0984	87100
Cremona	0372	26100
Cuneo	0171	12100
Enna	0935	94100
Ferrara	0532	44100
Firenze	055	50100
Foggia	0881	71100
Forli	0543	47100
Frosinone	0775	03100
Genova	010	16100
Gorizia	0481	34170
Grosseto	0564	58100
Imperia	0183	18100
Isernia	0865	86170
L'Aquila	0862	67100
La Spezia	0187	19100

City	Area Code	Postal Code
Latina	0773	04100
Lecce	0832	73100
Livorno	0586	57100
Lucca	0583	55100
Macerata	0733	62100
Mantova	0376	46100
Massa-Calatera	0585	54100
Matera	0835	75100
Messina	090	98100
Milano	02	20100
Modena	059	41100
Napoli	081	80100
Novara	0321	28100
Nuoro	0784	08100
Oristano	0783	09170
Padova	049	35100
Palermo	091	90100
Parma	0521	43100
Pavia	0382	27100
Perugia	075	06100
Pesaro	0721	61100
Pescara	085	65100
Piacenza	0523	29100
Pisa	050	56100
Pistoia	0573	51100
Pordenone	0434	33170
Potenza	0971	85100
Ragusa	0932	97100
Ravenna	0544	48100
Reggio di Calabria	0965	89100
Reggio nell'Emilia	0522	42100
Rieti	0746	02100
Roma	06	00100
Rovigo	0425	45100
Salerno	089	84100
Sassari	079	07100
Savona	019	17100
Siena	0577	53100
Siracusa	0931	96100
Sondrio	0342	23100
Taranto	099	74100
Teramo	0861	64100
Terni	0744	05100
Torino	011	10100
Trapani	0923	91100
Trento	0461	38100
Treviso	0422	31100

City	Area Code	Postal Code
Trieste	040	34100
Udine	0432	33100
Varese	0332	21100
Venezia	041	30100
Vercelli	0161	13100
Verona	045	37100
Vicenza	0444	36100
Viterbo	0761	01100

Index